Essays on the Poetry of James Wright

Edited by DAVE SMITH

The Pure Clear Word

UNIVERSITY OF ILLINOIS PRESS   Urbana   Chicago   London

Lines from "Captain Craig" are reprinted with permission of Macmillan Publishing Co., Inc., from *Collected Poems* of Edwin Arlington Robinson. Copyright 1915 by Edwin Arlington Robinson, renewed 1943 by Ruth Nivison.

"Those Winter Sundays" by Robert Hayden is reprinted from *Angle of Ascent, New and Selected Poems*, by Robert Hayden, by permission of Liveright Publishing Corporation. Copyright © 1975, 1972, 1970, 1966 by Robert Hayden.

I wish to thank the editors of the following magazines for permission to reprint essays which they originally published, sometimes in slightly different versions:

"James Wright: The Pure Clear Word," edited by Dave Smith, *American Poetry Review*, 9, no. 3 (1980).

"A Foreword to James Wright's *The Green Wall*," by W. H. Auden, is reprinted by permission of Mrs. James Wright.

"The Work of James Wright," by Crunk [pseud. of Robert Bly], *The Sixties*, no. 8 (1966).

"The Continuity of James Wright's Poems," by William Matthews, *Ohio Review*, 18 (Spring–Summer 1977).

"A World Immeasurably Alive and Good: A Look at James Wright's *Collected Poems*," by James Seay, *Georgia Review*, 27 (1973).

"The Rise and Fall of James Wright," by Edward Butscher, *Georgia Review*, 28 (1974).

"Open Secrets," by Stephen Yenser, *Parnassus*, 6 (Spring–Summer 1978).

"The Traditional James Wright," by Leonard Nathan, *Ironwood* 10 (1977).

"That Halting, Stammering Movement," by Dave Smith, *Ironwood* 10 (1977).

"James Wright," by Robert Hass, *Ironwood* 10 (1977).

"James Wright: Returning to the Heartland," by Bonnie Costello, *New Boston Review*, 5 (Aug.–Sept. 1980).

Library of Congress Cataloging in Publication Data

Main entry under title:

The pure clear word.

  Bibliography: p.
  Contents: James Wright / by Dave Smith—A foreword to James Wright's The green wall / by W. H. Auden—In the mode of Robinson and Frost / by Henry Taylor—[etc.]
    1. Wright, James Arlington, 1927– —Criticism and interpretation—Addresses, essays, lectures. I. Smith, Dave, 1942–
PS3545.R58Z74   811'.54   81-2976
ISBN 0-252-00876-6   AACR2

This book is dedicated to Michael Cuddihy and James Wright.

Contents

The kind of poetry I want to write is
    The poetry of a grown man.
The young poets of New York come to me with
Their mangled figures of speech,
But they have little pity
For the pure clear word.

James Wright (1927–80)

Introduction

DAVE SMITH

IN 1977, MICHAEL CUDDIHY published a special issue of his little magazine *Ironwood*, devoting it entirely to the work of James Wright. This collection of essays owes its genesis to Michael Cuddihy. My intention, however, has differed from Cuddihy's in that I meant to restrict this book to critical commentary and specifically to commentary which would reveal James Wright's struggle to become a contemporary poet, a struggle Wright understood to be the act of drawing closer the reader and the poem. This is an act of personality.

When I had assembled the book I realized that it lacked the authorizing pressure of biography. There is not very much public information about Wright's life and the essays here do not approach his poetry from that perspective. I decided to include an interview with Wright but found there was no suitable interview available.

In September of 1979, having just returned to the United States from Italy, Wright agreed to be interviewed. I sent him approximately 100 questions and then, in the company of poet Gibbons Ruark, went to New York for the interview which begins this book. I had particularly hoped it would provide an opening into Wright's future, a future certain to be as poetically unpredictable as had been his past. This hope was not to be realized. James Wright contracted cancer of the tongue and died March 25, 1980.

James Wright was by conventional definition a *contemporary* poet, even perhaps a second-generation contemporary if we think of Robert Lowell, Randall Jarrell, and Theodore Roethke as contemporary. Recently a graduate student told me that he could not consider Wright his contemporary and I realized this student was younger than Sylvia Plath's children. The point is that modernist poetics are falling farther into the past while Wright's generation has come to its maturity. T. S. Eliot and William Carlos Williams are names in books to the young and not the battle cries they were to poets born, like Wright, in the mid-1920s—including John Ashbery, Galway Kinnell, Robert Bly, Allen Ginsberg, W. S. Merwin, David Wagoner, and others. James Wright is, therefore, at least in part a representative man whose poetics demonstrate what we mean by *contemporary* as both an extension of and a rebellion against modernism. Wright had a proper contempt for pedestrian criticism which reduced a writer to a statistic or proof, but he hoped for the illumination of art which criticism has sometimes provided. He wanted, as he says in the following interview, "more genuine intelligent readers of good will." I hope that is what this book will engender.

We live in a time when critical theory has called into question not merely the function of art but the very existence of art. Theorists deny there can be an author. From Derrida to Culler to Fish, the talk is of the *text*, an impersonal object neither story nor poem. The desire of such criticism, whatever its Archimedean point, is to bring to literature the objectivity of scientific inquiry; that is, to codify what and how literature *knows*. This is the direction and legacy of New Criticism in part, of modernist rebellion in part—but it is largely the temperament of the industrial world. While criticism fabricates objectivity and impersonality, becoming at last not a way of experiencing art but a kind of parodic extension of Robert Frost's remark about free verse—that is, a game played without net, racket, or balls—poetry has gone in the opposite direction. To understand and to follow James Wright's development as a poet we have to search for the man in the poems.

There are, however, two James Wrights: one is the Wright created by and revealed in the poems and the other is a man who died in New York in 1980, a man about whom most of us know very little. We do not know very much because there are as yet few literary histories or biographies of Wright's generation and because Wright did not want his life made public. As William Faulkner remarked, the life was in the books and you could look for it there. James Wright believed that making one's life public and making public art of one's life were very different matters. When W. B. Yeats spoke about the need to choose between perfection of the art and perfection of the life, he touched upon the central issue in poetry since the emergence of romanticism. If he seemed to echo modernist doctrine, to take the side of art's perfection, Yeats's poems moved always toward the inseparability of life and art that seems and is particularly contemporary. His act, the contemporary act, is that of the personality of a man rising symbolically to become the personality of men. We can see exactly this process in the poetry of James Wright.

Wright began with poems remarkable for their facility in verse elegance and for their implicit homage to the modernist obsession with an ideal and an impersonal music which might create an art, as Flaubert had said, apparently about nothing at all. Wright's first book, *The Green Wall*, appeared in 1957. A winner of the Yale Younger Poets Prize, the book made far less splash that year than did the Russian satellite Sputnik. *The Green Wall* carried into the space age the approving introduction of the last major modernist, W. H. Auden. In style and in attitude it echoed Robert Frost and E. A. Robinson, Thomas Hardy and Edward Thomas. It was the kind of poetry that Wright has referred to as "quietist" but it did not entirely conform to Donald Hall's survivor's description of poetry in the 1950s: "Here was the ability to shape an analogy, to perceive and develop comparisons, to display etymological wit, and to pun six ways at once. It appealed to the mind because it was intelligent, and to the sense of form because it was intricate and shapely. It did not appeal to the passions and it did not pretend to."[1] Wright's was most unlike this paradigmatic poetry in that within his acceptance and practise of modernist restraint, decorum, and structure more received than evolved, he brought great passion to contend against historical constrictions. He spoke the modern dilemma in his poems: "Now we have coddled the gods away." But Wright had not yet coddled away what the gods of poetry had prescribed, though this was nevertheless an oddly personal book about the rural Ohio Valley where he had been born into depression economics and the countryman's struggle to stay alive. The poet of *The Green Wall* is capable primarily of conventional language and pastoral scenes of bruised beauty. Wright learned to call this glib. Even so he gave us a surprising mix of poems about mad girls, black prostitutes, George Doty the murderer, and Sappho the Lesbian. Sappho? From a Martins Ferry boy? That was the college influence, the books. The others were Wright's true subject, and his subject was the ghostly debris of the American promise (which was the local analogue of the Christian version of human experience).

James Wright understood the American promise to be life, liberty, and the pursuit of happiness. It was a vision of possibility, sometimes utopian but ordinarily practical. It was the vision of a small farm, a decently fed family, and the right to be responsible for one's self and one's own. It was the promise that life actually was dignity and hope, not the whim of the elect rulers. America, from the first, was the new world because it would not perpetuate the mistakes, the malevolence, and the dead-end *condition humaine* that was Europe and Asia. Emigration was, in main fact, a physical and spiritual rebirth. It required heroic figures and it got them. But what do the great tragic stories tell us if not that heroes are men, are flawed and doomed, are—as Wright says—sons of bitches just like us? Wright's subject was heroism, promise and failure and evidence. Even in the slicked-up poems of *The Green Wall* there are hints of the blunt, aggressive poetry he will come to, of the dream life he will dramatize, and of the fearful privation of the human spirit that will be his battleground. Yet, the poet who speaks *The Green Wall* is the composite voice of Wright's literary fathers. Wright himself is scarcely to be seen.

Saint Judas, published just two years after the first book, continues the neo-Georgian style, though there is a new urgency of personality. The book's initial poem, "Lunar Changes," suggests not so much an alteration in the way the poems will comport themselves—and indeed "Complaint" exhibits the smooth couplets of iambic pentameter which look backward in time—as the presence of deeper, more subtle changes. Wright had begun to abandon the pastoral hymn to Nature as the perfect Emersonian mirror. He had decided to know the reality of nature as he is in it and it is in him. As yet the attempt was rough and sporadic, but it was there. It was there stuttering through personality. Implicit in his lunar changes were the questions of what a poet knows and how he knows; that is to say, of facing the problem of what authority poetry might have in a post-*Wasteland* and post-Holocaust world. When poets or critics talk about the problem of form and content they are inevitably talking about the poet's *authority*, that which allows poetry to *do* anything or, as Auden says, "to make nothing happen."

The interjection of personality as the fundamental force of contemporary poetics drove against the cultural and critical lust for objective knowledge. To describe and evaluate the new poetry, criticism called it "confessional" and cited as primary examples Allen Ginsberg's *Howl* (1956), Robert Lowell's *Life Studies* (1959), W. D.

Snodgrass's *Heart's Needle* (1959), and others. It must have seemed to critics the poets had chosen to ignore Yeats and to perfect nothing at all. Confessionalism meant the recording and presentation of the raw data of biographical existence, the evidence of naturalistic decay. Everyone pointed out the extreme subjectivity and lack of shapeliness. It was, of course, a further rebellion against passionless modernism and the art about nothing. The poetry of personality, which had to have a confessional dimension but which might not be confessional, imagined that the details of the individual life might be drawn to a coherence and meaning that extended beyond the one life. The movement toward autobiographical art, whose beginning is at least with the *Confessions of St. Augustine,* finds that authority for the poet's work follows from the poem's sincerity, authenticity, and verifiability in a community of lives. The contemporary abuses which follow from this direction are many, among them the schooling of poets and critics, the socialization of art, and a schism between imaginative writers and critical theorists.

Because the direction of James Wright's poetry is confessional, his readers must determine to what extent he shaped art and to what extent he published raw data. In any such determination there is one problem: how may any of us know, short of biographical histories appended to the poems or of private knowledge, to what degree the poet has confessed and to what degree he has fabricated? What matters is the same thing we ask of fiction, the character of empirical truth and the fullness, complexity, and significance of character given to us as *real* in the poems. I mean here what history evidences as real.

With *Saint Judas* Wright began the invention of himself, his place, and of a poetry that would dramatize the life he had known, the American promise and the American nightmare. He began to feel that what he wrote and the way he wrote were historical lies. He wanted truth in his life and life in his poems. His poems underwent lunar changes and more. His titles pointed at guilt and innocence, purity and impurity; he called one poem "The Morality of Poetry," which meant, he said later, only that to write well is a moral act. Speaking of shame and humiliation, of revelation and accusation, Wright was a poet passing through learned abstractions toward finite places and things, what he called "secrets," that might constitute and define the individual life apart from and yet within a community. In "At the Executed Murderer's Grave," Wright believed that

"We are nothing but a man." This theme, Donne's and Coleridge's, of obligation and responsibility to man and being, which displaces the modernist obligation only to art, welled up. Wright had begun to allow his Ohio mythology to gleam forth from the details of his life, to allow his life to shape what was both immediately, verifiably true and also historically, mythically accurate. Here is the poem's first stanza:

> My name is James A. Wright, and I was born
> Twenty-five miles from this infected grave,
> In Martins Ferry, Ohio, where one slave
> To Hazel-Atlas Glass became my father.
> He tried to teach me kindness. I return
> Only in memory now, aloof, unhurried,
> To dead Ohio, where I might lie buried,
> Had I not run away before my time.
> Ohio caught George Doty. Clean as lime,
> His skull rots empty here. Dying's the best
> Of all the arts men learn in a dead place.
> I walked here once. I made my loud display,
> Leaning for language on a dead man's voice.
> Now sick of lies, I turn to face the past.
> I add my easy grievance to the rest:

Sylvia Plath and others would join Wright in portraying art as the instructor of how to die. Wright's employment of biographical details which are verifiable, the confessional element, was obvious and demonstrated the poetry of personality. However, the syntactical skill and suppleness, the suspensions and juxtapositions, the rigorous cadence and tight rhymes drove against the poem's spontaneity. Wright created a character in whom we could place trust, a mature and sympathetic and ironic voice. He wrote and published three versions of the poem as he worked it toward the illusion of veracity and away from the dead voices of the past. In "Three Stanzas from Goethe," included in his third book, *The Branch Will Not Break* (1963), Wright said "He kills his own life, / The precious secret." Wright's lunar changes and those of his contemporaries were directed at discovering, assembling, and giving cohesive authority to their secret lives. It is not difficult to see that the poets were regarding poetry as more nearly inspired than confessional. Their poet, logically, was an extension of the romantic corrective agent, though an agent virtually without power because their secret lives remained too often *merely* personal. Hence Wright could say in "At the Executed Murderer's Grave," in version three and with self-derision, "I croon my tears at fifty cents per line."

Wright's lunar changes did not happen in a vacuum. The contemporary movement toward personality is a romantic impulse, though it is an impulse finally as characteristic of modernism as of nineteenth-century art, with perhaps a renewed emphasis on a naked style capable of expressing experience in a world which had overnight hurtled into the space age. Of course Sputnik is only an image for a world spinning geometrically faster from its Cartesian birth. The critic George Steiner has suggested that poetry is anachronistic when men operate gas chambers by day and play Mozart by night. Pastoral visions and melodious verses were, in the new age, as unreal as bogeymen, and what life was there in seamless artifacts? Poetry, it seemed, was beyond passion, rather than made of passion. The contemporary poets responded by beginning to write what Donald Hall described as "the poetry of a man in the world, responding to what he sees: with disgust, with pleasure, in rant and in meditation."[2] If the result was art it would be the art of personal experience from which might rise a forged self, an empirical wisdom, a more tested vision of the real. The choice is, in retrospect, clear: the art about nothing at all or the life-roughened poem. Later there would be the third alternative of a neo-Emersonian nature poetry backed by quasi-scientific anthropological and psychological theorizing. As Louis Simpson said, "There is a great difference, however, between words that point to things and words that point to themselves."[3] And James Dickey had said in *The Suspect in Poetry*, published by Wright's friend Robert Bly in 1964, that "The secret does not, of course, reside in a complete originality, which does not and could not exist. It dwells, rather, in the development of personality, with its unique weight of experience and memory, as a writing instrument, and in the ability to give literary influence a new dimension which has the quality of this personality as informing principle."[4] From within and from without, James Wright was under pressure to bring his life, or an invented life, forth in his poetry.

Following the publication of *Saint Judas*, Wright wrote a letter to his publisher in which he said he would not do that kind of poetry

again. His third book, *The Branch Will Not Break*, showed radical
stylistic changes but not a complete break with the past. How could
there be, short of a conversion experience which alters the whole
man? He had undergone no conversion. The changes in Wright are
only the predictable steps taken by literary history away from modernist orthodoxy, and literary history is only what writers do. In general, the change is from a dispassionate, ironic, closed-form poetry
to Hall's poem in the world, to open form as it had been appearing to
Wright and others through non-English models. The usual argument
is that Wright was transformed by the influence of Robert Bly and
through readings outside of the Anglo-American tradition of poetry.
While this is a valid argument, we might be reminded that Wright
no more abandoned his native traditions in poetry than he abandoned his Ohio Valley.

Nevertheless, Wright's poetry was now marked by a turn toward a
private vision generally characterized by a juxtaposition of vivid and
disparate images, an abjuring of narrative or linear progression in
favor of an elliptical and spatial movement, and an economy of ad-
jective, adverb, or qualifying phrase, all of which produced a resonance from the particular as it was baldly felt. William Carlos Williams had said "no ideas but in things," but he had not said *no ideas*.
Wright did not abandon thought or thing in his new poems; he put
them in a different balance. If critics did not know quite what he was
doing, he did. In 1975 he published a poem to say so:

"Cold Summer Sun, Be with Me Soon"

I wanted to write something that you could understand, as
    Dr. Williams said.
So naturally the God damned kitchen light bulb burned out
    just as it got dark outside.
Here I am, sitting at day break, which is of course gray.
It is raining.
You haven't come out yet.
And neither have I.
Where does that leave me?
Where does that leave you?
Where are the God damned new light bulbs in this strange
    house?
Oh, come on out, for God's sake.
I can't write a damned thing, which was all I wanted to do.

And all I wanted to do was write something that you could
   understand.
Just as Dr. Williams said.
For his own good.[5]

The critics called Wright a surrealist and an imagist. He thought
himself neither. In time we are going to get what academics call the
definitive examination of what Wright was. We may get one after another and we may actually learn something about his lunar
changes—but it will be a small something. Critics are not very good
at understanding something any poet knows, which is that he contains multitudes because he lives by the imagination. Wright was
more and less than any label. Nevertheless he created a visible character, a personality, and a coherent art in which his individual poems
function as pieces of a mosaic.

In 1971 Wright published his *Collected Poems*, for which he was
awarded the Pulitzer Prize. It contained, in addition to most of his
previous work and a section of translations, thirty-one new poems
under the title "New Poems." This work showed Wright had come
far from his early conventional poetry, but it also showed that he had
moved away from the dream and nightmare image poems of his middle career. There was a renewed interest in narrative, or at least nar-
rativelike, poems. He did not abandon rhetoric or image, private or
public consciousness, screech or song, but he recombined these elements with an increasingly colloquial diction and an abruptly mod-
ulating tone. He tried to speak forcefully and plainly within the con-
straints of poetry, a poetry now identified with loosened rhythms,
circling syntax, repetitions of image and phrase, anecdotes daringly
dramatized and punctuated by authorial intrusion. In other words,
he tried to stretch his expectations for and his accomplishments in
poetry and he stepped even closer to the personal: he demanded the
right to speak not as persona or mask but as himself, a man in the
midst of chaotic experience who means to achieve a cohesive view
of the real. He wrote "We are men. / We are capable of anything."
Like Polonius's words to Laertes, that he should be true to himself,
Wright's words cut two ways. The foundation of Wright's vision of
man being, as he said, that most of us are selfish sons of bitches, he
still believed that no one was wholly without the evidence of hope
and possibility. Wright was, we should remind ourselves, making
these poems in an era of terrible racial struggles, of apparent social

fragmentation, and of the daily news delivered icily in body counts. Yet Wright's testimony was finally quite clear: life is good. Part of the tragic wisdom of Wright's poetry is the knowledge that men were never better, nor are they likely ever to improve. Therefore human history is the history of a man, a history not significantly altered by time, place, or circumstance. Grim as that history may be, it remained a promise of change.

Wright's awareness of the American dream of possibility, a dream which subsumes all other dreams, led him to rant and sing of kinsmen, waste, violence, betrayal, destruction, and love. He had written "Now sick of lies, I turn to face the past." But where was it? He seems to have felt he could not turn far enough. The past had been, in his poems anyway, mostly a style of writing for another James Wright. There was in "New Poems" and subsequently in *Two Citizens* (1974) a more raggedly personal style than ever. And in *Two Citizens*, which he came to reject, there was an open argument with country and kin. A surprising, shocking book, *Two Citizens* has been widely regarded as evidence of Wright's and contemporary poetry's failure to make art, a failure inherent in the exchange of art's distance for personal authority. Certainly there was an extension of Wright's decision not only to front the people, places, and ideas nearest to him but also to front his reader. Time will, of course, judge Wright's choice and the value of his writing but it is not irrelevant that his private argument has been felt by many to possess significant public resonance. What is so surprising about the book is that it surprised so many people, and that they thought it inconsistent with his poetry. It was not, as Wright demonstrates in a passage from a preface he provided in 1963 for a book of poems by Hy Sobiloff:

> The new poet is engaged in a search of his own, and he looks to the masters to provide him with living examples as well as the living precepts of their poetry. He tells us quite explicitly just what it is that he is struggling to learn: how to be true to his own self. And his entire book, particularly the opening sequence called "Speak To Me Child" demonstrates his awareness that the struggle to be true to one's own self involves a good deal more than the rediscovery of a childlike radiance and joy, though that rediscovery may lie at the end of the journey. The journey itself is a dark one. It is neither more nor less than the attempt to locate and reclaim those healing powers within one's

self that are able to provide sufficient courage and literal physical strength for one to confront and to overcome the agonies of
the world which exists beyond the womb and which, for better
or worse, does not happen to be shaped and arranged in a pattern
identical with the orchards and rivers and meadows of that earliest garden, sunken now almost below memory and, whether
wasted or redeemed, lost somewhere between the morning of
dancing animals and the tousled dusk of sorrowing human
faces. Beyond that garden we live a good deal of our death. We
may insist on returning to seek it by trying to ignore the shocks
and miseries that obstruct the only true way back home; and
such evasions really amount to a mere refusal to live. The refusal, the negation, the despair—these are our constant familiar
spirits in the twentieth century. They seem to be always claiming our souls even though we have not always made them any
promise. But there really seems to be a true path back to the lost
paradise, back home to the true child in one's self, back to the
source of healing strength—back to the Kingdom of God which,
we have been told, is within us. If there really is a true path
homeward, then it appears that certain heroic men found it
dark, sometimes yawning with dreadful pits of fire, sometimes
winding and confusing and heavy with the whispers of murderers, backbiters, and the unseemly contorted apparitions of
our own vanity. In short, there have been heroes on the earth,
whose heroism consisted in their willingness to face the facts of
pain; and their motive, as far as I can grasp it, was the motive of
Thoreau: to front life openly and to live it fully, and, if it proved
to be mean, then to get the true and genuine meanness out of it.
For such a hero, the worst kind of death is to discover, when he
comes to die, that he has not lived. And so, out of an abundance
of courage and an eagerness to live—not merely to survive, as
beetles and cynics survive, but to live—the heroes open their
arms to the world as it happens to have been arranged when
they were flung down into it without their suspicion or desire.
Thereupon they discover what Job discovered before them: that
agony and splendor often exist independently of a man's private
whims. Even so, the heroes live on, they throw themselves
headlong and live into the very teeth of the east wind. And apparently it is this decision which suddenly reveals to them certain resources of strength theretofore hidden from their eyes.

Confronting pain, they discover that they are able to confront the rest of creation also, in the magnificence of its first wakening life. They see the world as Thoreau did—as though they were the first men ever to lay eyes on it. And they discover themselves and what they contain. After so many false starts, they are alive at last.[6]

In speaking of Hy Sobiloff, Wright has virtually spoken of himself, and he has identified the fundamental task of modern art: the attempt to give coherence and objectivity to the subjectively real and all but ungraspable design of human experience. He moreover reveals the large and primary figure of his poetry by evoking the ubiquitous wandering exile whose journey is first shadowed in the Christian image of the lost garden and then echoed in the contemporary exile who is technocratically and industrially victimized. Wright has evoked Thoreau's fear of being ground up in the machine, processed, lost, made anonymous and irresponsible. In such a world, Wright knew, we belong not to the dead or the living but to the undead mass. How then shall we live—not merely survive as naturalistic motes—when to live is to see, to be fully conscious, able as Thoreau said to look another man in the face, to recall what the American promise was and to understand what it has come to? From this perspective it seems not surprising but predictable that Wright would woo a poetry of prosaic character and the emotional range of a Dickens, who not incidentally was the subject of James Wright's doctoral dissertation. Wright is devoted to Horace and the demands of Horatian craft, restraint, distance, humility, elegance—but it is the anger, humor, indignation, love, and ragged passion of Dickens in contention with that Horatian ghost that most identifies Wright's late poetry and his citizenship. Those who would examine Wright's poetry must determine how well he manages conflicting impulses and how well he reveals the universal in the temporal and local.

Indeed, few American poets have become so ruthlessly local, regional, and willing to address their arguments so directly as James Wright. In *Two Citizens* the mythical and real Ohio River Valley are one in contrast with Wright's adopted Italy, the country of Horace. His two citizens are himself and his wife Annie, but they are also America and Italy. Wright claims he loves Italy and hates America but he spits and blusters and does not believe that himself. He is like a father betrayed by a child, a loving father, and in "A Poem of Towers," he says "I am becoming one / Of the old men." Neither in memory nor in poetry could he abandon the source of his dreams, though in his life he had abandoned it. He understood that the artist cannot perfect life or art but must settle for a ragged interpenetration of both. When he wrote of his Appalachian country of steel mills, mines, factories, farms, and river towns, Wright showed us the suffering and horror and ugliness that Dickens had known, but after Horace the last words of Wright's *Collected Poems* are "I am so happy." And the last words of *Two Citizens* are "I love you so." Beyond all the false starts, for Wright, there had to be the journey homeward, the inside journey, where there would be courage and, more than courage, joy.

If Wright wrote searing indictments of blast furnaces, politicians, and hatred, if against the ambient purity of the natural world he portrayed men as murdered and murderers, if he seemed to denounce the feelings, convictions, and actions of those who had raised him, we need to remember he was a homeboy. He wrote "The only tongue I can write in / Is my Ohioan." His was art's most ancient ambition: the search for joy. And joy, he knew, was whatever "Ohioan" meant. We hear of nothing so frequently in his poems as the glint of that joy, the flash of happiness, the blossoming of beauty. Everything conspired toward joy. James Wright never thought of himself as a morbid or death-haunted poet, though some of his readers did. He was keenly aware of what it felt like to live in perhaps the most turbulent, confusing, painful, absurd, and incomprehensible time man has ever known. He had survived the hell of the Ohio River Valley and he had experienced firsthand the hell of destruction that the Atomic Age was in Japan. But he believed, as he wrote, that the branch would not break, that a man might lie still enough to watch a blue jay on that branch "abandon himself / To entire delight."

Wright's poems are counters to the fear and the ugliness that attack us all. The world of his poetry is one in which we may discover the heroic in ourselves, the secret life we hadn't known about. His poems tell only one story, the great story of finding the way home, and on the right terms. This is most significantly the American story, but it is not only the American story. We find him again and again standing in the place of darkness where the dream has died. Trying always to assume his individual responsibility for life, he leans like a compass needle toward the true place which is inside but which in the poems is Ohio, the place named after the river that is life itself. Wright knew that "The Winnebago gave you your name, Ohio, / And Ohio means beautiful river." In a poem that is central to Wright's feeling and thought, "Stages on a Journey Westward," we can see his intention even in the first stanza:

> I began in Ohio.
> I still dream of home.
> Near Mansfield, enormous dobbins enter dark barns in
>   autumn,
> Where they can be lazy, where they can munch little apples,
> Or sleep long.
> But by night now, in the bread lines my father
> Prowls, I cannot find him: So far off,
> 1500 miles or so away, and yet
> I can hardly sleep.
> In a blue rag the old man limps to my bed,
> Leading a blind horse
> Of gentleness.
> In 1932, grimy with machinery, he sang me
> A lullaby of a goosegirl.
> Outside the house, the slag heaps waited.

Here Wright mixes the personal particulars of dream, memory, and incumbent history so that the poem begins to speak with the organized power of myth. Refusing the least opaque language, Wright announces the home-journey and the distanced exile in the first two lines. Between the beginning and the end of the stanza all is a dream as, it may be, is life itself. This story is not different, really, from the lament of the Seafarer or the journeys of Huckleberry Finn, Gawain, or Nick Adams. Home is the light and tranquillity and ease and beauty of those horses, who have at least a barn and apples. In contrast the ghostly father, sustained only by obligation and dignity, prowls bread lines. Wright is headed for those slag heaps, as are we all, with scarce comfort but song. This is Wright's portrait of *destiny*, that grand and seemingly dead abstraction which has led to so much suffering. But destiny is the heart's desire and it remains translatable in the poet's dramatization of himself through time and in place. If the home-journey is only to slag heaps then we have wasted our lives, as well as the fabric of creation for which we bear continuing responsibility. That is why the father figure of genesis brings a way of being and a song to the poet dreaming Wright's poem. In language resides knowledge and love—which is responsibility. The language of poetry holds out the possibility of the home-journey as much as it reveals human limits.

In 1976 James Wright published what is commonly referred to as a collection of prose poems, *Moments of the Italian Summer*. He regarded these pieces as prose fragments but he also felt that the distinction between prose and poetry was irrelevant. The pieces, however defined, are reveries, testimonies to a joy immanent in the natural world. His language pours out like water from a broken dam and in contrast we become aware, as he must have, of how fitful and choked his poetry had sometimes been. In retrospect there is an impression that Wright spoke in spite of himself, that there was a joy in him he could not hide. He says in "The Secret of Light" that now "it is all right with me to know that my life is only one life. I feel like the light of the river Adige." Wright had learned that for the writer every life and every piece of creation was no less than the image of all creation. Through the struggle with language and for language, he had been given the gift of life that is the self. He had understood that he had to break down and scrape away the dead expression that sealed him from the living presence of the past in its pastness and from himself, from the actual world in which he and all men walked. Wright had discovered that history was not merely style; it was memory and power as the evidence of and the stimulus to ordinary human responsibility. The living past, shown forth by all that debris of the American promise, cries out to the poet. When he answers it is with poems. When the poems are true and strong they return us all to the dream of possibility. Only when language has turned as vital as life itself could James Wright's, or anyone's, poems be more than impotent against the waiting slag heaps.

Wright felt that, with the publication of *To a Blossoming Pear Tree* in 1977, he had succeeded. But in what? What would it mean to create a self? And how could it be given and to whom? Reinhold Niebuhr has a helpful answer:

Man is the kind of animal who cannot merely live. If he lives at all he is bound to seek the realization of his true nature; and to his true nature belongs his fulfillment in the lives of others. When this desire for self-realization is fully explored it becomes apparent that it is subject to the paradox that the highest form of self-realization is the consequence of self-giving, but that it cannot be the intended consequence without being prematurely limited. Thus the will to live is finally transmuted into its opposite in the sense that only in self-giving can the self be fulfilled.[7]

The hero that James Wright had described in 1963 had only one choice and that was to become himself, to undertake his destiny. He could not merely survive but must live, which is to say he must *know*. The man who has knowledge is paradoxically both gifted and giver. His gift is a vision of the way toward understanding and meaning, or love.

I said earlier that James Wright was not death-haunted. Still, Death is the main character in our fictions. Wright was like most of us God-haunted and self-isolated. This risked the refusal of life and the debasement of creation which he had described. Wright allows us to see that if we choose not to undertake our destiny and choose not to front life, which the choice to employ habitual language and gesture means, we effectively ignore communal responsibility. This is the responsibility each bears to all. It is the responsibility of courage. Wright's courage consists in his willingness to communicate the truth of his feelings at the risk not only of public failure but of failure before his masters, Dickens and Horace. Wright continuously praised writers for telling the truth boldly and powerfully but shied away from such claims for himself. The irony, though it is not very ironic, is that the more he brought his life into his poems, his emotional and ethical and biographical and mythical life, the more truth he made us feel in ourselves, the more courage he gave us. The one story he tells proceeds from the conviction to which he was always faithful, that however tragic life may be there is the beauty of joy within it and we must seek tirelessly for it. Wright speaks of this in the last poem of *To a Blossoming Pear Tree*, a poem in which he is remembering the flow of sewage.

"Beautiful Ohio"

Those old Winnebago men
Knew what they were singing.

All summer long and all alone,
I had found a way
To sit on a railroad tie
Above the sewer main.
It spilled a shining waterfall out of a pipe
Somebody had gouged through the slanted earth.
Sixteen thousand and five hundred more or less people
In Martins Ferry, my home, my native country,
Quickened the river
With the speed of light.
And the light caught there
The solid speed of that waterfall.
I know what we call it
Most of the time.
But I have my own song for it,
And sometimes, even today,
I call it beauty.

There are many ways to experience and value a poet, especially a poet as various, synthetic, and aggressive as James Wright. The essays included here can not and do not pretend to exhaust those ways. This is not, in fact, a book of scholarship so much as it is a book of responses, beginnings of responses, and a book written primarily by poets.[8] They are not accountable for what I have said in introducing Wright and I do not doubt they would be the first to offer alternative readings. That is as it should be. But I have no doubt that they also hope their remarks will draw readers to a renewed engagement with James Wright's poems, for that is where the true pleasure and beauty remains. Such pleasure and such beauty is, I think, what James Wright had in mind when he cited Samuel Johnson on the value of poetry. Wright would, I am convinced, have us remember Johnson's words when we are reading for or commenting on what Wright called the pure, clear word of poetry.

Nothing can please many or please long but just representations of general nature. Particular manners can be known to few, and few only can judge how nearly they are copied. The irregular combinations of fanciful invention may delight a while by that novelty, of which the common satiety of life sends us all in quest, but the pleasures of sudden wonder are soon exhausted and the mind can only repose on the stability of truth.

1. Donald Hall, *Contemporary American Poetry*, 2d ed. (New York: Penguin Books, 1972), p. 28.
2. Hall, p. 30.
3. Louis Simpson, *A Revolution in Taste* (New York: Macmillan, 1978), p. xvii.
4. James Dickey, *The Suspect in Poetry* (Marshall, Minn.: Sixties Press, 1964), pp. 55–56.
5. James Wright, "Cold Summer Sun, Be with Me Soon," *Paris Review*, no. 62 (Summer 1975), p. 64.
6. James Wright, "The Quest for the Child Within: Introduction," *Breathing of First Things*, by Hy Sobiloff (New York: Dial Press, 1963), pp. xxii–xxiii.
7. Reinhold Niebuhr, *The Children of Light and the Children of Darkness* (New York: Charles Scribner's Sons, 1945), p. 77.
8. All of the essays printed here were published before James Wright's death. Many of the writers have expressed concern about the tense, phrasing, or style of their essays in light of that fact. It has seemed proper to print the essays as they were written and published. They are, after all, responses to the life in James Wright's poems.

The Pure Clear Word

James Wright: The Pure Clear Word, an Interview

DAVE SMITH

Q. *Because you have written much about the landscape, culture, and activities of your youth, we would like to begin with some biographical questions. Did you play high school football?*

I didn't play on the high school team. I played a lot of football on a sort of semipro team. There was a lot of that in the Ohio River Valley, where I grew up. During the thirties and forties football was a very important activity in that community, all the way from Pittsburgh to Cincinnati. It was important in a way, I suppose, that it is still important to many communities in the United States. It is very difficult to say this, but I think you will know what I mean. The fall was a time when certain things began again. In nature this is the time, presumably, when things come to fruition, and it's the beginning of the end. But for people, after the long hot summer, certainly for children at school, this was a beginning again. I always felt that way myself. I loved to go back to school and it seemed to me that this was a kind of beginning with hope in it. The football season, then, was very intensely a communal activity, a communal occasion. Teams from the various towns along the Ohio River and back a little from the Ohio River met and provided a point of focus in which the members of the distinct communities would see one another. Sometimes this meeting, this confrontation with the ritualized, formalized violence of those football teams, would inspire a peculiar kind of violence in the spectators too. The game itself is formal and graceful, but people do sometimes behave very anarchically in the stands.

Q. *Thinking, in this context, of your poem "Autumn Begins in Martins Ferry, Ohio" do you mean to protest those games or are you pointing toward certain positive qualities which may emerge from such rituals?*

I think that there were positive qualities. Those games were occasions for the expression of physical grace. I still feel that any sport which is well played has a terrific aesthetic appeal. In high school I devoted most of my activities to track, and I still love track. I should say about football back in the Ohio Valley—Martins Ferry, Shadyside, and Bellaire, Ohio—that in the years when I was growing up there were some truly remarkable athletes. Lou Groza was on my high school team, for example, and he became one of the great place-kickers among the pros, playing for the Cleveland Browns. That was the quality of sport in that valley. This has some other significance. In my home town, Martins Ferry, Ohio, people were quite strikingly separated from each other along class lines. It is difficult to talk about class in America because we have the powerful myth of the common man, the myth of the absence of any class distinction. This troubled Henry James. Some later novelists who couldn't write as well as James, like James Jones, were able to deal in their novels with class issues and all the terrific drama that can rise from class confrontations by placing their characters in the army. What a startling experience it is to be a young American conditioned, to a certain extent, to believe we have no class distinctions in American society, then suddenly to get into the army and realize, if you are an enlisted man, that an officer, even a second lieutenant, for all practical purposes and down to the smallest detail, is regarded—and you regard him—as almost a distinct species. Even if, as in some cases during the Vietnam War, officers felt certain loyalties toward enlisted men, I'll bet there was something condescending about them. Officers aren't very democratic. You can find extreme instances of that in American life. The person who is born to privilege or who somehow has managed in his particular community to have attained to a position of privilege is often trying to show a common touch he does not really have. One of the most astonishing and, to me, fascinating examples of this is to be found in a photograph that appeared in a newspaper during the 1960 presidential election campaign. Henry Cabot Lodge, who was Nixon's running mate, was visiting Coney Island. Norman Mailer wonderfully said of him that probably no one had ever suggested to Lodge that he was not necessarily superb. Lodge knew that he was superb, but he had to contend with the fact

4

of electoral politics in the United States. There he stood at Coney Island and his beautifully pressed white shirt had the sleeves rolled up. He wasn't wearing a necktie. Hundreds of people were standing around him and staring with great interest. He had a hot dog in his hand and he stared at it. The expression on his face revealed profound conflict, the sort of thing that Jane Austen would love. I can't think of any other way to say it: he looked at that hot dog as if it were an obscene object which he *had* to eat.

Q. *In some respects it seems you still think of Martins Ferry, Ohio, as your town. Could you speak further about that?*

I have some places I feel especially devoted to. In a way some of them are in Europe, some in the United States. I have a peculiar kind of devotion to Martins Ferry, although I haven't gone back there in at least twenty-five years. I still have a brother there and I have friends from childhood who are still in the Ohio River Valley. I feel that I am stuck with it. It is my place, after all. My feelings about it are complicated. People in that place have gotten angry with me for things I've written. And I have always, when I have heard from people directly, written to them and insisted that I was simply trying to write about some times. I haven't always written about Martins Ferry but I have tried sometimes to write about the life that I knew.

Q. *What might a sense of place mean to a writer?*

D. H. Lawrence has a very beautiful essay about "The Spirit of Place." He is talking in particular of American places but I think that what he says is true of all places. There is a spirit of place. Virgil was aware of this. I think that he uses the word *imago*, which isn't simply image but is also presence. We still speak of the genius of a place. I believe James Dickey, in a wonderful poem of his which is plainly the idea for his novel *Deliverance*, speaks of a man who appears, a country person, a redneck I guess you'd call him, by the side of the Coosawattee River; he suddenly appears when Dickey and some friends in their canoes have got into some trouble. One has hurt himself, I think. They come over to the bank of the river and the man appears there. Dickey calls him the presiding genius of the place. There is such a genius of place, a presence, and because there is, people's feelings accumulate about it. You can share in that feeling when you become aware of particular historical events and the significance of monuments and so on.

The American Indians, the Sioux, had such a sense of place. Fred Manfred, a wonderful midwestern novelist, pointed this out to me, that the Sioux and other Indians as well had a sense that certain areas were holy ground. He said that more than once in writing his novels and in wandering around and doing research the way he does, not just reading old books but trying to get the feel of places he would write about, he realized that there was something special about certain areas of southern Minnesota. He later discovered the Indians considered it sacred ground. I think that this is, for some writers, an important way of participating in the life around them. I'm not saying that the value of poetry depends on writing about a place or not writing about a place, only that there is a kind of poetry which is a poetry of place. It appeals to me very much. There are so many different ways that language can come alive or be brought alive that it is silly to limit the kinds of poetry there could be. I think it is enough to say that there is, in our lives, a genius of place and so, appropriately, we sometimes value a poetry of place.

This suggests an interesting thing about poetry during the last fifteen or twenty years in the United States; leaving aside the effectiveness of it or the ultimate value of it, nevertheless there has been a willingness on the part of a great many writers, really, to deal with this fact of place. Earlier, we didn't see this so much, being an English-speaking culture which proceeded from Europe. This country has all sorts of places still to be discovered in it. With this idea has come the realization that, after all, anything can be the location of a poem as long as the poet is willing to approach that location with the appropriate reverence. Even very ugly places.

My feeling about the Ohio Valley is, again, complicated. I sometimes feel a certain nostalgia about the place. At the same time I realize that as my friend Tom Hodge, now a surgeon in California, wrote to me a few years ago our problem when we were boys in Martins Ferry, Ohio, in the industrial area enclosed by the foothills of the Appalachians on both sides, near that big river, was to get out. It has become plain to me that football helped many people to get out. And many of these people come from desperately poor families.

Martins Ferry, which is right across the Ohio River from Wheeling, West Virginia, is extraordinarily interesting in another respect. Ohio was a free state and this figures in *The Adventures of Huckleberry Finn*. Jim, as he and Huck go down the river, understands per-

6

fectly well that if only he can reach Cairo, Illinois, then he can go up the Ohio and find freedom. The Underground Railway went through the free state of Ohio. But Ohio is southern at the same time that it is northern, intensely so. What could be more intense than what happened in my own family background? One of my great-uncles fought for the Union and one fought for the Confederacy, members of the same family. I wrote about that in a poem called "A Centenary Ode: Inscribed to Little Crow, Leader of the Sioux Rebellion in Minnesota, 1862." My great-uncle Paddy Beck fought for the Confederacy. He got buried in the Old Soldier's Home in Tiffin, Ohio. He even managed to get the people, when he died, to give him a nice clean new uniform, which was a Union uniform.

Ohio is also eastern and western. I sometimes ask my students in New York how many of them have traveled across the United States. Most have grown up in New York and know the East Coast. Or some of them may have flown to California and back. I tell them they can't get a sense of how incredibly huge and varied this country is by flying; I tell them that after they graduate they might travel by bus straight across the United States, and stop off sometimes. I tell them to go and see what it is like to have a cup of coffee in Zanesville, Ohio. It is as far from New York to Pittsburgh as it is from Paris to Vienna, but when you've reached Pittsburgh you're not really yet at the beginning of the Middle West. And the Middle West is, itself, enormous. You have to go to the other side of Minnesota to start to get a hint of what the western United States is like. Then you go into the huge mountain region and on the other side of that is a vastness. Ohio is eastern and western while it is also northern and southern.

Martins Ferry, my particular town, has among its 16,000 people a Greek community, a Hungarian community, a Polish community, a Welsh community, a Black community, and a community of WASPs. All of these are distinct communities in one small town. Remarkable. They are communities in the sense that, for Europeans as well as WASP Americans, the family traditions, the religious traditions, and traditions of manners were maintained quite vividly. I remember that we had a May Day celebration. I was in the fifth grade and each grade, I guess, of all the five grade schools in town was to do a certain dance. I think my fifth grade learned how to do a Hungarian dance. I remember that my teacher told our class one day that when we all met down on the football field we would dance with our opposite numbers in the same grades from the other schools. She said that we must not feel bad that our costumes, which our mothers had carefully made up of crepe paper, were not as nice as the costumes worn by the kids from the northern part of town—because their parents had brought their costumes from Hungary. It turned out to be true. Their costumes were silk and they were gorgeous. I got so excited that May Day that I puked. It was beautiful.

Q. *Did you begin writing as a young man?*

I started to write when I was about eleven years old. My friend Tom Hodge was a year younger than I was and he belonged to a family that was fairly well off. His father was a businessman. My father was a factory worker. A friend of Tom's family, who was a minister, had gone to the war. Tom got access to this man's books and he gave me a book of poems by James Whitcomb Riley and also the complete poems of Byron. Hell, I'd never heard of either of them. I got very excited about Byron and I wrote a play in verse. I don't know what ever happened to that.

Q. *What did you do after high school?*

I spent two years in the army. I went in just after the war ended, and I moved around a lot in the army. I had never been out of the Ohio Valley. I went first to Fort Lewis, Washington. Then I was sent to Engineers' School at Fort Belvoir, Virginia. From Fort Belvoir I was sent overseas and was in the occupation army in Japan.

Q. *Does Japan influence your poems?*

Let me show you something. [Mr. Wright went to his bookshelf and pulled down a neatly wrapped package which, when he had carefully unwrapped it, was a book of his poems translated into Japanese.] I've been in correspondence with Professor Toshitada Iketani. He made this selection of my poems a few years ago. I've sent my last two books to him and he tells me he will do a selection from those. We were in the Japanese and the American armies at about the same time. Professor Iketani wrote to me several times before he could bring himself to admit that he had done this. Of course, I asked to see it and I am delighted with it. We were both enlisted men and we came, I suppose, within a few months of confronting one another. It could have happened. We might have tried to kill each other. I have been devoted to Japanese literature ever since I was in Japan. It seems to me there are several ways that a genuine influence can work. I have never, so far as I recall, referred in my printed writings to my experience in Japan as such. I have written about it. The Japanese spirit and the tradition of the poetry, I think, has influenced me from time to time—in the effort the Japanese writers make to get rid of the clutter of language, to conceive of a poem as something which, with the greatest modesty, is brought up close to its subject so that it can be suggestive and evocative. Japan was a revelation to me.

Q. *Upon leaving military service you enrolled in Kenyon College. Did you do so because of John Crowe Ransom and Kenyon's literary tradition?*

I had never heard of Kenyon College. It dawned on me while I was in the army in Japan, and I don't know why it didn't happen before, that I might be able to go to college. I had the GI Bill available to me. I applied to several schools in Ohio and they all said no except Kenyon College. So I went there. I did not know of John Crowe Ransom or any literary tradition. It was just a college. I think that with the family I came from, a very good people, there was no tradition of education in the family. I had one distant cousin who had gone to college but except for him no one else. My mother had to leave school when she was in the sixth grade, my father had to leave when he was in the eighth grade. He went into the factory when he was fourteen and my mother went to work in a laundry. All of my relatives were working people. Back in the thirties I would have called them working class. My older brother Ted, who is now a photographer in Zanesville, Ohio, was except for that distant cousin actually the first one of us who ever graduated from high school.

Q. *You speak with such respect for the "working class" that we wonder if there is a danger of sentimentalizing workers, a danger some have felt apparent in contemporary American poetry.*

I don't think that human sons of bitches are limited to this or that social class. I'm antipastoral. I've worked on farms and I would never work on another one. I've got up at four o'clock in the morning and shoveled the cow manure out of the barn and bailed away the horse urine. The hell with it. I worked for two nights in the factory my father had worked in, and I quit. I thought it was too much for me to handle. I couldn't live that kind of life. It was just as hard for my father. Before that summer was over I got a job in another factory elsewhere in Ohio, the old Mount Vernon, Ohio, Bridge Company. We chipped paint off girders and painted them with red lead. Do you know Robert Hayden's poem about his father?

"Those Winter Sundays"

Sundays too my father got up early
and put his clothes on in the blueblack cold,
then with cracked hands that ached
from labor in the weekday weather made
banked fires blaze. No one ever thanked him.

I'd wake and hear the cold splintering, breaking.
When the rooms were warm, he'd call,
and slowly I would rise and dress,
fearing the chronic angers of that house.

Speaking indifferently to him,
who had driven out the cold
and polished my good shoes as well.
What did I know, what did I know
of love's austere and lonely offices?

The word "offices" is the great word here. *Office*, they say in French. It is a religious service after dark. Its formality, its combination of distance and immediacy, is appropriate. In my experience uneducated people and people who are driven by brute circumstance to work terribly hard for a living, the living of their families, are very big on formality.

Q. *Would you describe your experience at Kenyon College? Were there other writers there with you?*

Well, it was exciting. There were only about 450 students in the school. They flunked out about half the freshman class every semester. They shocked us. We all went there, of course, thinking we were pretty smart and we found that they were going to show us pretty quickly that we were not all that smart. We had pretty vital relations with one another. The classes were exciting. I had to take freshman

English; I couldn't get exempted from it, but it was a splendid course. We read *Gulliver's Travels*, and essays by Matthew Arnold and Carlyle and Bacon. They wanted us to learn how to write critical essays, not just themes. Critical essays. I then took Ransom's course called "Poetic Analysis" and he was a splendid teacher, a great teacher. Anthony Hecht is writing an essay about Ransom as a teacher and it ought to be very fine. Tony had left before I got to Kenyon. He had been an instructor there. Once when I was an undergraduate I wrote him a letter because of a superb poem of his that had appeared in the undergraduate literary magazine. I don't think he has ever reprinted that marvelous poem in any of his books. It was an elegy for the builders of European cathedrals. Tony had been in combat in Europe and he saw many of those things he loved being blown up. His brother Roger was there when I was and is still, I suppose, as close a friend as I have. There was also a very gifted man named Jay Gellens. I don't know what has happened to him. George Lanning, the novelist, was there. Edgar Doctorow was there. E. L. Doctorow, who became a good novelist. And during my last year Robert Mezey came. He was just sixteen years old then. The first time I saw him I had been working very hard on a paper and he was there for prefreshman week in the spring. He was sitting with a friend in the student lounge, which was in the basement of the building where we lived. I remember throwing back the French doors and staring straight at Mezey. I didn't know who he was. Then I shouted, "I am a transparent eyeball." And I slammed the doors. That line from Emerson stuck in everybody's craw back at Kenyon. We were always trying to figure out what Emerson meant by that. Jarrell and Lowell, of course, had been at Kenyon earlier.

Q. *How do you now value Ransom's poetry?*

His poetry, as the years go by, seems to me to be finer than I had realized. I always liked it. Ransom is in slightly bad odor right now, partly because he writes the so-called square poem: you can glance at his poems on the page and see that they scan. If you look a little closer, unless you happen to be as tone-deaf as some of our reviewers apparently are—I don't say that in malice, I say it as a kind of curiosity, you can hear that his poems rhyme. Furthermore, Ransom plainly shows in his poems that he is willing to let his conscious intelligence operate in the poems and this is very much out of fashion. It's ridiculous that it should be out of fashion. It is part of the terribly self-flattering, self-indulging anarchic spirit of our times, the spirit of confusion.

Q. *What do you feel that you learned from Ransom?*

I think it was the ideal, what elsewhere I've called the Horatian ideal, the attempt finally to write a poem that will be put together so carefully that it does produce a single unifying effect. I still conceive of a poem as being a thing which one can make rather than as a matter of direct expression. It is true that I have written and published a good many poems that do manage to be nothing except direct expression of my own feelings about this and that. I regard those poems as failures. The fact that I've written them and published some just means that I ought not to have published them.

Ransom was a beautiful teacher because he was a beautiful reader of poetry. I'm not talking about the sound of his voice, although the sound of his voice was charming and students loved him. We parodied him endlessly. We imitated his voice, as in one old parody which I participated in. I'm still proud of the four lines we achieved, although there was a committee of five or six people in on it. Here it is:

"Balls on Joan Whiteside's Stogie"

There was such smoke in our little buggy
and such a tightness in our car stall—
is it any wonder her brown stogie
asphyxiates us all?

I went back to see Ransom when he was eighty-two years old. I finally told him this parody and he said he *knew* that. He knew all the gags. When I say he was a good reader, I mean he understood that humility is a necessary intellectual virtue, leaving its moral virtue aside. He tried to instill in us the recognition of how necessary it is to pay humble attention to what an author is trying to say. And behind that was his assumption about himself, that the first thought that popped into his mind was not necessarily coeval and coextensive with the mind of God. In other words, in Ortega's sense, Ransom was a noble man, as distinguished from a barbarian. He was very acute. He could be extremely funny. His genuine humility had quite a striking effect on students, in our occasional arrogance. He would let us undermine ourselves and he read poems with us and would take a long time reading them. It was marvellous because he could hear things in the poems that were there, in short.

Q. *Did you subsequently go to the University of Washington to study with Theodore Roethke?*

After I finished at Kenyon College I had a Fulbright Scholarship to the University of Vienna and I still had not decided whether I should go to graduate school. During the year I was in Vienna I did decide, finally, on something that I had thought a good deal about, that I wanted to be a teacher. Once I had decided to become a teacher, it seemed to me a serious matter to do graduate work and get a graduate degree. I was led to the University of Washington by a friend, Herbert Lindenberger. I knew practically nothing about Roethke. I didn't know his work. I had been at Kenyon College from 1948 to 1952. Roethke had not published very much at this time. I took one course from Roethke at the University of Washington, and only one course, because he got sick after that first semester and because I had literature courses to take. That was, however, a course in writing poetry. A course with Roethke was a course in very, very detailed and strenuous critical reading. Here was an assignment: he wanted us to go to the library and find ten or maybe even twenty iambic trimeter lines that had a caesura after the first syllable. He made us do that. For example, Robert Bridges's "Die, song, die like a breath." We tried. Remember that this was back in the 1950s and, though the people in that generation have been accused of being quietists, in any case it did not occur to us that our own immediate accidental opinions of things were not necessarily the everlasting truth. So, we knew Roethke was a very fine man, an intelligent and learned man, and when he asked us to do something we would do it. He was not trying to violate our psyches or something.

Of course, Roethke was only a part of my education at the University of Washington. I think that the most exciting and the most useful courses I took were medieval literature courses with David Fowler. I studied Chaucer with him; also the Pearl Poet and *Sir Gawain*. A few graduate students even persuaded him to give us a course in Langland and his contemporaries, so we read some Middle English in a dialect different from Chaucer's. Also I had a superb course from Maynard Mack, the eighteenth-century scholar from Yale, who came there and gave a course in Augustan literature. I still correspond with him. He was a great teacher. I retain a fondness for medieval literature though I haven't pursued it very much. I became very interested in the history of the English novel and it is my main academic subject. At Hunter College I'm teaching a course in the eighteenth-century novel and Cervantes's effect on it. I've given courses in Dickens, Hardy, even whole courses in the nineteenth-century novel.

Q. *You have been both an ardent supporter and a harsh critic of academic life, at least a critic of some of its attitudes. Could you discuss what kinds of approaches your teaching takes?*

I try to present to my students some of the necessary questions and problems of philosophical and historical background. For example, I have found that in presenting *Don Quixote* to my students it has been very important for them and for me to devote several class periods to a discussion of the philosophical terms materialism, idealism, the credibility of hypotheses and scientific method, logical positivism, and so on. I also occasionally teach a course called "Poetics, the Poetic Tradition." This is an attempt to introduce students to some of the problems and techniques of traditional poetry and when we have read individual poems it has been necessary and very useful, helpful to us all I think, for me to offer some historical background. For example, consider a poem I think is a great and important poem by Marvell, the "Horatian Ode on Cromwell's Return to Ireland." It is not possible to understand what is going on in that poem without some awareness of the political and social problems which obtain in England from the reign of Elizabeth through Charles II. That's a very complicated story, one of the most exciting. And it is one of the richest historical periods for the study of literature. On the one side we have Cromwell, who Marvell in his very intelligent poem characterizes so beautifully, and on the other side we have Charles I. Marvell shows that Charles I, in spite of his reputation as a frivolous playboy, actually had a profound understanding of power, the nature of political power and its uses, which even resembles that of Queen Elizabeth herself.

In the midst of this we sometimes read Robert Herrick and it is important to point out that Herrick was a Royalist who disappeared at one point in his life for thirteen years. Amazingly, in this period which historians as well as literary scholars have studied in such detail, nobody knows what happened to Robert Herrick for thirteen years. Then he emerges with his big book of poems—"I fain would kiss the calf of Julia's leg / Which is as white and hairless as an egg"—and at the end of his noble numbers he says, "Upon his gravestone these words he'd have placed / His muse was jocund but his life was chaste." He must have known we would say, no, no. Anybody but a monster would hope that he scored.

Well, this is the way I approach teaching. Of course we try to come down and see how particular works are constructed. I am also interested at least in the history of the novel with the meaning and the function of the particular language that the individual novelist uses. It is highly important. E. M. Forster says that there is a kind of novelist who can sing and a kind that can't. That doesn't mean that one is necessarily better than the other. George Eliot doesn't sing but Emily Bronte does. And her singing in that prose, sometimes, is artistically and intellectually very important. Say in *Wuthering Heights*. And the flat regular prose of Daniel Defoe is designed to give the texture, substance really, of factuality in the world that he presents. He means for us to forget that he is making the whole thing up. We now have the weird and interesting fact that Defoe is called matter of fact and prosaic by some very prosaic critics whereas Virginia Woolf regards him as a person of great poetic imagination. I think he is.

Q. *Does Dickens remain special to you?*

Yes, he does. I did my doctoral dissertation on Dickens. He has an almost insane poetic imagination, a power of invention, and an enormous intelligence. He is a compulsive writer and it would be silly to say he wrote too much; if he had not written so much he would not be Dickens. He can be very, very precise. But it isn't only Dickens who is special to me. It is also the prose of other novelists and the prose of essayists. I read often for enjoyment and some of my favorite writers, modern and otherwise, are themselves expository essayists. One of my very favorites, a writer I read for great pleasure, is H. L. Mencken. I have been reading with great pleasure the latest book of essays by Diana Trilling, called *We Must March My Darlings*. I admire Forster's essays. One of my favorite books, that I read the way some people read poetry, is Forster's *Two Cheers for Democracy*. In fact I think that among all modern writers I enjoy the expository essayist the most.

Q. *Does this reading of prose affect the nature of your poetry?*

I hope it does. What I hope to write is a poetry which is consecutive and clear. Sometimes I have written obscurely and sometimes I have written limply. But in these cases I know I have just written badly. That is not what I was trying to do or hoped to do. A valuable remark of Pound's is that a person who is going to write free verse should be careful not to write bad prose hacked into arbitrary line lengths. It seems to me, as I look around whatever little magazines are sent to me, that we are practically inundated with bad prose hacked into such lines. Eliot, too, argued that poetry has been most vital when it has been closest to good prose and yet has been able somehow to retain its own character. I take it that its own character finally has something to do with rhythm, a regularity of rhythm or a clear variation on regularity.

Q. *During the writing of your first collection of poems,* The Green Wall, *you said in a letter to Roethke that "I work like hell clipping away perhaps one tiny pebble per day from the ten-mile-thick wall of formal and facile 'technique' which I myself erected, and which stands ominously between me and whatever poetry may be in me." Can you comment on your meaning?*

I think that quotation is confused. I would enlarge on it by saying that I was starting to feel then, and I still feel, that the writer's real enemy is his own glibness, his own facility; the writer constantly should try to discover what difficulties there truly are inherent in a subject or in his own language and come to terms with these difficulties. If he does that, then he might be able to discover something in his own mind or in the language which is imaginative. I did not say very clearly what I was trying to think my way toward. What I was trying to suggest, trying to think, trying to realize is just that it is fatally easy to write in an almost automatic way. After you master certain gimmicks, whether in formal verse or in rhyme or in so-called free verse, then it is pretty easy to repeat them. I wrote a piece in my notebook about the purity and the force, really the great strength, of Richard Wilbur. He has always written regular verse and with wonderful purity and a beautiful music and great accuracy and clarity, and with great emotional depth. For a while during the fifties most writers were tending to write in too facile, too glib a way in regular meters and rhyme. Some of us turned away to free verse. Since then I think that whenever one opens a magazine nearly all the poems one sees will be in free verse. More and more they strike me as being just as facile and automatic in their way as the earlier poems had been in other ways. That is, it isn't a solution to one's artistic problems just to stop rhyming.

Here is one of my favorite themes. This is what I call "trite surrealism." The French surrealists, and there are some very good ones, understood that dadaism and surrealism were comic reactions to certain preestablished conventions of rationality in writing. They started to be deliberately irrational. They were able to write good poems when in one way or another they were comic. Americans who have tried to follow the surrealistic way don't get the joke. There are many bad surrealistic poems and there are horrible examples of the most automatic, unimaginable kind of thing. They are straining toward imagination and something new. They are like the Puritans in Dr. Seuss's old pocket book of boners. Some student wrote that the Puritans came to America to worship God as they saw fit and to see that everybody else did the same thing.

This matter of trite surrealism requires critical analysis. In a recent issue of the magazine *Kayak* [no. 51 (Sept. 1979), p. 38] there appears a letter by John Haines. I think he is a thoroughly admirable, serious man, one of the best poets now writing. What he says is so intelligent and important that I want to quote it at length:

> The greatest poetry has always shown abundant evidence of *mind*, of intellect directed toward a felt conclusion. The trouble with surrealism, as with many another modern mode, is that it is partial, a piece of a whole. The best efforts in our time have always been directed toward that whole, whether achieved or not. The liberation of thought and feeling granted to many modern poets through the influence of surrealism has been at its best a means to an end.
>
> One problem in all this, and it hardly needs saying, is the talent we display for trivializing everything, and by a mindless repetition, for turning even the most innovative ideas into cliches. (The trivialization applies as much to the objectivity of Williams and the ideogramic method of Pound as it does to the studied accidentals of surrealism.) It needed no great power of imagination to foresee that when a new poetry began to be written here in the early sixties, it would not be long before its characteristics would be imitated to the point of becoming just another promotional device. What we have seen, I suppose, is the

domestication of Surrealism. At this point, most efforts at surrealist poems strike me as pathetic. The offerings of the unconscious are only the beginning, and whoever takes those shadows for the truth will never see the daylight.

Another thing not brought out is the hidden motive, or hope, (implied anyway in surrealism) of making poetry relevant in the modern world, by claiming for it a significance we are afraid it no longer has. By taking over, in one way or the other, the material and terminology of psychology, by assuming a pseudoscientific approach to structure and meaning—by becoming finally a specialization—poetry would take its rightful place as a serious occupation. Or so, perhaps, the evidence indicates. The poet-interview, the many workshops and conferences, the solemn discussions of technique or "craft," are examples of what I mean by this, and destined perhaps to become the curiosities of an era.

Q. *How do you feel about your early poems?*

I haven't read them for a while. About three years ago I sat down and read my whole *Collected Poems*. Some of them I couldn't remember having written and some of them I didn't understand. It is true that I wrote to my publisher after *Saint Judas* and said I don't know what I am going to do after this but it will be completely different. This comment, and also Robert Bly's essay on my work, has given rise to some sort of assumption that I calculated that I was going to be born again or something, that I would become a completely different person. I think that this is nonsense. There was a good essay by Mark Strand, in *Field* magazine, regarding changes in poetry. He used my work as an example and he said the only difference, really, was that I don't rhyme so often now. I don't think that a person can change very quickly or easily. Well, there is such a thing as a conversion experience surely. William James has written formally about this in *Varieties of Religious Experience*. That change is a reality. Let me say that to change one's kind of poetry would be, in effect, to change one's life. I don't think that one can change one's life simply as an act of will. And I never wanted to. What I had hoped to do from the beginning was to continue to grow in the sense that I might go on discovering for myself new possibilities of writing.

I have written a good many prose pieces now and I did this because

I liked prose and I wanted to express myself that way. I put some prose pieces in my last couple of books and sometimes these have been called poems. They are not poems. They are prose pieces. Now whether they are well written or badly written is another question. I said before, in other connections, that we sometimes have a hard time discussing writing itself in the United States because we are constantly getting bogged down in nitpicking about technical terms. The French can talk about the prose-poem and do so effectively just because they can use a phrase like that and everybody knows that people may disagree with one another about these terms. But everybody in the controversy also knows that the prose-poem is a term of convenience. They know perfectly well that Flaubert wrote prose and that Baudelaire wrote in verse, and was a poet. With this distinction, then, they are free to go on and try new combinations of things. This is what I have always hoped for for myself. The trouble with it all in the United States is that sure as hell somebody's going to say, now which is it, prose or poetry?

Yvor Winters said a valuable thing in this respect. He said, poetry is written in verse whereas prose is written in prose. That is a help because I think it allows us to drop the nitpicking and then go on and try to see what the writing in question is. Then we can try to determine whether or not there is a way to understand it and, finally, to undertake the extremely difficult task of determining whether it is any good or not.

Good in relation to what, we may ask? Literary criticism itself, I think, ought to be as Matthew Arnold said: an effort to see the thing in itself as it really is. He went on to say it ought to be an effort to make reason and the will of God prevail. T. S. Eliot remarked that there was Arnold referring to that joint firm, Reason and the Will of God. Whether or not that particular phrase of Arnold's is useful to us still, he did see that observing the thing itself as it really is is only the first part of the task. The further task is the more dynamic one of trying to determine whether or not the thing itself was worth doing and what effect it can have—how far it is expressive, how far it is communicative, and finally whether it is any good. This requires us, as critics, to try to truly understand whether or not there is such a thing as the good or the bad. What do we mean by that? Can we make it clear? These are terrific and serious tasks for literary criticism.

I said at one point that there can't be a good poetry without a good criticism. I did not mean that there has to be a great body of formal criticism in print. I meant that a person who is writing and reading is going to be able to write better and more truly if he tries to think about language, if he tries to imagine what his own writing is going to look like and smell like and sound like to an intelligent person of good will. These are critical efforts. Or if he tries to determine what relation he has or can have to the authors whom he, himself, genuinely considers to be great and enduring. What do I have to do with Horace? It is a question that I have to ask myself if I am a serious man. Well, I can try to understand what Horace says, many of the things that he says, for example his pieces about the art of poetry. I can try to be true to them in the immediate terms of my own work. He says valuable things. This is not to say that I have ever written anything or could write anything within a thousand miles of Horace's excellence. To know this, and to know as I do know, that the assumption of my equaling Horace, the least thing by Horace, is an illusion—this is a help to me in understanding my own limitations and my possibilities. I am a traditionalist and I think that whatever we have in our lives that matters has to do with our discovering our true relation to the past.

Q. *Can you talk about why you wrote poems about George Doty, a convicted and executed murderer?*

I was preoccupied with that because it startled me for a while, the whole notion of how little we human beings understand one another. I was preoccupied with how, back in Ohio, a taxi driver named George Doty from Bellaire drove a girl out in the country and made a pass at her, which she resisted, so he banged her in the head with a tree branch and killed her. I was convinced that he didn't really know what in the hell was happening. He had stumbled into something evil, a murder he had committed, but I don't think that he understood anything about the legal proceedings. Many people in that community thought he was terribly wicked, but he did not seem to me wicked. He was just a dumb guy who suddenly was thrust into the middle of the problem of evil and he was not able to handle it. I thought it was ridiculous to execute him and, further, I thought that murder is murder whether the state commits it or some stupid, retarded taxi driver. That is what I was trying to say. The epigraph of the second poem, "At the Executed Murderer's Grave," is from Freud. Many people thought the epigraph referred to execution. I was a little calculating about this. It is interesting to do this with critics and reviewers, to say something and see how they will go on rattling about it and will show with every damn word they write that they haven't the faintest idea of what you mean. Freud was not speaking of capital punishment there. It is taken from his book *The Future of an Illusion* and he is referring to the idea we call the Golden Rule. Freud says "Why should we do this? What good is it to us? Above all, how can we do such a thing? How can it possibly be done?" Notice how Freud, who was very precise and careful, is repeating himself compulsively. He's staggered by this idea. Knowing what he knows about human beings, it is a staggering idea to him.

Q. *How do you respond to the assertion that "A Poem about George Doty in the Death House" has an ugly, unfeeling conclusion?*

I can understand that. Some people believe that I was sympathizing with the criminal rather than with the victim. Well, I sympathize with the victim all right. As I have replied at least ten times to people from Martins Ferry who have written to me to protest that poem, I sympathize with the victim. I'm just saying that I sympathize with George Doty, too. I think what annoyed them is somehow that the person who committed this crime ought to be cut off from human fellowship; that is, they believed this and I did not believe it.

In the same sense I believe that *The Adventures of Huckleberry Finn* is a genuinely subversive book. It is subversive not because it uses bad grammar and not because it takes an ornery little boy as its hero; what is subversive about it is that it doesn't say each human being is complex and valuable. It demonstrates in scene after scene, action after action, with absolute finality that the slave Jim is a complex human being with a high moral intelligence. Mark Twain makes that undeniable. And this is unbearable to a person who has to regard somebody as a thing, as property. The idea of slavery still lurks powerfully. The idea that some men are no more than things, the idea that if you give some men bathtubs they will only fill those tubs with coal. This still lurks powerfully in spite of our liberal rhetoric. In recent years everybody in America has taken over liberal rhetoric. But the idea of slavery remains. It is not so much the racists as people who are comfortably off.

This is exactly the appropriateness of Cyra MacFadden's good novel, *The Serial*. She sees that the comic imagination is required to examine the influence of Freud and psychoanalysis in the United

States, an influence which has turned into a rhetoric that Americans have seized upon so that we can tell one another how neurotic we are instead of facing our genuine human tragic problems. Her novel is about life in Marin County, California, and nobody can say or do anything without saying "create your own space" or "build up your karma" and so on. In one scene a child goes into the bathroom and locks itself in and turns on the water and is drowning in the bathtub. They can't get in and the kid is screaming. Instead of doing anything—they've all been divorced about five times through creative divorce—they sit there and talk about creative parenting. They hang loose in their own space.

Q. *Was "At the Executed Murderer's Grave" a watershed poem for you?*

Yes. And it was that in its language too. The previous version of it was very, very overblown and rhetorical. That version had appeared in *Poetry*. When I came to try and put it into *Saint Judas* I was completely dissatisfied with it, so I sent it to Jim Dickey. He and I had had a misunderstanding and a disagreement earlier, followed very rapidly by an exchange of letters. We became good friends and have been so ever since. I sent him the *Poetry* version of the poem. It was a mess, full of mythological and biblical references and so on, very Victorian. He made comments all over it and sent the poem back. I studied his comments in Minneapolis. Then I had to go up to Seattle to defend my Ph.D. dissertation, which I did, and on the way back, on the train, I didn't have his comments with me but I remembered them. I didn't have the poem either. So I sat there and rewrote it without looking at the previous version, from the beginning, and rewrote it as straight and direct and Robinsonian as I could make it. That is the way it came out. It was important to me. I felt as if I had shed something.

Q. *Have you forgotten this [showing a poem to Wright] earlier, first version which was published in* Botteghe Oscure?

"At the Executed Murderer's Grave"

Reflective calm, you tangle, root and bone,
Fang, fist, and skull, that huddle down alone.
Sparrows above him, sneaking like police,
Peck at the lawn, the hedge, the careful trees.

Man's wild blood has no heart to overcome
Vengeance and summer and the lily's bloom.
Henceforth, so long as I myself shall live,
Earth will be torn, the mind be fugitive.
My shadow flees me over mattocked stone:
Father and citizen, I killed this man,
This man who killed another who might kill
Another who might slay another still
Till the tall shadows of mankind are cast
Bodiless on the empty stars at last.
Rage and destruction trouble me, and fade.
The casual flocks of sunbeam round my head
Flutter away to dusk, and I am dark,
Peering between the granites for his mark.
Slow hills away, the milch-cows pause and yawn,
Wondering when day will go, and man be gone:
That one man, angry at the heart's release,
This brutal pastoral, this unholy peace.

Well, I'll be damned. This is still pretty rhetorical. It was a stage. What I would do today would be to just keep that in my notebook. I know Robert Bly feels that the third, finished version that is in *Saint Judas* is very much a failure. I don't think that one is a failure. I think it is clearly what I wanted to say. Robert feels that it is a failure, I believe.

Q. *What good is a poem, finally?*

I don't know. A poem is good because of the pleasure that it provides us. Samuel Johnson argues in his preface to the 1765 Shakespeare that a work endures if it gives pleasure but then, very acutely, he says that there are different kinds of pleasure. Some are more frivolous and occasional. There is nothing wrong with that, except such pleasure wears out. There is a deeper pleasure we can find in trying to see the truth, by which Johnson means to imply something about the tragic complexity of life. Shall I state Johnson's remark? He says it with such force: "Nothing can please many or please long but just representations of general nature. Particular manners can be known to few, and few only can judge how nearly they are copied. The irregular combinations of fanciful invention may delight a while by that novelty, of which the common satiety of life sends us all in quest, but the pleasures of sudden wonder are soon exhausted and the mind can only repose on the stability of truth." Johnson is, of course, as thoroughly aware of the multiplicity of truth as Shakespeare is. But there is a difference between the truth to be found in what T. S. Eliot very brutally calls birth, copulation, and death, and what Johnson means. There is more pleasure, Johnson says, in being able to understand those tragic complexities than there is to be found, say, in concrete poetry. Thom Gunn said the same sort of thing a few years ago while reviewing a book-length poem. He said, "This must be the first full-length *Wasteland* that I have read in a couple of years."

Q. *You have said that when your own work fails it does so because of a lack of clarity. What do you mean by clarity and why is it difficult?*

I would like to write something that would be immediately and prosaically comprehensible to a reasonably intelligent reader. That is all. That is all I mean by being clear, but it is very difficult for me. This is a Horatian idea. It is the attempt to write, as one critic said once of the extraordinarily and beautifully strong writer Katherine Anne Porter, so that "every one of her effects is calculated but they never give the effect of calculation." We read a story like her "Noon Wine" and it is what we call seamless. It is almost impossible to pick that story apart and find her constructing a beginning, middle, and end. When you read the whole thing you do realize, and not just with your feelings but with your intelligence, that what you have just looked at is a living thing. It has a form. She hasn't written in bulk, never in such bulk as, say, Edward Bulwer-Lytton. And yet, her work has a certain largeness about it because it is so alive. I think that she has thought very clearly and carefully about the need to make things clear to a reasonably intelligent reader of good will. As for other kinds of readers, well there are fools in the world, and bastards.

Q. *You said this once: "One thing a person tries to do is to discover the appropriate form for whatever he is saying." What do you mean by* form?

I don't mean form in the abstract. I mean what anyone would mean when he talks about true rhetoric. I mean the proper words in the proper places. That's all. We have mentioned Robert Creeley's idea that form is no more than an extension of content. I think I follow what Creeley is saying and as far as I follow it, I think it is sound. Beyond a certain point, however, it gets confusing and starts to sound vague. It is easiest to talk about such matters when one is dealing with comic poetry because there, as Auden pointed out, the form is predominant and the joke comes out of discovering in the following of certain strict forms. This is true even when one writes a parody in free verse like that one in William Harmon's *Oxford Book of American Light Verse*, which is a wonderful parody of Whitman in long-line Whitmanesque catalog form. There is a housewife present and her husband is drunk and comes in singing, "We won't get home until the morning" and at the end of this long line, which takes about five lines of print, the husband is finally inside and the parodist says, "He inebriate, chantant." And consider Whitman's great bad line, one of the great bad lines in the world, I think, and yet like some lines in Dickens only Whitman could have written it. It's this: "How plentious, how spiritual, how resumé." Isn't that nice? It reminds me of Dickens. David Copperfield, after he's gotten hung over, knows that the pure Agnes Whitfield has seen him drunk, so he goes and asks her forgiveness. She forgives him and he says, ... It is just staggering. A mediocre writer could never have written this. It has the whole of Victorian taste in it. He says, "Oh Agnes, you are my good angel, beast that I am." Isn't that fine? I know it is horrible, but it has genius in it.

Q. *Would you speak about your life in Minnesota, after you had left Seattle?*

I taught at the University of Minnesota for six years and at Macalester College for two years. I was not given tenure at the University of Minnesota, so I was invited over to Macalester. I taught there for two years and then I felt I had been in Minnesota long enough. I had a Guggenheim Fellowship that next year and this enabled me to look around. I finally found a job in New York and I have been here since.

Q. *Would you speak about Allen Tate and John Berryman, your colleagues at the University of Minnesota?*

I knew Tate pretty well. I went to his house many times and we were good friends. I knew his wife at that time, Isabella Gardner, and we are still good friends. She is in New York, too. I got along with them very well. I did not know Berryman so well, personally. But formally I knew him and admired him. I still admire Tate's poetry very much. I realize that at the moment there isn't very much discussion of it, but I believe that his best poems are good enough to survive beyond fluctuations of fashion. "The Ode to the Confederate Dead," some of the sonnets, "The Eagle"—these are wonderful. Berryman, after his death, of course, provoked all sorts of speculation, his alcoholism, and so on. I think we are going to come back to Berryman's poetry in a few years when the smoke has cleared and someone will set about making a good selected poems and will discover the work is extremely fine. He was a very rattled man. He was desperately sick and I think his achieving so much was really quite heroic, amazing.

Q. *Was Robert Penn Warren at Minnesota during this time?*

No, he was there earlier. I have got to know him somewhat, personally, since then. We have corresponded and met a couple of times. He certainly is a fine man. There is an interesting thing about Warren. In America we have a very powerfully operative myth about, and not only about, writers who burn themselves out while young. This comes to us, I suppose, from the twenties and from, or back of, F. Scott Fitzgerald. We have also still, perhaps from grade school and high school, a kind of confused notion of literary romanticism. People don't express this so openly and directly, but I believe that it is somehow in the air. It is the notion that it is actually very desirable for a young person to create a big hullaballoo and die very young. But we have also had, in America, the extremely fine possibility of the writer who continues his search and is steadfast. He continues his effort to learn how to write well and to be true to life as he understands it. This is the writer who in spite of his steadfastness may occasionally write clumsily, but who nevertheless is not dull. This is the writer who in his advanced age is able to bring so many of his good-hearted, I think you can use that word, good-hearted and steadfast efforts to fruition. That is what has been happening in the work of Warren with his most recent books. If you did not know he was seventy-four years old, you would think he has the vigor and freshness of someone who is perhaps thirty.

Another author who is able to do this, who is a little plodding and not perhaps so startlingly gifted as Warren has obviously been as a novelist and as a critic and as a teacher, as well as a poet, who nevertheless wrote poems to the end of his life, poems of great beauty, is John Hall Wheelock. I told Mr. Wheelock once that I hoped he understood how much his very life meant to somebody like me and to many people my own age. I told him that Galway Kinnell agreed with me, that by being true to himself he really had given us some hope. He had demonstrated to us that to try to be true to whatever poetic gift we might have, large or small, really did mean something. It was not a stupid vain effort. Of course this is obviously not the same thing as saying we can't fail; most of us probably will fail, but the failure isn't total.

Warren right at the moment, it seems to me, is an inspiration. Another interesting thing is that he seems to have no hostility toward writers younger than himself. He will do anything to help people.

Q. *Thinking specifically of your review-essay of Warren's* Promises, *which appeared in the* Kenyon Review *in 1958, it appears that you suggested something in Warren's development that was, perhaps, also occurring in your celebrated shift of form at about that time. Can you discuss the importance of Warren's influence on your work?*

Yes. The way I see things now, Warren has been more important to me than even I realized at the time. What I take it that he was doing, what I tried to write in that essay, however clumsily, was important to me. It was important for me to write that essay and Mr. Ransom understood that. Ransom and I were corresponding and I had said that my friend Morgan Blume and I were reading Warren again. Morgan, who was a very, very close friend of mine at Minnesota, died three years ago of a stroke. A terrible loss, he was just forty-three years old. Morgan was very bright and a passionate student of literature. He wrote some poems and essays, but mainly he was a superb reader and a good critic. He and I were going through Warren. We met and talked often and we were talking about the novels, the poems, and we read a great deal in these. We were sort of speculating about the relationship between them. I told Ransom this and he wrote back and said why don't you do a piece on Warren's new poems and get Blume to do his fiction. So we did that. We wrote our essays and showed them to each other and talked about them. Then they were published in consecutive issues of the *Kenyon Review*.

I think that you can speak legitimately and reasonably and necessarily, about the craft of writing. Well, I think that Warren is as much a master of the craft as Ransom and Tate. People who have split their poems, Warren's and Tate's and Ransom's, away from emotion are just wrong. Who could be more passionate than Tate? Sometimes he's so passionate in his poems that he is almost inarticulate. He had the boldness to do this. "The Eagle," is, I think, a great poem and yet there are parts of it that are just about gibberish. But the rhythm is so powerful that it goes over you and through you.

Warren had become a technical master, a master of craft, and in *Promises*, knowing this, he tried deliberately to be craftsmanlike and constantly to reach out in terms of his rhythm and his diction. And also, by the way, in terms of place; he was trying to write a poetry of place. They are Italian poems. And all of this is what moved me, what seemed to me exciting. It seemed bold and original and also helpful. One could learn something. One could learn first the necessity of trying to master a craft and then to recognize that, as I was arguing a little earlier, that there was a danger of glibness, of an excessive facility. Then one could learn to try and keep one's language and one's rhythms open to new possibility. Of course this kind of poetry can lead to clumsiness, which is embarrassing and asinine and unintentional. I suppose that there is no escape from the charges of sentimentality and asininity so long as you are willing to try. It has seemed to me in my own life, in my own attempt to write, and within my own narrower limits—I don't have Warren's learning or range or anything like Warren's intelligence—but within my own limits it seemed to me necessary and sensible to discover new ways of writing for oneself. The discovery of such new ways surely has something to do with discovering the possibilities of one's life. It is something like Thoreau's remark. He said, "I have never met a man who was entirely awake. How could I have looked him in the face?"

In Warren's *Promises* language had been taken to a formal extreme only to be broken and reshaped. You could feel him doing it in the book. It is a ragged sort of book, yet it has such life in it. And where does that life consist? How can we find it? How do we find it, if it is not in what I would call the entirely finished and polished poem? It is in his ability to show us the struggle going on as he writes, so that each poem in that book is very dramatic even if it is just a piece of straight description.

Q. *When people speak of the change in your poems after your first two books they speak of the surrealism and often refer to "Lying in a Hammock at William Duffy's Farm in Pine Island, Minnesota" as not untypical of your change. You have said of this poem, "All I did was describe what I felt and what I saw, lying in the hammock. Shouldn't that be enough? But no, there's your American every time, goddamnit, somebody's got to draw a moral." Would you comment further?*

Well, I think that the poem is a description of a mood and this kind of poem is the kind of poem that has been written for thousands of years by the Chinese poets. I can't read Chinese but I certainly can read Soames Jennings and Robert Paine and Witter Bynner and Arthur Wailey. And that poem, although I hope it is a description of my mood as I lay in that hammock, is clearly an imitation of that Chinese manner. It is not surrealistic. I said, at the end of that poem, "I have wasted my life" because it was what I happened to feel at that moment and as part of the mood I had while lying in the hammock. This poem made English critics angry. I have never understood what would have so infuriated them. They could say the poem was limp or that it did not have enough intellectual content. I can see that. But I hope that it did not pretend to. It just said, I am lying here in this hammock and this and that is happening.

American critics think that last line is a moral, that it is a comment which says I have wasted my life by writing iambics, or that I have wasted my life by lying in the hammock. Actually, behind everything in my general thoughts and feelings was the idea that one of the worst things in American life is waste. I think that our tendency to waste is a truly dreadful one. I have told my students that one of the most horrifying things to me is to stand, being my age, and look at a class of nineteen- and twenty-year-old people who are trying to read a passage of, say, Milton or Shakespeare and to see their faces saying it is a waste of time. They don't see how precious their lives are.

Q. *One of your poems is called "The Morality of Poetry" and another is called "The Idea of the Good." Can you speak of the difference between drawing a moral and the ideas implied in these titles?*

I only used the phrase "the morality of poetry" once and it is the title of that poem in *Saint Judas*. What I meant there was that there are different kinds of forms in poetry which are possible and to try to write any of them well is a good thing. That is the morality of poetry, as far as I am concerned. "The Idea of the Good" is a very, very confused poem. I don't have the faintest idea what it means. I can't imagine how anyone could find a meaning in it. It is just badly written. I forget what I was thinking of at the time. I feel this way about almost everything in my book *Two Citizens*. The book is just a bust. I will never reprint it. Let me put it this way, I ought not to have published that book the way it stands. I should have taken possibly six poems in it and tried to wait a year, to see if I couldn't revise them and see what else I had. That is what I ought to have done and I didn't. I made an ass of myself. It seems to me a bad book because most of it is badly written. Obscure and self-indulgent, it talks around subjects rather than coming to terms with them. It is impossibly ragged. It is just unfinished. If I were ever going to reprint any of it, I would take maybe six poems and write them out again in longhand and see what might happen. I would try to think about them as thoroughly as I could.

Q. *Do you have a specific feeling about that book's initial poem, "Ars Poetica: Some Recent Criticism"?*

It has some strong possibilities in it, but it is still confused. I am not quite sure what it means. That can be a glib answer, an evasion of responsibility, but I mean that when I go back and look at it I can't quite figure out what it is about. I called it "Some Recent Criticism" because I had in mind to write the kind of poem that could not be glibly disposed of by some reviewers and critics who were interested in facility alone. I made that conscious effort. Suddenly I called it "Ars Poetica" as if to say here is a piece of raw life. I think artistically that was a mistake, but that is what I was trying to do. I meant to introduce something that would be difficult for certain glib reviewers to solve.

Q. *Is it possible that in spite of your intention and present evaluation of that poem that it could have its own myth and meaning?*

If it has those I am not aware of them. I wasn't thinking of that. You can't always tell, though. You might write something and think

as clearly as you can that you have said a certain thing. Then someone else will find something in it, an intelligent person of good will,
and maybe he will explain to you what is really there. There is something about language that can be very surprising, and words we
use—even in conversation—sometimes can have implications, very
colorful ones, that we haven't been aware of consciously. We find examples of this in our public life. I really do believe that there is, in
language, something like a power to heal itself, to right itself. Language is a living thing, a part of ourselves, and, as such, I think that
the notion among the evangelists of the word as flesh is a very, very
complex and important living idea. I am not enough of a philosopher
or critic or theologian to spell it out, yet I feel it has a certain truth.

Language can convey a meaning we were not aware of. There are
staggering examples of this. One of my favorite Americans, and I
have a poem about his death, was Mayor Daley of Chicago. By favorite, I mean as an example. Mayor Daley used to say to his constitu-
ents such things as: If I am reelected the great city of Chicago will
rise to an ever higher platitude of achievement. He did not mean to
say *that*, but he did say it. And the meaning is there. There is another example in New York's Mario Procacino. In earlier years Mario Procacino would emerge to run for mayor and then disappear. He
had a pencil-thin moustache, black hair slicked down and parted in
the middle, and somebody once said he looked like a face painted on
a balloon. He did various things. Once he went to Israel and told people that he was the President of Verranzo College. Of course, there is
no Verranzo College. Once when he was running for mayor he went
to Harlem and met a large constituency, a big crowd. All Black people. And Mario Procacino, part of whose manner was to be sort of
weepy and yearning like a hack obstetrician from Martins Ferry,
Ohio—oh help this woman have her baby!—said to that audience
. . . . I can hardly bring myself to say this, it is so good. If it were
consciously controlled, Shakespeare could have written this line,
though first he would have had to create Procacino and that audience. Procacino said to that Black audience: My heart is as black
as yours! Now he didn't mean *that*. He didn't intend it to sound the
way it sounded to that audience and to you and to me. But he said it.
It is almost as if the language cried out, save me. Somebody save me.
We do have a wonderful language in America and we still haven't
really gotten to it. Some people have approached it.

We were speaking earlier of my poem "Lying in a Hammock at William Duffy's Farm in Pine Island, Minnesota." Let me read a parody of that poem. It was sent to me by Ron Smith, from Richmond, Virginia.

"Righting the Love Boat"

Over my head I see blood flecks
dropped like gnats and flies
dark in the dust webs.
Beyond the kitchen table, the scraps from
last week's dinners follow one another out
the back door to the anthill.
To my left, behind the white leg wearing
pepper-like holes, a small fire blazes up
in the overflowing trashcan.
I lie back on the cold tile
as the siren howls and comes on.
A chicken wing hangs from the chandelier
looking for home.
I have wasted my wife.

Isn't that good? I love that sort of thing. Maybe Ron Smith will send a copy to Robert Bly and Henry Taylor. Robert, in earlier years out on the farm in Minnesota, had a big file-folder which was stuffed with parodies people had sent him. It was wonderful.

Q. *What value do you place on humor in poetry?*

I could not do without it. Robert Bly gets annoyed at the phrase "light verse." Nevertheless, he likes parodies. He likes silly songs. I think what he really objects to is triviality and superficiality. I feel that a great deal of what you have to call light verse is very beautiful and very exciting. I'm grateful for it, for good humor in poetry. There is a great poem by Ben King, of whom I had never heard. It is a knockout and I like it just as a poem. I found this in William Harmon's new *Oxford Treasury of Light Verse*. Ben King lived from 1857 to 1894, a funny time for prose writers but some funny poems got in too. Here is Ben King's poem:

"If I Should Die"

If I should die tonight and you should come
to my cold corpse and say
weeping and heartsick o'er my lifeless clay,
if I should die tonight and you should come
in deepest grief and woe and say
"Here's that ten dollars that I owe,"
I might arise, in my large white cravat
and say, "What's that?"

If I should die tonight and you should come
to my cold corpse and kneel
clasping my beard to show the grief you feel,
I say, if I should die tonight
and you should come to me
and there and then just even hint
'bout payin' me that ten,
I might arise a while,
but I'd drop dead again.

Q. *Why do you so insistently use certain words such as* alone, lone-ly, dark, *and so on in your poems?*

Somebody wrote to me once and said, speaking particularly of the "New Poems" section of my *Collected Poems*, that anybody who used the word *lonely* and the word *loneliness* that often must not really know what the experience is. I do overuse certain words. These words all meant something to me at the time I was writing them, but how they relate to one another in different poems written over a period of years would be, as far as I can tell, accidental. They may reveal something about me that I have not been aware of con-sciously. I see no reason to be opposed to a word so long as it is help-ful in an individual poem.

Q. *What do you mean by the "abounding delight of the body"?*

I don't know. As it stands, it is a very vague and frivolous remark. I don't know. I think behind it is the notion that I simply came to like myself much better after I met Annie. It certainly doesn't mean a rejection of American Puritanism. I think it is just a pompous remark.

Q. *You often refer in poems to "rising." Does this have a particular meaning?*

I don't know. I haven't thought it through.

Q. *One of the changes in your poems has been a move from a formal to a more colloquial diction. It has been suggested that this is like Wordsworth's demand for a language of the common man. Is this your intention?*

No. I have never been able to figure out what Wordsworth means. I don't think that one can generalize about it. It depends on the needs of the particular poet. In the arrangement of the words I would like to be very formal but I would like the effect of having a certain ease. That is the Horatian notion. I do think any language is available to poetry. My brother, who lives in California and works for IBM, told me that they fed things into a computer out there. They got a computer to translate Keats's "Ode to a Nightingale." It was nutty. But in itself, it seemed to me to make a wonderful woozy kind of poem. They translated it into other terms. They tried to clarify it. I remember Ransom reading the "Ode on Melancholy" and saying "Nor suffer thy pale forehead to be kissed by nightshade." Ransom pointed out that in the *Oxford English Dictionary* one of the meanings of nightshade is a night-walking prostitute. Well, the computer would get some of that made clear.

Q. *Do you consider that there is any distinction to be made between the way you have used the image in poems and the way delineated by the imagist poets?*

I do not understand any such distinction. I am simply trying to write as clearly as I can. Sometimes I use figures of speech and sometimes I don't. I do not operate according to a set of principles or manifestos.

Q. *You have referred frequently to the musical quality of poems. Granting that each ear may perceive this music differently, can you say what you mean by the music of poetry?*

It is first of all the movement of language. This includes pauses and everything meant by timing. There is the actual sound of the words, the syllables in relation to one another. And there is something beyond that which moves literally toward the condition of music. One thing that has pleased me very much is that there are at least five composers who have set things of mine to music. It has pleased me that professional musicians would find that quality in my poems.

Q. *Can you speak of the relationship of timing to form?*

Yes. Auden says it is often the timing, especially, the rhymes, that will dictate the meaning. He says that Byron suddenly became aware of this and became a great poet in "Beppo," that wonderful piece about Venice. Also in *Don Juan*.

Q. *Is the speaker of your poems an artificial, or created, speaker? Or is it the actual James Wright?*

Sometimes it is an artificial voice and sometimes it is a direct voice. There are some poems that I have written which are more like dramatic monologues in the sense that Browning conceived of that form. Sometimes I have simply made things up. Sometimes people have called me a confessional poet. I don't see that. I feel perfectly free to make up something that never happened to me. There is not a point to point reference between the events of my books and the events of my life. Not at all. I have said that I regarded writing poetry as a curse, but that remark was a silly affectation. With me, to be as realistic as I can, I would say that writing poetry has been what one could reasonably call a neurotic compulsion. I have not made that much money from it. It is not that useful. To some extent, it has made me notorious. Notoriety makes me extremely uncomfortable. This sounds like an affectation, too, but honest to God it is not. Poetry is not a curse. Often it is a pleasure to write but I think that I have written, as I say, sort of neurotically. I have gone on writing because it has made me feel, from time to time, more emotionally safe.

Q. *What do you mean by the remark that "the value of a poet's life is going to depend on the truth of the language and the truth of his life"?*

That is another pompous remark. I don't know what it means. It reminds me of Robert Benchley's maxim from the Chinese. He says, "It is rather to be chosen than great riches, unless I have omitted something from the quotation." A remark like mine is, I think, hot air. It sort of sounds nice though. We don't have to be bullied by our own asinine remarks that have got into print.

Q. *Do you construct your books in a certain way? Do you think of a poem or a book as having a statemental or communicative function?*

Yes, I do think of the construction in a certain way. Frost said somewhere, I have forgotten where, that if there are twenty-five poems in a book, the book itself ought to be the twenty-sixth poem. That is, in presenting a group of poems in the hope that someone will read them, one ought to be aware of a relation between the poems as well as of inner relations that exist in the individual poems. It is an idea of shapeliness that appeals to me. There are blossoms all over *To a Blossoming Pear Tree*, my latest book. And I think that this book is more tightly organized than any of my previous books. Whether or not it comes through that way, I don't know. This is what I felt, anyway.

As for the second half of your question, I think that the kind of thing that a person writes will depend partly on his own interests and concerns as a human being. Those things will come out in his poems inevitably. In the poem called "To a Blossoming Pear Tree" I am talking about addressing the beauty of nature, which is nonhuman. It suggests to me sometimes the perfection of things and I envy this perfection of things, or at least this nonhumanity, precisely because it is not involved in the sometimes very painful mess of being human. Yet I say at the end of the poem that this is what I have to be, human. Human life is a mess. This is something I wanted to say, and I said it.

Q. *You have said in other places that you consider yourself a nature poet. What does this mean?*

I care very much about the living world, the organic and the inorganic world. It comforts me more and more to realize and to observe and to feel the great self-restoring power that the creatures in nature have while we human beings are making such a mess of things. I hope that poetry, and the poetry of nature, has a similar power. Roethke said a beautiful thing once when he talked to a class about the poetry of nature. He said that we ought to remember that there is an inner nature, and I think he was suggesting something about poetry. That, perhaps, poetry could remind us of the need for restoration through the inner nature. Also, I think that in the poetry of nature there is the willingness to approach the living creatures with the kind of attentiveness that is almost a reverence. In Robert Bly's poems about nature he is at his best and most beautiful. Many of his ideas, political or religious or whatever, are absorbed into the attention that he is paying visually and spiritually to the things he writes about. The ideas are all there in the poems about nature.

Q. *Does poetry help to move us toward the good and away from the bad?*

I think that it sometimes does. Sometimes it can. But there are plenty of poems, and good poems, that wouldn't necessarily do that. They would still be good poems. Take Gavin Ewart's little poem about Miss Twye. I feel like a better person when I read that poem because it delights me.

Q. *Do you believe that there is such a thing as a good man and a bad man?*

Yes. I can read you a passage that defines the bad man about as well as anything I have ever seen. Over in Chapter 15 of *The Adventures of Huckleberry Finn* Jim and Huck get lost in the fog and are separated from each other. A steamboat goes between them. Huck goes off in the canoe and Jim remains on the raft. Then Huck returns and shows himself to Jim. Jim was so exhausted he had fallen asleep. When he wakes up, he is very glad to see Huck and says "I thought you were dead." Huck pretends that none of this has happened, that Jim has had a dream. Then he asks Jim to interpret the dream in which all these horrible things have happened and Jim gives an elaborate interpretation of it. Then Huck points out that there is some trash, dead leaves and dirt and rocks and so on, stuck on the raft. This proves that all those things really did happen. Huck was just trying to joke with Jim and make fun of him a little bit. Well, here's what Jim does.

Jim looked at the trash, and then looked at me, and back at the trash again. He had got the dream fixed so strong in his head that he couldn't seem to shake it loose and get the facts back into its place again right away. But when he did get the thing straightened around he looked at me steady without ever smiling, and says:

"What do dey stan' for? I's gwyne to tell you. When I got all wore out wid work, en wid de callin' for you, en went to sleep, my heart wuz mos' broke bekase you wuz los', en I didn' k'yer no' mo' what become er me en de raf'. En when I wake up en fine you back ag'in, all safe en soun', de tears come, en I could' a'got down on my knees en kiss yo' foot, I's so thankful. En all you wuz thinkin' 'bout wuz how you could make a fool uv ole Jim wid a lie. Dat truck dah is *trash*; en trash is what people is dat puts dirt on de head er dey fren's en makes 'em ashamed."

Then he got up slow and walked to the wigwam, and went in there without saying anything but that. But that was enough. It made me feel so mean I could almost kissed *his* foot to get him to take it back.

It was fifteen minutes before I could work myself up to go and humble myself to a nigger; but I done it, and I warn't ever sorry for it afterward, neither. I didn't do him no more mean tricks, and I wouldn't done that one if I'd a' knowed it would make him feel that way.

That is a good definition of a bad man.

Q. *Thinking of your statement in* Field *magazine about the poetic line, can it be inferred that you do imagine a principle which distinguishes a line of poetry from a line of prose?*

I do not understand much of that piece of mine in *Field*. What I was really trying to say was that I am impatient with arguments of this kind. I don't think that, in any deep sense, it makes a damn bit of difference whether or not one is writing in prose or in verse, just so he's trying to be imaginative and true to what he is hearing. But I also think there is a principle such as you suggest. It is the way a line sounds, its musical structures, the conception of a line as being a musical unit itself. Of course this doesn't mean that it has to be either iambic or noniambic because there are other metrical and musical possibilities in our American language. I don't mean that the specific pattern of the line has to be repeated either. But it has to have, somehow, a musical shape. At least that is what I have tried to achieve. I think that, essentially, a poem is distinguished from a prose piece in terms of song. A piece is to be identified and enjoyed as a poem in so far as it is closer to a song.

Q. *Why did you include prose pieces in* Moments of the Italian Summer *and* To a Blossoming Pear Tree?

I felt like trying to learn how to write a clearer prose. A better prose. It grew out of my notebooks. I found I was taking more and more pleasure in writing prose. Its rhythm and its music are different from that of my poems, really.

Q. *You have been very strong in your condemnation of* Two Citizens. *How do you feel about* To a Blossoming Pear Tree?

I feel that *To a Blossoming Pear Tree* is the best book that I have ever published. It is the best written and, whatever it says, whatever the value of the book, it is the book that I wanted to write. I wrote it over a long period of time, and carefully. I had about 500 pages of manuscript in that book. I struggled with it a lot.

Q. *Looking back over your career, you have stated often that you were strongly influenced by Robert Frost and E. A. Robinson. Can you say a little more about that?*

Yes. I meant that what I was trying to do was to learn how to write poems in a simple syntax and also to write in a musically very precise way that had some ease to it. Here I mean something like the sound of Frost, although I also like the sound of Robinson and have tried to get close to that too. The subject matter, perhaps, had closer affinities to Robinson. Robinson felt, and this is what he portrays in his poems, that there is no verifiable justification for hope in this world. And, along with this, there was his recognition, you could call it psychological or moral, that hope in human beings is absolutely necessary for us to go on living. His characters are always trying to live as if there was some hope, some kind of hope, and at the same time they know that there isn't. There they are. You don't find the same kind of thing in Frost. Although, at bottom, Frost is very much a tragic poet. Yet, I don't think he explores this kind of darkness as consistently as Robinson does. Shall I say some lines of Robinson's from "Captain Craig"? The old man says, when the young man asks him how it is that he can be old and a failure and still act happy, or as if he is happy. Isn't he aware of the terrible things in life?

> I cannot think of anything to-day
> That I would rather do than be myself,

Primevally alive, and have the sun
Shine into me; for on a day like this,
When the chaff-parts of a man's adversities
Are blown by quick-spring breezes out of him—
When even a flicker of wind that wakes no more
Than a tuft of grass, or a few young yellow leaves,
Comes like the falling of a prophet's breath
On altar-flames rekindled of crushed embers,—
Then do I feel, now do I feel, within me
No dreariness, no grief, no discontent,
No twinge of human envy. But I beg
That you forego credentials of the past
For these illuminations of the present,
Or better still, to give the shadow justice,
You let me tell you something: I have yearned
In many another season for these days,
And having them with God's own pageantry
To make me glad for them,—yes, I have cursed
The sunlight and the breezes and the leaves
To think of men on stretchers and on beds,
Or on foul floors, like starved outrageous lizards,
Made human with paralysis and rags;
Or of some poor devil on a battle-field
Left undiscovered and without the strength
To drag a maggot from his clotted mouth;
Or of women working where a man would fall—
Flat-breasted miracles of cheerfulness
Made neuter by the work that no man counts
Until it waits undone; children thrown out
To feed their veins and souls with offal . . . Yes,
I have had half a mind to blow my brains out
Sometimes; and I have gone from door to door,
Ragged myself, trying to do something—
Crazy, I hope.—But what has this to do
With Spring?

Q. *To expand the context of your remarks slightly, does it bother you that the audience for poetry in America seems a small and an academic one?*

No. I like that very much. At least I like a comparatively small audience. If indeed we can say that there is an audience for poetry. Galway Kinnell and I were sitting together at the only conference I've ever attended, the National Poetry Conference up near Grand Rapids, Michigan, about three years ago. We were going to give a little course there, to be called "The Pleasures of Poetry." But we found the students hadn't actually read anything. They reminded me of the old Pogo comic strip. Richard Hugo loves this bear, too. There was a bear in the strip and he discovered he could write. He wrote some stories, but he couldn't read. So he would take them to Albert the Alligator and he would ask Albert to read them to him. As Albert read the stories, the bear would sit nearby saying things like "I was young when I wrote that."

We had a hard time conveying to that class what we meant. We'd ask somebody to say a poem he liked and somebody would stand up and say something he himself had written. Don't you like anything by John Donne? Who? We ran into a great deal of that, a great many people who don't read. I don't think we have a very big audience for poetry. We can get big audiences for poetry readings but this is something else entirely. I am sure that people do believe that there is a greater interest in poetry in other countries, but I wonder. A few years ago in Yugoslavia, with some other writers, I spoke. The entire town of Struga turned out seated all up and down the river. Still, I'm getting suspicious of that kind of public performance and the notoriety and the celebrity that goes with it. I am sure that these are social forces and powers in themselves. What they have to do with the practice of poetry, I wonder.

We hear a lot about the great Russian audiences, but I think sometimes that the Russians like to get one up on us by telling us how much goddamn soul they have got. This is a pain in the neck. It is a way of being superior. We are told by *Time* magazine that a writer like Yevtushenko has to do nothing except appear in a town and he will have an audience of 50,000 people. All right. I don't know what his poems look like in Russian but I've seen several translations into English, and I just hope that they don't look that way in Russian. They were ungodly awful. And not even funny.

Neruda conceived of poetry as a very popular thing and he drew great numbers of people. But this was partly due to his public recognition as a Chilean legislator and diplomat. Of course in Latin American countries the tradition of the popularity of poetry is greater and stronger than it is in the United States. I do not object to the popularity of poetry as such. In Latin America, the people actually read poetry, themselves, in privacy. This is not the same thing as being a camp follower at poetry readings. We could use more genuine intelligent readers of good will.

A Foreword to James Wright's
The Green Wall

W. H. AUDEN

CONSCIOUSLY OR UNCONSCIOUSLY, every poet draws a frontier between the poetical and the nonpoetical; certain objects, persons, events seem to him capable of embodiment in a poem, even if he has not yet discovered how, while there are others which it would never occur to him to consider himself, whatever other poets may have done with them. Further, among the various moods of feeling of which he is capable, he has preferences as a poet which may have little to do with his preferences as a man; a feeling which he enjoys may make little appeal to his imagination; a state of unpleasure may excite it.

Some of these distinctions are peculiar to himself, but most he shares with his contemporaries. From time to time a poet or a group of poets proclaim that the existing frontier is unjust and should be redrawn; when this happens, a new "period" of poetry begins.

One of the problems for a poet living in a culture with a well-developed technology is that the history of technology is one of perpetual revolution, whereas genuine revolutions in the history of art (or society) are few and far between. He is tempted to imagine that, unless he produces something completely novel, he will be unoriginal. The reading public, too, may be similarly misled and attach undue importance to the individual differences between one poet and another, which, of course, exist and matter, ignoring that which is characteristic of them all, though this may really be of greater interest.

For example, Mr. Wright uses as an epigraph to this volume the well-known medieval carol "Adam Lay Ibounden." It is as impossible to imagine a poet of the twentieth-century writing this as to imagine a fifteenth-century poet writing these lines by Mr. Wright:

She was aware of scavengers in holes
Of stone, she knew the loosened stones that fell
Indifferently as pebbles plunging down a well
And broke for the sake of nothing human souls.

A modern poet might perfectly well be a Catholic, believing in the divine plan for human redemption of which the medieval carol sings, but his consciousness of historical earthly time is so different that he could never strike the same note of naive joy in the present; should he attempt it, the note struck would almost certainly be false, expressing not Christian hope but a sort of Rotarian optimism.

A medieval poet, on the other hand, might have written an elegy on the death of a friend, though he would be more likely to choose a public figure, but it would never have occurred to him to celebrate the melancholia of the deceased; he would have described her beauty, her actions, he might even have portrayed her as a mourner, provided that the reason was some objective suffering, but a subjective illness like melancholia would have seemed to him unpoetic.

One way of perceiving the characteristics of an age is to raise certain fundamental questions which human beings have always asked and then see how the poets of that age answer them, such questions, for example, as: "What is the essential difference between man and all the other creatures, animal, vegetable, and mineral?" "What is the nature and human significance of time?" "What qualities are proper to the hero or sacred person who can inspire poets to celebrate him and what is lacking in the churl or profane person whom poetry ignores?" A man in the Middle Ages would have said that the difference between man and other creatures is that only man has an immortal soul eternally related to God. He has, therefore, a goal, salvation or damnation, but this goal is not in time nor is reaching it a matter of time. A baby who has been baptized and an old man who repents after a lifetime of crime die and both are saved; their ages are irrelevant.

On the other hand, so far as his temporal existence, individual or social, was concerned, like anyone who lives in a predominantly rural culture without machinery, he would be conscious of little difference between himself and other creatures, that is to say, he would be mainly aware of their common subjection to biological time, the endless cycle of birth, growth, and decay. Of man as creating irreversible historical time so that the next generation is never a repetition of the last, he would be scarcely, if at all, conscious. But to a modern man, whether or not he believes in an immortal soul, this is the great difference, that he and his society have a self-made history while the rest of nature does not. He is anxious by necessity because at every moment he has to choose to become himself. His typical feelings about nature, therefore, are feelings of estrangement and nostalgia. In "A Fit against the Country" Mr. Wright sees nature as a temptation to try and escape human responsibility by imitating her ways, in "The Seasonless" he contrasts the rotation of the seasons with a human figure to whom no season can ever return, in "The Horse" and "On the Skeleton of a Hound" he contrasts the "poetical" animal and its unchanging identity with the "unpoetical" man who can never say who he is.

Poets have always reflected on the passage of time, comparing the present and the past, but before the modern period this usually meant expressing a sorrow because the present was less valuable than the past, what was once strong is now weak, what was beautiful has faded, and so forth, but past and present were felt to be equally real. But in Mr. Wright's poems, as in nearly all modern poetry, the present is not unhappy but unreal, and it is memories, pleasant or unpleasant, which are celebrated for their own sake as the real past. The present can only be celebrated, as in "A Girl in a Window" or "To a Hostess Saying Good Night," by showing it as pure chance; what makes the present moment poetical is an awareness that it is related to nothing so that nothing can come of it.

Two of Mr. Wright's poems, "The Assignation" and "My Grandmother's Ghost," are about the dead coming back to haunt the living.

In earlier times the motive for doing this would have been malignant and ghosts were regarded as evil. The good dead were thought to be much too happy in their present state to wish to return to their earthly life; in their thoughts about those on earth whom they had loved they looked not backward but forward to the future when their loved ones would join them. On earth past and present had seemed equally real; in eternity both seem equally unreal.

Given the circumstances of modern life, the feeling that only memories are real is to be expected. When a man usually lived in the house where his father and grandfather had lived before him, the past still existed in the present, not just in his memories but objectively about him. Today when men change not only their house but their part of the world every few years, their present circumstances become more and more impersonal, subjective memories more and more important.

Even more striking than its attitude toward nature and time is the kind of person whom modern poetry chooses to speak of. Aside from love poems and poems addressed to relatives, the persons who have stimulated Mr. Wright's imagination include a lunatic, a man who has failed to rescue a boy from drowning, a murderer, a lesbian, a prostitute, a police informer, and some children, one of them deaf. Common to them all is the characteristic of being social outsiders. They play no part in ruling the City nor is its history made by them, nor, even, are they romantic rebels against its injustices; either, like the children (and the ghosts), they are not citizens or they are the City's passive victims.

His one poem to a successful citizen is, significantly, to a singer, that is to say, to someone whose social function is concerned with the play of the City, not with its work.

Mr. Wright is not alone in his imaginative preferences. It is difficult to find a modern poem, unless it be a satire, which celebrates a contemporary equivalent of Hector or Aeneas or King Arthur or the Renaissance prince. To the poetic imagination of our time, it would seem that the authentically human, the truly strong, is someone who to the outward eye is weak or a failure, the only exception being the artist or the intellectual discoverer, the value of whose achievements is independent of his contemporary fame.

There are many reasons for this change, and everyone will be able to think of some for himself. One, obviously, is the impersonal character of modern public life which has become so complex that the personal contribution of any one individual is impossible to identify and even the greatest statesman seems more an official than a man. Another, I think, is the change effected by modern methods of publicity in the nature of fame. Formerly a man was famous *for* something, for this great deed or that which he had done; that is to say, the deed was the important thing and the name of the doer was, in a sense, an accident. Today a famous man is a man whose name is on everybody's lips. Their knowledge of what he has done may be very vague and its value, whether it was noble or shameful, matters very little. So long as he is in the news, he is a famous man; the moment he ceases to have news value, he becomes nobody.

We should not be surprised, then, if modern poets should be drawn to celebrate persons of whom nobody has heard or whom, at least, everybody has forgotten.

I have not said anything about the quality of Mr. Wright's poems because assertions have no point without proofs, and the only proof in this case is reading. I will content myself with one or two quotations to illustrate his handling of imagery and rhythm and the variety of his concerns.

> Behind us, where we sit by trees,
> Blundering autos lurch and swerve
> On gravel, crawling on their knees
> Around the unfamiliar curve . . . .

> . . . The flop of wings, the jerk of the red comb
> Were a dumb agony,
> Stupid and meaningless. It was no joy
> To leave the body beaten underfoot;
> Life was a flick of corn, a steady roost.
> Chicken. The sound is plain.

> And through the windows, washing hands,
> The patients have the mattress made,
> Their trousers felt for colored stones,
> The pleasures of the noon recalled:

> For some were caught and held for hours
> By spiders skating over a pond,
> Some parted veils of hollyhocks
> And looked for rabbit holes beyond.

> But now the trousers lie in rows,
> She sees the undressed shadows creep
> Through half-illuminated minds
> And chase the hare and flower to sleep.

> But now I fumble at the single joy
> Of dawn. On the pale ruffle of the lake

The ripples weave a color I can bear.
Under a hill I see the city sleep
And fade. The perfect pleasure of the eyes:
A tiny bird bathed in a bowl of air,
Carving a yellow ripple down the bines,
Posing no storm to blow my wings aside
As I drift upward dropping a white feather.

In the Mode of Robinson and Frost: James Wright's Early Poetry

HENRY TAYLOR

WHEN A POET'S CAREER has lasted long enough for us to start talking about his early work, we face some problems of critical perception. We may not be able to solve them, but we should at least keep an eye out for the traps they set for us. This is especially true in the case of James Wright, who set his earlier work apart from the rest with unusual ostentation.

Almost anyone can avoid the absurdity of referring to *The Green Wall* and *Saint Judas* as apprentice work, as if the poems in them were written with an eye toward *To a Blossoming Pear Tree*. But it seems harder to avoid the equally fallacious tendency to think of *The Branch Will Not Break* as the moment when Wright "found his real voice," as if the first two books constituted some sort of ventriloquism.

Certainly *The Green Wall* contains some poems which got in because this was a first book, and certainly Wright's poetry has developed along lines most obtrusively introduced in *The Branch Will Not Break*. But in this discussion of the first two books, I hope to keep in mind the following points.

First, *The Green Wall* and *Saint Judas* are anything but false starts. In the poetic climate during which they appeared, they displayed, in their way, the self-reliance that characterizes most of Wright's work. The problem of perception here is that it is hard to recreate, imaginatively, the climate of the late fifties; but I will set down a few reminders.

Second, Wright's well-known shift in style was a necessity, a survival tactic. *Saint Judas* is a splendid book, but it contains considerable evidence of Wright's growing impatience with the style in which most of it is written. Moreover, the shift seems to have been more stylistic than thematic. I do not deny the new subtlety of per-

49

ception, the new sensitivity, in Wright's later work, but I am suspicious of claims that the shift was a cataclysmic transformation of the whole man. The problem of perception here is insurmountable; time has condemned us to hindsight.

Third, many of Wright's early poems may still be ranked among his best. As Richard Howard has suggested, Wright's having declared a moratorium on his earlier manner ("whatever I write from now on will be completely different") is not the same thing as declaring that he should never have written those poems in the first place. In assembling his *Collected Poems*, Wright discarded only five, all of them underachieved pieces from *The Green Wall*. The rest were brought forward, and they can still stand the light.

Finally, it will be noticed that Wright's abandonment of rhyme and meter has not been absolute. Each of his books contains at least a few poems in traditional forms. But it must be noticed, too, that these are inheritors, not only of the early style, but of the new style as well.

We cannot go back to the days when Wright was putting together his first two books, but we can spend a little time among relics of the period. There is the first edition of *New Poets of England and America*, which appeared in 1957. One reads vast stretches of it with half-amused bafflement, wondering what has happened to some of these people, noticing that all five of the selections by Robert Bly are metrical, and agreeing, mostly, with James Dickey, who said of these poems, "It is easy to like them, but difficult to care about them."

There are also such reference works as *The World Almanac*, which reminds us that from 1956 through 1960, the Pulitzer Prizes for Poetry went to Elizabeth Bishop, Richard Wilbur, Robert Penn Warren, Stanley Kunitz, and W. D. Snodgrass. The National Book Awards for the same period went to Auden, Wilbur, Warren, Roethke, and Lowell. That is how things seem to have been. Other important forces were at work, but they were not widely felt until the early sixties.

In his introduction to another anthology, the Penguin *Contemporary American Poetry*, Donald Hall, writing in 1961, took some notice of these other forces:

One thing is happening in American poetry, as I see it, which is genuinely new, and so new that I lack words for it. In lines like Robert Bly's:

> In small towns the houses are built right on the ground;
> The lamplight falls on all fours in the grass.

or Louis Simpson's:

> These houses built of wood sustain
> Colossal snows,
> And the light above the street is sick to death.

a new kind of imagination seems to be working.

It is tempting to say, with Flannery O'Connor's Mrs. Crater, that "they wasn't as advanced as we are." This is nonsense, of course; things change, for better or worse, whether we like it or not. In 1960, Gregory Orr was thirteen, and Carolyn Forché was ten.

In the fifties, despite the commandments that came down from the Black Mountain, it was quite usual for young poets to try to accommodate their own voices to forms inherited from England. Wright, though he began with a strong talent and notable independence, was not exceptional in this respect. In *The Green Wall*, the process of accommodation is tentative and slow; several of these poems, successful in many ways, sound like no one in particular:

> And though she made a leaflet fall
> I have forgotten what she said:
>
> Except that spring was coming on
> Or might have come already while
> We lay beside a smooth-veined stone;
> Except an owl sang half a mile
> Away; except a starling's feather
> Softened my face beside a root:
> But how should I remember whether
> She was the one who spoke, or not?
>> "Witches Waken the Natural World in Spring"

Wright early acknowledged an indebtedness to E. A. Robinson, and this passage reveals some of the things that master could teach, though the awkwardly enjambed *away* is not one of them. Here are the careful setting, the question that deepens the mystery by being somewhat baffling in itself, and the significant details which are sometimes hard to visualize, despite the specificity of the words ("except a starling's feather / Softened my face beside a root").

Something more fully achieved appears in a short poem called "To a Hostess Saying Good Night." It combines formal craftsmanship with occasional clichés and colloquialisms, to produce an interestingly low-keyed extravagance:

> Shake out the ruffle, turn and go,
> Over the trellis blow the kiss.
> Some of the guests will never know
> Another night to shadow this.
> Some of the birds awake in vines
> Will never see another face
> So frail, so lovely anyplace
> Between the birdbath and the bines.
>
> O dark come never down to you.
> I look away and look away:
> Over the moon the shadows go,
> Over your shoulder, nebulae.
> Some of the vast, the vacant stars
> Will never see your face at all,
> Your frail, your lovely eyelids fall
> Between Andromeda and Mars.

This is the courtly tradition in somewhat modern dress, allowing itself several nods toward its forerunners: the careful parallelism of the two stanzas, the shift from earthly to astronomical praise, the *O*. Yet under all this runs a diction flexible enough to include a word like *anyplace*.

This flexible diction, expanding at times to an enormous inclusiveness, soon found a subject or a set of subjects to which it was appropriate. Throughout his career, Wright has been concerned with "social outsiders," as Auden called them in his introduction to *The Green Wall*—bums, drunks, whores, murderers, homosexuals, and so on. He also returns often to the vast, gritty landscape of his youth in Ohio, and the nature of love and death in such a place.

The union of style and subject approaches perfection in many of Wright's poems; some of them, though not as ambitious as others, transcend the manner of their time, and remain durable. Such a poem is "An Offering for Mr. Bluehart," the third poem in *Saint*

Judas. It is a model of formal organization, its three-part narrative falling without excessive tidiness into three tightly rhymed stanzas of iambic tetrameter. The first two stanzas evoke a boyhood time and place, when the speaker and his friends raided an orchard while "the lean satanic owner" cursed them, even shot at them. But now that the old man is dead, and the speaker has grown up, there is touching honesty in a small gesture:

> Sorry for him, or any man
> Who lost his labored wealth to thieves,
> Today I mourn him, as I can,
> By leaving in their golden leaves
> Some luscious apples overhead.
> Now may my abstinence restore
> Peace to the orchard and the dead.
> We shall not nag them any more.

The surprisingly appropriate last line is brilliantly prepared for, even metrically: in the first two stanzas, the rhyme scheme is *a b a b b c b c*; but in this stanza the poet goes to a fourth rhyme in the fifth and seventh lines, thus avoiding *grieves* at the same time that he leads us to expect it.

If Wright brought his early style to a high degree of excellence in several poems, he was also finding in other poems, both good and bad, that the style could betray him, or he the style. His oft-quoted statement on completing *Saint Judas* reveals his impatience: "Whatever I write from now on will be completely different. I don't know what it will be, but I am finished with what I was doing in that book."

It is evident that this statement was made some time before its use in promoting *The Branch Will Not Break*; when it appeared on the jacket of that book, Wright had learned something about what his new direction would be. But when he made the statement, he was apparently more interested in quitting a style than in defining a new one.

Mastery of traditional forms can sometimes be accompanied by the illusion that within those forms there is a finite way of doing things. Clearly articulated, the idea is not very convincing; but as a

sneaking suspicion in the mind of the poet, it can have unhappy results. Certain habits of phrase, rhythm, and rhyme come along more
often than the poet cares to notice, and some poems seem less themselves than versions of earlier poems. The poet is able to apply too
much prior experience to each new poem, and not enough fresh experience. (I wish it could go without saying that all these traps await
the worker in open forms as well; but in this century the opponents
of traditional form have produced the stronger propaganda.)

That Wright's poetry had reached some such impasse can be de-
duced merely from the ends of the lines in his first two books. The
following words appear anywhere from nine to thirty-four times
each: *snow, bird(s), dead, down, gone, ground, stone(s), tree(s),
face(s),* and *air.* Every one of the sixty-six poems carried forward
from the first two books into *Collected Poems* uses at least one of
these end-words; a few use almost all of them. *Stone* and *air* are durable, but not indestructible.

"All the Beautiful Are Blameless" is a fine example of various uses
of these habitual moves. It is one of my favorite poems in *Saint
Judas;* I came upon it when I was an undergraduate, and I still read it
with an echo of that first surge of certainty that this was the kind of
poem I liked. It is an account of a girl's drowning in a lake, and of the
recovery of her body. Much of the tension in the poem arises from
the intrinsic power of the subject matter, but even more is produced
by the two views of what happened. One point of view is unswerv-
ingly romantic, and the other is realistic, sometimes to the point of
brutality. "Out of a dark into the dark she leaped / Lightly this day,"
the poem begins, but the tone quickly moves into its rapid alterna-
tion of tones and viewpoints:

> Two stupid harly-charlies got her drunk
> And took her swimming naked on the lake.
> The waters rippled lute-like round the boat,
> And far beyond them, dipping up and down,
> Unmythological sylphs, their names unknown,
> Beckoned to sand bars where the evenings fall.

These shifts in diction are deftly modulated, and establish a wide
range of sensitivity. The voice launches a few lines later into something close to preciosity, as the imaginative attraction of the subject
is clarified:

Slight but orplidean shoulders weave in dusk
Before my eyes when I walk lonely forward
To kick beer-cans from tracked declivities.
If I, being lightly sane, may carve a mouth
Out of the air to kiss, the drowned girl surely
Listened to lute-song where the sylphs are gone.
The living and the dead glide hand in hand
Under cool waters where the days are gone.
Out of the dark into a dark I stand.

Orplidean is interesting, not least because I have seen no dictionary which contains it. But it has the sound of a real word, all right, and it turns up again in *To a Blossoming Pear Tree*, where Wright gazes lovingly across a part of Italy he calls "my orplidean country." The word seems to be a coinage based on Orplid, an imaginary country of fantastic loveliness invented by the German poet Eduard Mörike. This word, then, strikes an extraordinarily literary note, which reverberates through *declivities*, *lute-song*, and *sylphs*, to the last line of the stanza, where the distinction between *a dark* and *the dark* is echoed from the first line of the poem. The sensibility thus depicted is brought up short in the next two stanzas:

The ugly curse the world and pin my arms
Down by their grinning teeth, sneering a blame.
Closing my eyes, I look for hungry swans
To plunder the lake and bear the girl away,
Back to the larger waters where the sea
Sifts, judges, gathers the body, and subsides.

But here the starved, touristic crowd divides
And offers the dead
Hell for the living body's evil:
The girl flopped in the water like a pig
And drowned dead drunk.

As in the passage quoted from "Witches Waken the Natural World in Spring," there is a small syntactical mystery in the first sentence above. "Down by their grinning teeth" is hard to visualize: does *by* mean *beside*, or *by means of*? To the speaker, it does not matter; the violence of the image, blurred as it may be, is enough, and its very confusion is a symptom of the speaker's state of mind; he can see what he wishes to see only if he closes his eyes. In the final stanza, a reconciliation between the two ways of seeing is almost achieved:

> So do the pure defend themselves. But she,
> Risen to kiss the sky, her limbs still whole,
> Rides on the dark tarpaulin toward the shore;
> And the hired saviors turn their painted shell
> Along the wharf, to list her human name.
> But the dead have no names, they lie so still,
> And all the beautiful are blameless now.

The long second sentence of this stanza is a fine fusion of the romantic's way of talking and the realist's way of seeing. But the first and third sentences tilt the balance in favor of a romantic fuzziness. "So do the pure defend themselves" is an interesting summation of the girl's leap; it seems also to reach out farther into the poem, and speak for the romantic visionary's defense as well. And the last two lines demand more assent than they quite deserve. They are prepared for in several ways: the unknown names of the "unmythological sylphs," and the "ugly" who "[sneer] a blame," give the lines a ground to grow from. At the same time, however, the lines fail to make quite enough literal sense; we are free to take or leave their assertions. All this leads to a suspicion that the lines may have been written earlier than other parts of the poem, and were worked toward. This cannot be proven in the absence of worksheets, but that is not the point; that they *sound* like a prearranged conclusion is a considerable deficiency in the poem, even though the lines themselves have a memorable loveliness.

Another illustration of Wright's increasing frustration with his early style is the trio of poems about men condemned to death: "A Poem about George Doty in the Death House," from *The Green Wall*, and from *Saint Judas*, "American Twilights, 1957," and "At the Executed Murderer's Grave." All three poems are somewhat oratorical, and contain passages of inflated rhetoric. The last of them is explicitly concerned, not only with the executed murderer, but with the problem of poetic style and posturing.

"A Poem about George Doty in the Death House" reveals Wright's early style at something close to its best. Formally, it consists of almost inappropriately delicate eight-line stanzas of rhymed iambic trimeter, but within that framework Wright masters his flexible diction. The speaker begins by describing the prison, and then imagines in more detail one prisoner, George Doty, an Ohio rapist and murderer. Beside his cell, "hardy perennial bums" are said to complain of hunger and cold, while Doty's desperate need for love, and his pathetic failure, are the occasions for the speaker's sympathy:

> Now, as he grips the chain
> And holds the wall, to bear
> What no man ever bore,
> He hears the bums complain;
> But I mourn no soul but his,
> Not even the bums who die,
> Nor the homely girl whose cry
> Crumbled his pleading kiss.

The unusually exclusive sentiment in this stanza is implicitly rejected in "American Twilights, 1957," which is dedicated to Caryl Chessman, famous for staving off execution at San Quentin until he finally went to the gas chamber in 1960. The poem is in two parts, the first a description of the hopeless routine of prison life; the second takes the oratorical stance, pointing to public obliviousness, and calling for God's mercy on the public as well as on the outcasts. The tone is somewhat artificially elevated by means of repetition ("God, God have pity") and occasional poeticism ("Lo now, the desolation"). However, it mourns, not one soul to the exclusion of others, but everyone caught in the human predicament.

"At the Executed Murderer's Grave" returns to the subject of George Doty, and "by occasion," as Milton said, takes up the situation of the poet, identified in the first line as James A. Wright. Most of the poem is in irregularly rhymed iambic pentameter, but the lines are often violently colloquial, stronger even than the "realistic" sections of "All the Beautiful Are Blameless":

> I walked here once. I made my loud display,
> Leaning for language on a dead man's voice.
> Now sick of lies, I turn to face the past.

One could hazard a guess that "the dead man" is E. A. Robinson, in whose mode Wright had "tried very hard" to work; but the tone is enough to tell us, not what Wright thinks of the dead man or his voice, but what he thinks of his earlier "loud display":

> Doty, if I confess I do not love you,
> Will you let me alone? I burn for my own lies.
> The nights electrocute my fugitive,
> My mind. I run like the bewildered mad
> At St. Clair Sanitarium, who lurk,
> Arch and cunning, under the maple trees,
> Pleased to be playing guilty after dark.
> Staring to bed, they croon self-lullabies.
> Doty, you make me sick. I am not dead.
> I croon my tears at fifty cents per line.

This passage repudiates not only the earlier Doty poem, but also "She Hid in the Trees from the Nurses," an excessively wistful characterization of a girl in a sanitarium evading the curfew. Wright works himself up to brutal energy in the next section, describing Doty as an idiot, a thief, a piece of filth; then he makes a double-edged declaration:

> I waste no pity on the dead that stink,
> And no love's lost between me and the crying
> Drunks of Belaire, Ohio, where police
> Kick at their kidneys till they die of drink.
> Christ may restore them whole, for all of me.
> Alive and dead, those giggling muckers who
> Saddled my nightmares thirty years ago
> Can do without my widely printed sighing
> Over their pains with paid sincerity.
> I do not pity the dead, I pity the dying.

The anger in this passage seems to radiate in all directions, until the last line focuses the poet's rage. Wright himself is among "the dying," as he makes clear in the fourth and fifth sections of the poem. In the fifth section, the meter expands surprisingly, as does the vision, and we are given a glimpse of things to come:

> This grave's gash festers. Maybe it will heal,
> When all are caught with what they had to do
> In fear of love, when every man stands still
> By the last sea,
> And the princes of the sea come down
> To lay away their robes, to judge the earth

And its dead, and we dead stand undefended everywhere,
And my bodies—father and child and unskilled criminal—
Ridiculously kneel to bare my scars,
My sneaking crimes, to God's unpitying stars.

"The last sea" is like those "larger waters" in "All the Beautiful
Are Blameless," "where the sea / Sifts, judges, gathers the body, and
subsides." That all will be judged leads the poet to the poem's conclusion where, as he reverts to meter, he faces the realization that he
cannot fully separate himself from

the rotted face
Of Doty, killer, imbecile, and thief:
Dirt of my flesh, defeated, underground.

Though it sometimes skirts the edges of self-indulgence, the flexibility and unpredictability of this poem mark it not only as a recognizable precursor of Wright's later style, but also as one of his best
poems in either style.

But if Wright came to distrust his early manner, and could even
articulate that distrust in good poems, there are other poems in
which the form is simply there, not visibly separable from the poems, which are as good as anything Wright has done. These very successful poems tend to be concerned with the same themes that
Wright has always returned to with some regularity.

"The Assignation," for example, still ranks as one of Wright's
most impressive achievements. It may be that few poets now under
forty will admire it; certainly few enough of them have the skill to
have carried it off, even on a dare. Like "My Grandmother's Ghost,"
"Come Forth," "The Ghost," "The Alarm," and "But Only Mine,"
the narrative concerns revenance or resurrection, presented in this
instance not as a dream, but as the thing that really happens. The
poem is surprisingly controlled, given its length—eighty-eight
lines—and the melodramatic nature of the story. By an intricate
spell, a ghost rises and is enabled to return to a picnic ground, a place
significant to her and her lover when she was alive. She fails to find
him, and takes a demon as a surrogate; but still the pain of her loss
keeps the ghost yearning for her lover, and accusing him of failure to
keep an old promise:

You sat beside the bed, you took my hands;
And when I lay beyond all speech, you said,
You swore to love me after I was dead,
To meet me in a grove and love me still,
Love the white air, the shadow where it lay.
Dear love, I called your name in air today,
I saw the picnic vanish down the hill,
And waved the moon awake, with empty hands.

In one view, this poem may be taken as a *tour de force*, a contemporary attempt at Coleridgean evocation of the supernatural; as such, it is successful, which is remarkable enough. But in the particularity of its details, the poem becomes a convincing character study as well, taking hold of the reader and not letting go until it has made a point; the reader senses the unimaginable permanence of the separation between the living and the dead.

The poems about revenance, or the "graveside" poems like the second one about George Doty, are almost all quite moving in their presentation of the impossibility of communication between living and dead. In one case, "Devotions," there is a hard and honest edge to the speaker's frustration, as he stands before the grave of a childhood enemy, regretting that it is too late even to gloat:

I cannot even call to mind so clearly,
As once I could, your confident thin voice
   Banishing me to nothing.
Your hand crumbles, your sniffing nostrils barely
   Evoke the muscles of my loathing;
And I too die, who came here to rejoice.

In the presence of his enemy's bodily deterioration, which of course he can only imagine, the speaker is "shaken" by the same realization of futility that overtakes the final address to George Doty. In language quite similar to that of his later work, Wright addresses to the dead enemy a final stanza of unusual power, evocative of losses which cannot be regained; at this cemetery, there is

Nothing to mark you off in earth but stone.
Walking here lonely and strange now, I must find
   A grave to prod my wrath
Back to its just devotions. Miserable bone,

Devouring jaw-hinge, glare gone blind,
Come back, be damned of me, your aftermath.

At its most extreme, Wright's early-mastered ability to combine traditional form and colloquial diction sounds increasingly like his later poems. "A Note Left in Jimmy Leonard's Shack," for example, arises from the same grimy background that has produced such later poems as "Autumn Begins in Martins Ferry, Ohio"; the speaker is a boy, apparently a recreation of the young Wright, who has had to deliver a message to a drunken bum. Jimmy Leonard's brother Minnegan has been found unconscious beside the river. The boy is afraid to try rousing Jimmy out of his stupor, and is already apprehensive about having broken family rules in "coming up this far, / Leaving a note, and running as I came." Here is how the voice sounds at the end of the poem:

Beany went home, and I got sick and ran,
    You old son of a bitch.
You better hurry down to Minnegan;
He's drunk or dying now, I don't know which,
Rolled in the roots and garbage like a fish,
    The poor old man.

And here, from the end of a poem published almost fifteen years later, is the voice of a man recalling another unsavory episode; the poem is "Ohio Valley Swains," from *Two Citizens* (1973):

You thought that was funny, didn't you, to mock a girl?
I loved her only in my dreams,
But my dreams meant something
And so did she,
You son of a bitch,
And if I ever see you again, so help me in the sight of God,
I'll kill you.

What is notable here is not merely the shared epithet, but the continued inclusiveness of diction; Wright's later manner is sometimes said to be free of old-fashioned rhetoric, but it can still put in the right place a line like "I loved her only in my dreams."

The publication of *The Branch Will Not Break* elicited various reactions, most of them extravagantly favorable. And now that Wright has mastered his open forms, retaining in them the voice and character which have always given his poems their extraordinary strength, it is not hard to conclude that he moved in productive directions. But two things need to be remembered. First, as I have said, Wright has not completely abandoned traditional forms; and, second, many of the earliest poems in the new manner are boring, derivative failures. At the same time that Michael Hamburger was claiming that "it is only in the new collection that Wright has found this wholly distinctive voice," George Garrett, in a virtuoso essay called "Against the Grain: Poets Writing Today," was less certain about the distinctiveness of this voice: "The triumph of Bly is all too obvious in the 'new' James Wright. Wright began as a disciple of Frost, developed as one of the finest poets we have. But *The Branch Will Not Break* is quite close in style and mannerism and even subject-matter to Bly's *Silence in the Snowy Fields*; and, in fact, one of the poems is called 'Mary Bly,' after Bly's daughter."

Sure enough, there are some poems in Wright's third book which are virtually indistinguishable from most of the poems in Bly's first book. There is the insistent absence of meter, the flatness of statement, the heavy dependence upon image alone; this is a kind of poem that absolutely anyone could write, after having seen a few examples:

> "In the Cold House"
>
> I slept a few minutes ago,
> Even though the stove has been out for hours.
> I am growing old.
> A bird cries in bare elder trees.

It can be argued that this little poem is held together by the contemplation of time; it moves from *minutes* to *hours* to *growing old*. Unfortunately, it goes on from there to *elder*, which suddenly becomes a pun that must be explained away somehow, like the end of this sentence from Frost's "Mending Wall":

> Before I built a wall I'd ask to know
> What I was walling in or walling out,
> And to whom I was like to give offense.

But of course Wright was more often successful with the new style, especially when he made it his own; poems like "A Blessing" still stand up very well, and the fierce gentleness of vision in Wright's subsequent books has kept him in the first rank of poets writing today.

The rhymed and metered poems which continue to appear are interesting, not merely because they are there, though that is something; but even in that mode Wright has developed and extended his art. "Two Horses Playing in the Orchard," included in *The Branch Will Not Break*, may possibly be left over from years when *Saint Judas* was being written; but its delicately truncated grammar, especially in the final stanza, is unlike anything in the first two books. The first two stanzas describe the horses, raiding the apples in an orchard where they do not belong; the poem begins, "Too soon, too soon, a man will come / To lock the gate, and drive them home." The last stanza echoes this beginning, expresses a view somewhat different from that taken in "An Offering for Mr. Bluehart," and achieves a magical ambiguity in the last line:

> Too soon, a man will scatter them,
> Although I do not know his name,
> His age, or how he came to own
> A horse, an apple tree, a stone.
> I let those horses in to steal
> On principle, because I feel
> Like half a horse myself, although
> Too soon, too soon, already. Now.

From this point onward, it is almost safe to say that the vagueness goes out of Wright's poetry. In later poems in traditional forms, there is a new kind of bluntness in the tone acquired during the mastery of open forms. There is also a new willingness to speak somewhat cozily about the problems of the formalist poet, as in "Speak" (*Shall We Gather at the River*) or "To a Dead Drunk" ("New Poems," *Collected Poems*). In the first of these, the tight form is abandoned momentarily ("rhyme be damned"), and in the second, a line which ought to rhyme with *miracle* is a parenthetical aside: "(Listen, what rhymes with miracle?)" There are other examples of this calculated lapse into self-consciousness, even the use of metrical terminology such as *hendecasyllabic* and *amphibrach*. At the same time, Wright continues to turn faultless stanzas to good uses, as in "With the Shell of a Hermit Crab" (*To a Blossoming Pear Tree*).

It appears, then, that certain features of Wright's career are less important than has sometimes been claimed. Many poets of Wright's generation—Rich, Merwin, Kinnell, among others—shifted from closed to open form at about the same time. Some poets simply find it necessary to keep moving. What is extremely unusual in Wright's career is that through great industry, independence, and vision, he has evolved an increasingly large and flexible command of technique. His flexibility has saved him from the rigid allegiances to open or closed form which are sometimes declared by other poets, and that often make current American poetry seem less artistic than political. Through all of Wright's poetry, though there have been some underwrought failures and some ill-suited postures, there has continued to run a strong thread spun of compassion and technical brilliance. It is a tough combination.

James Wright: The Quest Motif in *The Branch Will Not Break*

PETER STITT

> "what is the relation between my brief and tragic life and this force in the universe that perpetually renews itself?"[1]

I

JAMES WRIGHT'S THIRD volume of poems, *The Branch Will Not Break* (1963), is generally regarded as marking his transformation into an important and path-breaking contemporary poet. It has been described by various critics as "the real watershed in Wright's work," "one of the key books of the early 1960s," and as containing poetry "unlike anything being written in America at the time."[2] More than anything else, these reactions are based on the new way of writing which Wright exhibited in the book, a style and structure best described by James Seay, who suggests that after *Saint Judas* (1959), Wright began "concentrating on simplifying the individual line, sharpening the imagery within a given line, making it more obviously receptive to the irrational, and reducing exposition to a minimum. In this new spareness there was no room for rhetorical impulses. In general, the imagery took on a more luminous nature and a dreamlike fluidity. As for the development of the total poem, he gave himself more freedom to depart from a strictly 'logical' progression and introduce the unexpected, the unpredictable."[3]

The last quality mentioned by Seay—a deemphasis of logic and a corresponding reliance upon the unexpected and unpredictable—has made Wright's newer poems difficult and obscure for many readers. At times this would seem to be Wright's fault; one critic, after quoting this passage—

And the moon walks,
Hunting for hidden dolphins

            Behind the darkening combers
            Of the ground

—justly comments: "These lines really don't mean anything. At times Wright deludes himself into believing he has a poem when he really hasn't anything."[4]

More often, however, the fault belongs to the reader, who has been either too lazy or too inattentive to penetrate beyond the surface difficulties of style. For example, in a recent book, this assertion was made: "We can infer . . . that the inscription, 'My life was never so precious / To me as now,' [from "Inscription for the Tank"] was scrawled on the wall of the drunk tank by the Sioux speaker of 'In Terror of Hospital Bills,' who utters the phrase also in that poem."[5] The speaker of these two poems, which appear in *Shall We Gather at the River* (1968), is not a Sioux Indian, but the poet himself. The critics have misinterpreted the statement "I am a full-blooded Sioux Indian," which appears in "In Terror of Hospital Bills," and which is simply part of an unreal monologue which the poet imagines himself addressing to an ordinary, respectable citizen (which the poet, in this book, is not).

If otherwise intelligent critics can go this wrong—and the example is by no means an isolated one[6]—then it seems likely that ordinary readers are also misreading the poems. While the world probably does not need yet another discussion of Wright's style, it does seem to need a full discussion of the structure of meanings implicit in some of his books. In this essay, I propose to show what *The Branch Will Not Break* is about—its thematic concerns and thematic strategies.

       II

    The basic strategy Wright employs in *The Branch Will Not Break* is that of a quest. In his search for happiness, for comfort, for consolation, and for sustenance, the poet turns from the city to the country, from society to nature, from human beings to animals, and from a fear of the finality of death to a trust in immortality. The struggle has the stamp of authenticity; the speaker of the poems is the poet himself—not some persona he has created—and the poems are based on his own life.[7] Speaking of the time when these poems were written, Wright has said that, after his second book, *Saint*

Judas, was published in 1959, he "had come, for personal reasons but also for artistic reasons, to something like a dead end. I was in despair at that time, and what usually has consoled me is words. . . . But suddenly, it seemed to me that the words themselves had gone dead."[8] In his despair Wright happened to come across a copy of Robert Bly's then-new magazine, *The Fifties*: "I wrote him a letter. It was sixteen pages long and single spaced, and all he said in reply was, 'Come on out to the farm.' I made my way out to that farm." Wright at this time was teaching at the University of Minnesota and living in Minneapolis, and Bly was living on his farm near Madison, in western Minnesota. What Wright said he eventually found there was a twofold resurrection. It was artistic, for Bly "made it clear to me that the tradition of poetry which I had tried to master, and in which I'd come to a dead end, was not the only one. He reminded me that poetry is a possibility, that although all poetry is formal, there are many forms, just as there are many forms of feeling." The resurrection was also personal: "I'm a member of [Bly's] family too. I'm Mary's godfather. They love me and they saved my life. I don't mean just the life of my poetry either."

The Branch Will Not Break, as Wright has told the story, grew out of his frequent visits to the Bly farm: "At the center of that book is my rediscovery of the abounding delight of the body that I had forgotten about. Every Friday afternoon I used to go out to Bly's farm, and there were so many animals out there." He goes on to tell how he would sometimes sit looking out over the prairie in the company of Simon, the dog, and David, the horse: "One afternoon, a gopher came up out of a hole and looked at us. Simon didn't leap for him, David didn't kick him, and I didn't shoot him. There we were, all four of us together. All I was thinking was, I can be happy sometimes. And I'd forgotten that. And with those animals I remembered then. And that is what that book is about, the rediscovery."

The personal nature of these poems and of the poet's quest is reflected in form as well as in content. John Logan has pointed out that the book is made of "images where what is imaged is a gesture of the inner life of man."[9] There is also an attempt, in individual poems as in the volume as a whole, to make "the poetic revelation in its unfolding . . . more closely approximate the actual sequentiality of images and ideas that led the poet to a given conclusion."[10] In a sense, we see the poet's actual quest taking place before us as we read the poems—his conclusions are sometimes tentative rather than firm, the stages in his progress are sometimes vague and inconclusive rather than clear and final. In short, the poems seem more nearly to reflect the pattern found in life than that found in well-made works of art.

In the book itself, Wright sets up the idea of a quest in his epigraph, two stanzas from German which may be translated:

> Oh, if I could go there,
> And there gladden my heart,
> And be free of all torture,
> And be free and blissful.
>
> Oh, that land of bliss!
> I often see it in my dreams.
> But with the coming of the morning sun,
> It melts like sea foam.

This kingdom must not, of course, be identified explicitly with any specific place, real or imagined. It represents the heart's desire, any paradise where one may find his ease, joy, fulfillment. The lines express the spirit of longing present in the first half of Wright's book, and the spirit of temporary attainment found in the second half.

In his first poem, "As I Step over a Puddle at the End of Winter, I Think of an Ancient Chinese Governor," Wright locates his sense of longing in Po Chu-i—"balding old politician" and minor poet— who, late in life, was sent to a new post in a small city far up the Yang-Tze. That Wright views the journey of Po as a quest is indicated by the quotation—from Po himself—that he has chosen for an epigraph to the poem: "And how can I, born in evil days / And fresh from failure, ask a kindness / of Fate?" A quest can fail as easily as it can succeed, and the poem ends inconclusively:

> Did you find the city of isolated men beyond mountains?
> Or have you been holding the end of a frayed rope
> For a thousand years?

Wright is obviously presenting his own indeterminate situation through or behind that of the Ancient Governor, and all that is established thus far is the necessity for the quest; we cannot as yet know its outcome.[11]

68

III

The negative side of the poet's quest—that from which he wishes to escape—has two general aspects. First, his separation from nature, a result of being human, has made him conscious of death, fearful of death, and self-absorbed. Second, the society of which he is a part—America—is seen as sterile, soulless, and destructive. Wright has explained his general view of man's place in nature (a view which will be modified toward the end of *The Branch Will Not Break*) in this way: "Human beings are unhappily part of nature, perhaps nature become conscious of itself. Oh, how I would love to be a chickadee! But I can't be a chickadee, all I can be is what I am. I love the natural world and I'm conscious of the pain in it. So I'm a nature poet who writes about human beings in nature. I love Nietzsche, who called man 'the sick animal.'"[12]

This statement gives an accurate description of the position man occupies with respect to nature in the early poems in *The Branch Will Not Break*. Wright always sees American society as out of phase with nature, but here even the poet functions as a "sick animal." A striking example of this discordance is "A Message Hidden in an Empty Wine Bottle That I Threw into a Gully of Maple Trees One Night at an Indecent Hour." The poem begins with an image in which no two elements are harmonized: "Women are dancing around a fire / By a pond of creosote and waste water from the river / In the dank fog of Ohio." The phrase "waste water from the river" even pits nature against nature, as the river expels part of itself. The poet is in no better shape than the women: "I am alone here," he writes, "And I reach for the moon that dangles / Cold on a dark vine." The image is not a comfortable one, romanticism turned on its head. The poem ends with a fearful prayer:

Come out, come out, I am dying.
I am growing old.
An owl rises
From the cutter bar
Of a hayrake.

The first two lines here are addressed to whoever is intended to pick up the wine bottle mentioned in the title. And who is that? An imagined lover perhaps, or, as seems more appropriate, a nymph, a nature goddess. The last three lines reemphasize the feeling of mortality—owls are predators, and the cutter bar on a hayrake is akin to the scythe carried by the figure of death. Finally, as the owl lifts off, it is as if nature were deserting man, as well it should in a poem like this. Similar poems from this part of the book are "In Fear of Harvests" and "In the Face of Hatred," both based on natural mortality.

Wright communicates his sense of egotistical self-absorption— characteristic of the man cut off from nature—in his translation or adaptation, "Three Stanzas from Goethe." The poet views himself from the outside here, as a man "lost in the thicket," one "whose balm" has "turned poison," who "kills his own life, / The precious secret. / The self-seeker finds nothing." The concluding stanza is a prayer which reiterates the quest motif that underlies this book:

> Oh Father of Love,
> If your psaltery holds one tone
> That his ear still might echo,
> Then quicken his heart!
> Open his eyes, shut off by clouds
> From the thousand fountains
> So near him, dying of thirst
> In his own desert.

The poet is aware of the sustaining glories that surround him, but is still cut off from them.

Whenever he is asked about his position among the poets, Wright says something like this: "I am a minor poet. All I can hope to do is lodge a couple of poems where they will be hard to get rid of."[13] Wright's modesty is authentic, whether we wish to accept his judgment or not. Surely "Lying in a Hammock at William Duffy's Farm in Pine Island, Minnesota" has to fit Wright's criterion. The poem has been misunderstood by readers who don't recognize its context, but the fact that it is mentioned so often indicates how hard it has been to forget. The poem is thirteen lines long, and, though it exhibits neither rhyme nor regular meters, has the effect of a sonnet. It is divided into four groups of lines, each of which presents a different scene. The first, second, and fourth are three lines long, the third is four lines long. Each of the first three groups consists of a single, flowing sentence and deals with an observation of the natural world which surrounds the poet. The fourth consists of three separate sentences—a change which lets us know the end is coming and prepares us for the dramatic close. The entire poem is subjective—we are always conscious of the poet's interpreting eye—though it is not until the final line that he comments explicitly on himself. And it is this line which has caused the noncomprehending consternation of some readers.

Each of the first three groups of lines presents an image of nature that emphasizes its beauty, its balance, its magic, its happy rightness. The third group is typical:

> To my right,
> In a field of sunlight between two pines,
> The droppings of last year's horses
> Blaze up into golden stones.

In the final group the lines turn slightly darker, as the poet builds to his dramatic conclusion:

> I lean back, as the evening darkens and comes on.
> A chicken hawk floats over, looking for home.
> I have wasted my life.

The complaint usually made against the poem is that the last line comes from nowhere, has nothing to do with the rest of the poem, and is totally unprepared for. In truth, the poem is perfectly coherent and easily explained. Throughout this part of the book, Wright is disturbed by his separation from the glories of nature and longs to be integrated into them. In the face of all this self-sufficient beauty, the poet, who feels neither self-sufficient nor beautiful, has to feel that he is wasting his life.

However, he is not yet ready to join nature; first he must escape from the dominant factors in American society, one of which he presents in conjunction with nature and with his beloved animals in "Fear Is What Quickens Me." The first three lines present an image of the predatory destructiveness of America:

> Many animals that our fathers killed in America
> Had quick eyes.
> They stared out wildly.

In the concluding line of the poem, Wright identifies himself with the fear felt by the animals: "I look about wildly." It may be that this identification is with the animals themselves (rather than just with their fear), but this still would not be health-giving for the poet. What he is searching for is a sense of positive harmony with the natural world, but in this part of the book even the animals themselves are out of phase with that world.

The theme of America has always been an important one in Wright's work, and has a climax of sorts in *Two Citizens* (1973). In *The Branch Will Not Break*, America is associated primarily with two qualities: hopelessness and political repression. The book contains five explicitly political poems, grouped together beginning with "Two Poems about President Harding" and ending with "The Undermining of the Defense Economy." "Eisenhower's Visit to Franco, 1959" states clearly the theme of these poems in its first two lines: "The American hero must triumph over / The forces of darkness." Light and whiteness are here (though not everywhere in the book) associated with an industrial, military mentality that wishes to suppress the "darker," more natural, earthy, and humanistic way of thought and life exhibited by peasants—"Wine darkens in stone jars in villages. / Wine sleeps in the mouths of old men, it is a dark red color"—and poets. Surely by design, the poem which follows this one is "In Memory of a Spanish Poet," which contains this positive evocation of "the forces of darkness": "I dream of your slow voice, flying, / Planting the dark waters of the spirit / With lutes and seeds." When Eisenhower arrives in Spain in Wright's poem, he is greeted by Franco, who significantly "stands in a shining circle of police" and "promises all dark things / Will be hunted down."

Whereas ordinary citizens in a country like Spain are presented as living fulfilling lives, despite oppression by their government, the lives of ordinary Americans are almost always seen as hopeless in this book. A desperate coal miner in Ohio, for example, "Stumbles upon the outside locks of a grave, whispering / *Oh let me in*." For the American woman especially life is a series of broken dreams, as in "American Wedding":

> She dreamed long of waters.
> Inland today, she wakens
> On scraped knees, lost
> Among locust thorns.

Water is a positive and longed-for essence throughout the book, representing a kind of fecund fulfillment.

But life is not fulfilling for this representative American wife, whose only defense becomes a form of hibernation:

> Now she is going to learn
> How it is that animals
> Can save time:
> They sleep a whole season
> Of lamentation and snow,
> Without bothering to weep.

American society represents a dead-end road in these poems, and must be escaped. Some of Wright's characters move—as does this American wife—from one form of hopelessness to another. Wright's protagonist—himself—is luckier; his journey to the farm returns him to nature and provides, in the process, a balanced, fulfilling, even a beatifying life.

IV

When he recognizes in nature not fear but those positive, sustaining features so absent from society, and when he recognizes in his own intimate kinship with the animals a release from self-consciousness and death-consciousness, then does the poet begin to succeed in his quest. The first instance of a positive identification with an animal comes in the second of the "Two Hangovers," where Wright watches a blue jay "springing up and down, up and down, / On a branch." "I laugh," says the poet, "for he knows as well as I do / That the branch will not break." A strong break is, however, made with society, as in "Depressed by a Book of Bad Poetry, I Walk toward an Unused Pasture and Invite the Insects to Join Me," where Wright ends up preferring the "clear sounds" of grasshoppers and crickets to the cluttered sounds of the bad poet. A similar renunciation is made in "A Prayer to Escape from the Marketplace"; and "Snowstorm in the Midwest" ends with this clear rejection of society in favor of nature:

> Escaping in silence
> From locomotive and smoke,
> I hunt the huge feathers of gulls
> And the fountains of hills,
> I hunt the sea, to walk on the waters.

Early in this book, as we have noticed, most of the images drawn from nature had, despite their beauty, threatening undertones, as in the owl rising from the hayrake. Here such images are used positively and give reassurance of immortality. This theme strikingly enters the book in "Today I Was So Happy, So I Made This Poem":

> As the plump squirrel scampers
> Across the roof of the corncrib,
> The moon suddenly stands up in the darkness,
> And I see that it is impossible to die.
> Each moment of time is a mountain.
> An eagle rejoices in the oak trees of heaven,
> Crying
> *That is what I wanted.*

Wright's concept of death here is similar to Whitman's, though it surely is not religious in any traditional sense. Whitman believed both in spiritual immortality—as the soul rejoins the oversoul at the moment of death—and in physical immortality—as the body rejoins the earth, thus remaining part of the life cycle within nature: "I bequeathe myself to the dirt, to grow from the grass I love; / If you want me again, look for me under your bootsoles." Indeed, the spirit of Whitman is strong everywhere in these concluding poems.

The final poem in the volume, "A Dream of Burial," seems also to owe a debt to Emily Dickinson. It ends:

> I listened for the sea.
> To call me.
> I knew that, somewhere outside, the horse
> Stood saddled, browsing in grass,
> Waiting for me.

The theology—if there is any—is extremely vague in these poems, but the affirmation is not. From his new sense of nature the poet has gained many things, not the least of which are these intimations of immortality.

Perhaps the most remarkable poem in this volume, one which embodies all of the positive themes enunciated so far, is "A Blessing." The negative statement which concludes "Lying in a Hammock . . ." was a result of the poet's essential separation from nature. Here, all is unity. The poet and a friend stop their car in order to greet two horses grazing in a pasture. Neither fear nor hostility is expressed, but only welcome: the horses "can hardly contain their happiness / That we have come." The horses are as affectionate to the humans— "she has walked over to me and nuzzled my left hand"—as the humans are to the horses—"the light breeze moves me to caress her long ear / That is as delicate as the skin over a girl's wrist." Given this preparation, the last three lines—

> Suddenly I realize
> That if I stepped out of my body I would break
> Into blossom

—do not come as a surprise. The poet by now recognizes that he is a natural creature and that he has cleansed himself of the sullying features of mankind; thus he is as open to apotheosis as any flowering plant.

The penultimate poem in the book, "Milkweed," could have been used as an epigraph to the volume, so completely does it evoke both sides of Wright's quest. It begins with the poet "lost in myself"; then, suddenly, "It is all changed," and he gains magical powers, the ability to create: "At a touch of my hand, / The air fills with delicate creatures / From the other world." The result of this process is a series of beautifully descriptive, clear and imagistic, poems describing delicate creatures drawn from nature. Because of their simplicity, such poems do not require the mediations of a critic; but it is important to point out that, without a successful end to the poet's quest, none of them would have been possible. "March," which describes the end of a season of hibernation for a mother bear, is typical:

> A bear under the snow
> Turns over to yawn.
> It's been a long, hard rest.
>
> . . . .
>
> When the wind opens its doors
> In its own good time,
> The cubs follow that relaxed and beautiful woman
> Outside to the unfamiliar cities
> Of moss.

The mood of poems such as this is thoroughly positive, and shows the poet at peace with himself and his world. The mood is also quite different from that encountered at the beginning of the book. The poet's quest has taken him from man to nature, from city to farm, from solipsistic self-absorption to identification with the animals, from an end-stopped despair at death to an inherent faith in natural immortality. The speaker who greeted us from a web of neuroses has left us in buoyant good health. Since *The Branch Will Not Break*, James Wright has mostly retreated from nature in his poetry (his own life has taken him from Minneapolis to New York, thus intensifying his experience of the city)—except in some of his most recent poems based on the Italian and French landscapes. He has not, however, abandoned the quest motif, which underlies both his *Collected Poems* (1971), the basis of which is love,[14] and *Two Citizens*, the basis of which is America.

NOTES

1. Peter Stitt (Interview with James Wright), "The Art of Poetry XIX: James Wright," *Paris Review*, no. 62 (Summer 1975), 37.
2. Marjorie G. Perloff ("Poetry Chronicle: 1970–71," *Contemporary Literature*, 14 [Winter 1973], 125); Paul Zweig ("Making and Unmaking," *Partisan Review*, 15, no. 2 [1973], 270); James Seay ("A World Immeasurably Alive and Good: A Look at James Wright's *Collected Poems*," *Georgia Review*, 27 [1973], 71).
3. Seay, "World Immeasurably Alive," p. 72.
4. Crunk [pseud. of Robert Bly], "The Work of James Wright," *The Sixties*, no. 8 (1966), 76.
5. George S. Lensing and Ronald Moran, *Four Poets and the Emotive Imagination: Robert Bly, James Wright, Louis Simpson, and William Stafford* (Baton Rouge: Louisiana State University Press, 1976), p. 120.
6. See also Marjorie G. Perloff's misreadings of "Many of Our Waters: Variations on a Poem by a Black Child" in her "Poetry Chronicle: 1970–71," pp. 126–27. To cite one instance: Gemela, the little girl in the poem, is not the poet's daughter, as Perloff thinks; she is Garnie Braxton's little sister.
7. For a discussion of the notion of personal authenticity in Wright's poetry, see Peter Stitt, "James Wright: Poetry of the Present," *Ironwood 10* (1977), 140–53.
8. This quotation and the several which follow on this topic are from Stitt, "Art of Poetry XIX: James Wright," pp. 48–50.
9. John Logan, "Poetry Shelf," *The Critic*, 22 (Aug.–Sept. 1963), 85.
10. Seay, "World Immeasurably Alive," p. 72.
11. For an interesting discussion of this poem, see Paul Carroll, "The Lone-

liness of 1000 Years or the Poet as Emmett Kelly," in his book *The Poem in Its Skin* (Chicago: Follett Publishing Co., 1968), pp. 190–202.

12. Stitt, "Art of Poetry XIX: James Wright," p. 47.
13. Conversation between the poet and the author.
14. For a discussion of the quest motif in *Collected Poems*, see Peter Stitt, "The Poetry of James Wright," *Minnesota Review*, 12 (Winter 1972), 13–32.

The Work of James Wright

ROBERT BLY

I

WHEN WE OPEN the first book of James Wright, we find ourselves in the presence of a man who is climbing over a wall. In *The Green Wall*, published by Yale University Press in 1957, he does not get all the way over the wall. One reason is that the American and English poets upon whom he modeled his poems were actually climbing the other way.

Mr. Wright was born in Martins Ferry, a steel-mill town on the Ohio River, and brought up there. After several years in the army during the war, he went on the G. I. Bill to Kenyon College. He therefore found himself moved from the incredibly ugly landscape of strip-mining to a sort of pre–Industrial Revolution pastoral enclosure. Kenyon College resembled a walled castle, surrounded by Americans crying to climb over the wall, from the disheveled South into the ordered poem.

Almost all Americans at the time imagined the writing of poetry as a climb somewhat like that—leaving the vicious, chaotic world behind, the poet finds himself abruptly in a walled enclosure with fairly tame animals as decoration. When people praised order in a poem, as they did much in those days, they were praising the ordered world possible to them only in a poem.

It is interesting that Lorca's image for the act of writing a poem suggests a journey in the opposite direction. Lorca says that when he was about to write a poem, he felt a strange excitement, like that of a man about to go hunting in a forest. To him then, writing a poem was a climb from his own world into a wilder world.

Here are two views of poetry, absolutely irreconcilable. Americans never really take a choice, because they keep arguing about form. The fault of our metered poetry does not really lie in its order. A poem may have order—Lorca's poetry is an example—and still have terror and ferocity in it—or rather, inklings of them. A poem can't hold in itself all the wildness in the world—grudges that last for forty years, populations that are killed in ten minutes, hundreds of men suddenly going out to live in caves in the Egyptian desert, horses slipping in blood. It is the world which has all these things in their full force. The work of art shows their tails escaping under the door, and we know by this that they are in the next room.

But when the poet imagines, as American poets under the influence of English poetry and American scholasticism did, that poetry is a climb over a wall into an enclosure, then the poet must abandon all possibility of ferocity and terror, even the inklings of them. Yet the colleges still understand poetry in that way—as a climb into a walled garden. They imagine the garden as poetry's world.

In the first poem of *The Green Wall*, "A Fit against the Country," Mr. Wright declares his intention to go to some other world:

> Odor of fallen apple
> Met you across the air . . .
> Both of you had your share . . .
> Of the dark tang of earth.
>
> Be glad of the green wall
> You climbed across one day,
> When winter stung with ice
> That vacant paradise.

He immediately begins to introduce into poems the scarred and the hated. American poetic heroes were usually graceful even in their defeat, for example, Ransom's "I am a gentleman in a dust-coat trying," or Eliot's "Shall I turn back and descend the stair." Instead of these heroes, Mr. Wright brings in a stupid criminal who "stopped his car and found / A girl on the darkening ground / And killed her in the snow." He has more respect for those who break laws than those who keep them. This comes out in a certain affection for rowdy dogs and people:

> The earth knows how to handle the great dead
> Who lived the body out, and broke its laws,
> Knocked down a fence, tore up a field of clover.

He has a poem for a fugitive who got away:

> Hurry, Maguire, hammer the body down,
> Crouch to the wall again, shackle the cold

Machine guns and sheriff and the cars:
Divide the bright bars of the cornered bone,
Strip, run for it, break the last law, unfold,
Dart down the alley, race between the stars.

The speakers in *The Green Wall*, who make a series of "voices," have no pretense to literary education. At the same time, the language of the poems is conventional literary, full of such elaborate syntax that the voices are smothered. "The Assignation" is an example. Others, like "Three Steps to the Graveyard," and "My Grandmother's Ghost," partly escape from it. In a poem describing a wake for a small town Ohio whore, the language suddenly clears entirely at the end:

I saw the last offer a child a penny
To creep outside and see the cops were gone.

Wright's second book, *Saint Judas*, published by Wesleyan University Press in 1959, could have been called "The Branch Will Not Break" as well. The book expresses a fierce, almost ferocious, will to survive. The way to survival, the book says, cannot be found by changing roads, or climbing over obstacles in the road, but only by swallowing the stones in the road, gobbling down what is dark and heavy.

That angel, wheeled upon my heart, survives,
Nourished by food the righteous cannot eat
    And loathe to move among.

The body of the imagination grows stronger, more able to take in terrible griefs:

underground
Where Homer's tongue thickens with human howls.

Poe said that the best subject for poetry was the death of a beautiful woman. James Wright has several poems in this book about women dying. One dies by drowning. The girl

Rides on the dark tarpaulin toward the shore.

The death was senseless:

Two stupid harly-charlies got her drunk
And took her swimming naked in the lake.

But James Wright is interested not in a poetic grief, as Poe was, but in an insupportable grief. The death happens among beer-cans, in some steel town in Ohio, among professional body-divers.

The spirit, ready to pit itself against all harsh things, leaps out into strange alleys of air. In one poem the spirit imagines leaving the body, and returning at dawn to find the body still lying there on the bed. Forced at last to reenter it, the spirit considers the possibility it is something frightful:

One of the living buried like the dead.

In a poem on mourning, he writes against ordinary lamentation, and preachers who claim the earth is comforting. Rather than trust the preacher or the undertaker, we are better off trusting the moon, "blown among the stars." Life is pain without possibility of comfort: some of the living who are honest know it. The poem ends with a moving line:

The hard stones of the earth are on our side.

One of the most beautiful things in *Saint Judas* is a tone of goodwill toward others. American self-hatred is everywhere present in the book, but existing side by side with it is a remarkable and rare goodwill. This emotion is sometimes described by Buddhist teachers as "friendliness toward yourself." This friendliness toward yourself is not very common in the United States. Most Americans, as American writing makes clear, live all their lives with a vigorous hatred of themselves; others look on themselves with skepticism, as if they were an employee of themselves; finally, others live with a sort of impenetrable and cruel self-worship. Goodwill toward yourself is one of the fundamental emotions of great art. In the best Chinese poetry, it is present in almost every poem. Yet it is very seldom discussed in poetry criticism in the U.S. At any rate, Mr. Wright's poems embody a calm conviction that his self is significant and worthwhile, which he affirms quietly. This conviction becomes one of the deepest emotions in *The Branch Will Not Break*.

The most pronounced emotion in *Saint Judas* is guilt. The title itself shows Mr. Wright is aware of it. He has taken the man who is, in Western literature, the most guilty man in the world, and used him as an emblem for himself. He suggests that when one is totally without hope, as Judas was, one forgets the advantages of money:

when Judas sees a man being beaten, after the betrayal of Christ, Judas says he held "the man for nothing in my arms."

The poem is moving; at the same time it is clear it is not a good poem. The transformation of Judas from a criminal who did something despicable into a saint is too quickly done—it is as if a man were to claim he dug a hole for one day and immediately comes out of the other side of the earth. Kierkegaard and others have defended awareness of guilt as one of the most valuable sensitivities. To say, however, that taking acts which increase guilt is a way toward sainthood is to give impossible directions. The poem is really an attempt to bend together, with his imagination, two ends of an iron bar—Wright's conviction that he is in some sense a criminal, and his conviction that he is somehow a man of goodwill.

The first conviction, that he is a criminal, is expressed with much more power in the poem just before called "At the Executed Murderer's Grave." The poem is a final attempt to weld a savagery and intensity to the old literary iambic line, and it has an air of foredoomed failure.

It begins:

> My name is James A. Wright, and I was born
> Twenty-five miles from this infected grave,
> In Martins Ferry, Ohio.

He describes his own guilt:

> . . . "I burn for my own lies" . . . .
> . . . I run like the bewildered mad
> At St. Clair Sanitarium.

In this poem he has finally slipped all the way over the wall, among people who do not fit into the literary paradises mankind constantly makes up. He comments once more on the old innocent world:

> Nature-lovers are gone. To hell with them.

He restates again that he is on the side of those who break laws, not those who keep them.

> Order be damned, I do not want to die,
> Even to keep Belaire, Ohio, safe.

At the same time it is clear that he has not climbed over the wall only for a simplistic Algren-like walk on the "wild side," visiting golden-hearted whores and drunks.

> And no love's lost between me and the crying
> Drunks of Belaire, Ohio, where police
> Kick at their kidneys till they die of drink.
> Christ may restore them whole, for all of me.

A certain ferocity of emotion sets him apart from other poets of his generation. The intensity produces fine lines, though the poem as a whole is again not really a good poem. Too much of it is a typical American paranoia—the feeling that someone somewhere regards you as a criminal, and will imprison and kill you if he can. He identifies himself with the rapist-murderer less out of compassion for the murderer than out of fear of the authorities. The only other poet who compares with Wright in this intensity of guilt is Allen Ginsberg. The same paranoiac fear of authority leads Allen Ginsberg to say America treats marijuana smokers exactly as the Nazis treated Jews. Both poets are expressing the feeling that someone wants to kill them, but their comparisons are inaccurate. A Jew who had really been in Dachau could set Allen Ginsberg straight about the resemblance, just as a convicted rapist-murderer is a different piece of goods from James Wright. Both Mr. Wright and Mr. Ginsberg are trying to imagine circumstances that will respond to the enormity of their guilt, since circumstances in real life refuse to.

II

At the time Mr. Wright finished *Saint Judas*, it is clear that he considered his work to be a failure. He says this in one of the early poems of *The Branch*, "Goodbye to the Poetry of Calcium":

The sight of my blind man makes me want to weep.

. . . .

Look: I am nothing.
I do not even have ashes to rub into my eyes.

During a year's stay in Vienna in 1952–53, he had come to know Trakl's poems. Comparing Trakl's poems to his own, he came to the conclusion that his own work was not actually poetry; it had not helped anyone else to solitude, and had not helped him toward solitude: "Mother of roots, you have not seeded / The tall ashes of loneliness / For me. Therefore / Now I go." He felt the discrepancy enough so that he decided to stop writing poetry entirely.

American criticism in the '50s had been almost worthless in helping the younger poets to get a clear view of their work. Mr. Wright's work, even the weakest of it, was praised to the skies, along with everyone else's. One of the first attacks came from James Dickey, when he reviewed *New Poets of England and America* (I) in 1958 for the *Sewanee Review*. Dickey ripped the book to shreds, lumping Wright in with the others of the "school of charm," and referred contemptuously to his "plodding sincerity." Wright replied. The *Sewanee Review* undertook to print an exchange of letters, lengthy and angry on both sides. The exchange was finally canceled when Wright decided that those who had criticized his work harshly, Dickey among them, were right. He had already concluded that the poetry he had written so far was not poetry, but verse, and if it were possible for his generation to write only verse, it would be better to write nothing at all.

Rereading Trakl gave him the hope that poetry in the next decade could be something more than verse. When he did return to poetry, the influence of Trakl brought in a new tone. The new tone did not mean an obvious correspondence between the two poetries. Rather, the poems begin to come from farther back in the brain. "In Fear of Harvests," for example, goes this way:

> It has happened
> Before: nearby,
> The nostrils of slow horses
> Breathe evenly,
> And the brown bees drag their high garlands,
> Heavily,
> Toward hives of snow.

Dying in this poem is presented as something desirable, not to be hated: snow becomes warm, like beehives.

D. H. Lawrence mentions how rare it is that any new tone appears in language. When this new tone does appear, it has the effect of a new sound suddenly heard in a forest. The sound may be low, but the animals all perk their ears up, and listen with great care.

In "I Was Afraid of Dying" Mr. Wright touches again on the possibility of being free of the fear of death. The walker finds out that

the insects get their freedom from this fear of death from some secret elixir which they find in cast-off things—in things thrown
away: "In empty snail shells, / And in secret shelter of sparrow
feathers fallen on the earth." There is something strengthening in
these things precisely because they have been abandoned by the living creature as it went on to something else. They are like the psychic shells the human being throws away.

His poems no longer concentrate on sensational faults of murderers or rapists, but instead Wright looks back on his own life, and
moves to discard without hysteria old ideas that proved wrong.

At the same time a subtle and eccentric thought comes in. "Undermining of the Defense Economy" is an example. The political
and military world is represented curiously by pumpkins and animals. "A pumpkin / Lies on its side / Turning yellow as the face / Of
a discharged general." The watcher notices that there are things
alive that can't be added up economically, in terms of the gross national product: "Girls the color of butterflies / That can't be sold."
These holdouts bring a tension, an anxiety, that is destructive, that
hollows out humans:

> Only after nightfall,
> Little boys lie still, awake,
> Wondering, wondering,
> Delicate little boxes of dust.

"Milkweed" describes the realization that the longing to be loved,
the demanding of love, the insistence that everyone around us show
their love, was all wrong. All the time, the walker was being loved
by something unknown, "the small dark eyes / Loving me in secret."
The poem suggests that when we realize this, the world of the saints
and mystics becomes real and visible to us. He uses the image of the
milkweed.

> . . . At a touch of my hand
> The air fills with delicate creatures
> From the other world.

The poem most clearly influenced by Trakl is the poem called
"Rain." Trakl has a confidence in the spiritual unity of the world. He
therefore makes statements with qualification.

"Where the skulls are, God's eyes silently open." In Trakl a series of images makes a series of events. Because these events appear out of their "natural" order, without the connectives we have learned to expect from reading newspapers, doors silently open into unused parts of the brain. Here is Wright's poem, "Rain":

It is the sinking of things.

Flashlights drift over dark trees,
Girls kneel,
An owl's eyelids fall.

The sad bones of my hands descend into a valley
Of strange rocks.

III

The book in which those poems appear, *The Branch Will Not Break*, meant an intensification of certain habits of Wright's work, and outright elimination of others. One thing that has infested American and English poetry for years like the death-watch beetle is moral and philosophical truisms. In his new book, Wright has put these aside. Many reviewers, especially academic ones, watched this move with hostility. Larry Rubin, Jr., American scholar from Hollins College, reviewed *The Branch Will Not Break* in *The Nation*, and brought the issue clearly into the open. Rubin's review contrasted Wright's work with the work of Howard Nemerov, whom Rubin takes as the model of a really good poet. He said of Wright: "In *The Branch Will Not Break*, James Wright has gone way off on a tangent, it seems to me. He has completely abdicated the job of giving meanings to what he describes, and is trying to show things as things, after the manner of pictorial art. It is a kind of willful refusal to enter into the business of interpreting experience. . . . Why Mr. Wright has chosen to back off from attempting to show relationships, I don't know. But given his past work, I hope that he soon returns to the business of trying to make things add up in verse" (*The Nation*, July 13, 1963).

How dominant business is in America is suggested by Rubin's bizarre use of business language to describe poetry: writing poetry is a "job," "the business of trying to make things add up in verse."

Rubin makes it clear in his review that he is insisting that James Wright do what Nemerov does, namely, relate what he is describing to the great ideas of the Western world. This is called "giving meanings." If the poet has done his job of "interpreting experience," we will meet in his poem ideas familiar to us from our course on Pope. Let's examine a stanza from Nemerov's well-known poem "On the Murder of William Remington" as an example of a poem that provides the required "relationships." Remington was killed in prison by some self-appointed anticommunists:

It is true, that even in the best-run state
Such things will happen; it is true,
What's done is done. The law, whereby we hate
Our hatred, sees no fire in the flue,
But by the smoke, and not for thought alone
It punishes, but for the thing that's done.

In other words: 1) where there's smoke there's fire; 2) the law punishes the deed, and reserves judgment on the thought. William Remington's death has now been related to the larger world of ideas. The rhythm is a tedious metrical trot picked up from Pope, the language has been constructed from abandoned newspapers and textbooks. The banality of language numbs our senses, and keeps us from seeing how little the various cliches have to do with one another. The rhyme does its part, shaking everything up, like square wheels on a cart; the poem finally becomes fused into a single mass, like an old jelly sandwich.

Rubin can talk confidently of a poet's "going off on a tangent," since he already knows, from reading English poetry, *what poetry is*. He knows it is 20 percent philosophical thought, 30 percent imagery, and 50 percent personal perceptions. One appalling characteristic of American academics is their ignorance of literature. Wright shares his refusal "to show relationships" with 3,000 years of Chinese poetry. Even bad translations into English make this refusal perfectly clear, but the idea never penetrates to people like Rubin.

Thom Gunn also drops crocodile tears on the same issue, mourning that in Wright's poems "the operation of the discursive reason is deliberately excluded." The attack here is coming from the same quarter as Rubin's. Gunn's remarks in the *Yale Review* (Spring 1964) are interesting: "In *The Branch Will Not Break*, (Wright) has pretty well reversed his attitude to style and content. . . . He is far from being interested in moral questions now, and there is a deliberate avoidance of anything resembling thought." Gunn has actually redefined "thought" here, and shrunk it until it is identical with a certain kind of discursive reasoning. Discursive reasoning as understood by Winters and his followers is, like Rubin's "meanings," merely the ability to handle moral platitudes; the ability of the poet to think is proved by the presence of such platitudes in the poem. Critics of this sort are unable to find any thought content in Trakl either, for example, since they are unable to find any recognizable moral and philosophical platitudes in his lines.

What are battling here are two different definitions of thought, which are linked to two different definitions of what a poem is. It is obvious that we have seen only the beginning of this battle. The poetry of the generation of '62, poetry of Creeley, Wright, Snyder, etc., represents a watershed in American poetry—two different views of poetry fall away to each side. On the one side the poetry of "relationships," written to, for, by, and about the conscious mind, which still dominates English and American poetry, and on the other a different sort of poem entirely.

The advocates of the poem of discursive reasoning, those who have a vested interest in it, have not really begun to fight. They will fight tenaciously because they believe they are fighting for nothing less than reason and ultimately—they carry it all the way—for civilization itself. Winters spoke for the earlier generation with his *In Defense of Reason*. Hulme spoke for a still earlier generation; A. Alvarez and Gilbert Sorrentino are among the guardians of the past now.

The idea of "reason" was once used to distinguish between human intelligence and animal intelligence. It is clear the "reasonless" poems we are speaking of were not written by animals, so the critics must be using the word in a narrower sense than the ancients did. Reason has come to mean the part of the intelligence that deals with the areas of consciousness already mapped out, areas like the old Canadian wilderness that has now become "rationalized. The Hulme-Sorrentino-Winters critics deny that ideas can appear expressed in images. To them an idea is only expressed when it is suitably dressed in philosophical language—that is, language without the senses. For that to happen, however, the idea must have been around for a while. The discursive reason then really deals with ideas which have been thought by so many men that the ideas have become petrified into a wide path, like an asphalt road. The winterized critics are really more interested in science than in poetry. Discursive reasoning is important in science, and it is valuable for writing clear essays, but when the poet is in the interior of a poem, discursive reasoning is of little use. There is another part of the intelligence dealing with unexplored consciousness, for which we really have no name.

The great poem differs from the great essay precisely in that the intelligence used to write the poem is the same sort of daring intelligence that discovered the new ideas in the first place. When we see a man bringing up into consciousness what has been hidden, we are seeing a man thinking with that second sort of intelligence. Darwin found such an intelligence available; Freud used it with massive energy.

Thom Gunn would agree with all this. He would merely add that a poet ought to use and reconcile both kinds of intelligence in his work. But they are irreconcilable. The discursive reason he talks of deals with groups of accepted ideas; but the second sort of intelligence comes into play only when none of the accepted ideas are acceptable. Freud's work is a good example of this second sort of intelligence extending itself into medicine and healing. Freud's first effort was the rejection of all accepted ideas in medicine. His new intelligence then came forward. Trakl's and Rilke's work is very like Freud's in that their poems move by a kind of "original reasoning" which carries the reader far back into the brain.

When the reader, and the poet before him, gets back there, he usually finds something painful, some bad news about himself, some anguish that discursive reasoning had for a long time protected him against. Trakl's poetry is made of these painful visions. Rilke with infinitely graceful steps, like a cat's, arrives with great surprise at the wounded area.

Occasionally in James Wright's poems, the speaker comes upon a wounded area in the same way. An example is his poem, "Lying in a Hammock at William Duffy's Farm in Pine Island, Minnesota":

> Over my head, I see the bronze butterfly,
> Asleep on the black trunk,
> Blowing like a leaf in green shadow.
> Down the ravine behind the empty house,
> The cowbells follow one another
> Into the distances of the afternoon.
> To my right,
> In a field of sunlight between two pines,

> The droppings of last year's horses
> Blaze up into golden stones.
> I lean back, as the evening darkens and comes on.
> A chicken hawk floats over, looking for home.
> I have wasted my life.

The mind here seems unnaturally, preternaturally, awake. It sees everything in delicate detail. The cowbells are like magic caravans; the dung of horses blazes up like alchemical stones. The poet leans back, goes deeper into himself. A glimpse of a chicken hawk reminds him that he has found nothing in his life to be sure of, that he has arrived nowhere, that he is still floating. The question the poem never asks directly is this: how is it possible for there to be so many spiritual emblems, signs, reminders of the path, everywhere, and yet for the man who sees them to have gotten nowhere, to have achieved none of the spiritual tasks that those emblems suggest?

The poem is related to the three stanzas from Goethe that come two pages before it. The poem asks who will heal the pain of this man:

> Who drank nothing
> But hatred of men from love's abundance?
> Once despised, now a despiser,
> He kills his own life,
> The precious secret.
> The self-seeker finds nothing.

His eyes are

> shut off by clouds
> From the thousand fountains
> So near him, dying of thirst
> In his own desert.

"Lying in a Hammock" has provoked a great amount of discussion. Some consider the last line, "I have wasted my life," great; the academic critics, almost without exception, consider the final line a failure. Thom Gunn speaks as well as any for the second point of view. He says the poem is made up of several images, "loosely connected by situation, followed by a general observation that may well have occurred to the poet after he perceived the images, but is for us connected with them by neither logic nor association . . . the final line is perhaps exciting because we are surprised to encounter something so different from the rest of the poem, but it is certainly meaningless. The more one searches for an explicit meaning in it, the vaguer it becomes. Other general statements of different import could well be substituted for it and the poem would neither gain nor lose strength."

It is clear Gunn does not understand the poem, or rather, it is not the poem he doesn't understand, but the emotion. He can't bring himself to understand how an intelligent man could have such an emotion. After all, too, Gunn is an educated man; he has trained his intelligence; other people, chaotic ones, may have wasted their lives, but not he. What prevents Gunn from understanding is his habit of discursive reasoning, his rationalism. The rationalistic mind has strong defenses against any harsh view of itself. The rationalist mind works best in mathematics, or geometry, figuring angles of triangles, far from any question of threatened self-worship. The success of mathematics in invading and dominating nature never threatens the self-esteem of the mathematician. But if a man wants to pursue an avenue of thought that undermines human self-esteem, he will have to find a way of thinking other than rationalism! Freud, in fact, used the same dim linkages of intuitions and half-understood images that good poets use. He also realized, and said, that the ultimate result of his work, like Darwin's, would be to reduce the self-esteem of man. In poems the deepest thoughts are often the most painful thoughts, and they come to consciousness only despite the rationalist road-blocks, by slipping past the defenses of the ego. In most men, the inner thoughts are never able to slip by these defenses of the ego. The ordinary mind has pickets everywhere, who make an impregnable ring.

In Mr. Wright's poem, this impregnable ring is broken. Its firm ending reminds one of the close of Robert Creeley's fine poem, "The Hill":

> But that form, I must answer,
> is dead in me, completely,
> and I will not allow it
> to reappear—
>
> Saith perversity, the willful,
> the magnanimous cruelty,

which is in me
like a hill.

Most people would be willing to agree that they are cruel or perverse for a little while each day, for a few minutes. But Creeley uses as an image a hill, which is there all the time. Both of these poems, then, by avoiding discursive reason penetrate to a deeper and more painful level. In each case the poem follows its own path, refusing the supposed duty of relating itself to the great ideas of Western man.

American criticism generally does not understand the distinction between discursive reasoning and original reasoning, and tries to deny the name of intelligence to any but the first kind.

IV

Two energies have been trying to get free in James Wright's work; the first is natural American speech, the second images.

In Wright's first book, it is rare to find lines that actually sound like someone speaking. Frost and Eliot gave tremendous emphasis to natural speech. Frost made it the basis for his poetry—"the most important thing I know." In *The Wasteland*, convincing voices of neurotic upper-class women and pugnacious barflies contribute most of the drama. The absence of these voices in Wright's early work obviously did not come from inability to hear speech. Lines like:

I saw the last offer a child a penny
To creep outside and see the cops were gone

show that he heard voices well. What prevented the natural speech from coming free was a nest of syntax in which the speech became hopelessly entangled. For example:

Nightfall, that saw the morning-glories float
Tendril and string against the crumbling wall,
Nurses him now, his skeleton for grief,
His locks for comfort curled among the leaf.

No whole voice could come through this cat's cradle of grammar. In the second book the voices are stronger, though the syntax is often still literary:

> His daughter struck him in her grief
> Across the face, hearing her lover dead.

If the syntax had not been twisted to accommodate the meter, it would probably go: "So he was dead. His daughter hit him in the face."

As he writes more, Wright's poems depend less and less on elaborate syntax to give the illusion of form, and as the syntax retreats, hearable voices come forward:

> Well, I'll get hell enough when I get home
> For coming up this far.

He describes a woman who:

> smacked the kids for leaping up like beasts.

> Defeated for re-election,
> The half-educated sheriff of Mukilteo, Washington,
> Has been drinking again.

> I can hear my father downstairs,
> Standing without a coat in the open back door,
> Calling to the old bat across the snow . . .
> She has to meet somebody else, and
> It's no use, she won't listen,
> She's gone.

Another buried energy constantly trying to come out in Wright's work is the energy of the image. These three lines are fairly typical of his first book:

> But now I fumble at the single joy
> Of dawn—on the pale ruffle of the lake
> The ripples weave a color I can bear.

The image is smothered by cotton wool. The writer is obviously too mushy. A thought begins, is hardly half-expressed, then the language shifts to another thought. It is curious that the syntax is what encourages this mushiness. The syntax can't wait for the thought to be fully expressed—it is already hurrying on to its next clause. The syntax in turn is pushed along by the meter. So we have the curious possibility that the initial decision to use iambic meter causes the images to be stillborn. Despite all the voices to the contrary, the iambic meter is not suited to the English language. The language may fall naturally into *tum te tum*, as conservatives repeat at every beanfest, but in order to maintain iambic meter, an elaborate syntax is necessary. It is the elaborate syntax which is unnatural in English. Thinking of the artificial syntax so often imported into English, we return again to the vision of the poem as a nicely ordered, universal world, in which all the best things—Latin brevity, German syntax, and Greek lightness—all live together in fortunate community. This Paradise is entirely made up.

Wright has had a heavy struggle with syntax. Through *Saint Judas* one can see his determination to keep the modest syntax of Robinson, at least, and still bring in the living voice. He throws himself at the problem again and again, like a caged bear at a wall. When he finally realizes what he is trying to do is impossible, the syntax clears, and the image begins to be visible.

> Now twilight gathers,
> A long sundown.
> Silos creep away toward the west.
>
> A horse grazes in my long shadow.

The poem "Eisenhower's Visit to Franco, 1959" is a triumph in the simple use of images. Everything is said with images. The poem is obviously one of the best political poems written in the U.S. for several years, and it becomes so without the use of political language. It is certainly one of his very best poems. The poem begins:

> The American hero must triumph over
> The forces of darkness.

The contrast between darkness and light, expressed entirely in images, gradually dominates the poem.

> Franco stands in a shining circle of police.
> His arms open in welcome.
> He promises all dark things
> Will be hunted down.

Throughout the poem, Eisenhower and Franco are associated with a kind of hideous, brutal light, a light that can't bear darkness. The contrast of images is so well established that the image becomes the content. Details that would otherwise be merely description have, by the care taken with the image, turned into some sort of image themselves:

> Clean new bombers from America muffle their engines
> And glide down now.
> Their wings shine in the searchlights
> Of bare fields,
> In Spain.

V

If we begin to pay attention to the faults in James Wright's work, we find that we are constantly aware of a kind of softness. In the early poetry, the softness is a vague, romantic mist that wraps everything. From the beginning his tendency has always been to make his own experience more literary than it really is. For example, the girls tend to be dark, gentle, and romantic; even though he saw, all through his childhood, the ugliest Industrial Revolution land-scapes, that does not come out in the poems as often as one would expect. When slag heaps do come in, a lot of literary language is embedded:

> For two hours I have been dreaming
> Of green butterflies searching for diamonds
> In coal seams.

It is difficult for Wright actually to live in the present. He sees him-self surrounded by a world so entirely hostile that writing poetry be-comes for him at times a sort of step sideways into another dimen-sion—the dimension of beauty, rather than a wrestling with ugliness.

Yet he has an extraordinary gift for bringing alive pool hall fail-ures, drunks gone to pieces, Ohio whores sneered at by business-men, failed wives who are "clucking for love." The searchlights in the airfield as Eisenhower lands are a symbol of the hostility of the world. The poems are best when they make a place for the hostility that he feels in the world. As for his paranoia, it is finally expressed memorably in a few lines from *The Branch Will Not Break*:

> The only human beings between me and the Pacific Ocean
> Were old Indians, who wanted to kill me.

In *The Branch*, the poems about animals tend to be weak. The animals are often unreal. Evidently what happens is that, tired of his own vision of the hostility of things, Wright assumes in animals a gentleness that is not there. Poems like "Trying to Pray," "To the Evening Star," and "Beginning" are weak in that way. The trouble with those poems is that the bulls are too delicate; even the ants are well-read.

He seems to be able to write poetry about almost anything. In one poem he is describing a hatred of industry, and a desire to get away from it. This comes out:

> Escaping in silence
> From locomotive and smoke,
> I hunt the huge feathers of gulls
> And the fountains of hills,
> I hunt the sea, to walk on the waters.

Beauty suddenly blows up, from nowhere, like a storm. Despite his great gift, he often settles for easy effects; for example, he uses words with a kind of literary perfume on them. That is the trouble with his butterflies in coal seams, and occasional poetic animals like doves, stallions, white birds, small winds, etc. Their literary associations are built-in, and the muscles of the poem get soft from not having to work.

The grammar also tends to be too repetitive. In *The Branch*, there are too many *of* phrases: inhuman fire of jewels, hallways of a diamond, pillows of the sea, happiness of small winds, oak trees of heaven, waters of air, shores of melting snow, etc. Some of this is inevitable: when a writer leaves the rhetorical and artificial syntax of baroque English poetry, he discovers that the English sentence, particularly as it is spoken, is held together mainly by *and* and *of*.

Some of the *of* phrases are more interesting than others. There are actually two types: the first, purely descriptive: "Graves of Chippewas and Norwegians," which could be rephrased as "graves *belonging* to Chippewas, etc." The second sort is quite different. When a man says "ruins of the sun" he is imagining a substance that is neither ruins nor sun, but some third substance, which has never existed before, created by the words. Other examples are "daylight of the body," "black waters of the suburbs," "heaven of my skull." These constructions cannot be rephrased. They are a kind of vision, rather than a description. Nevertheless, the reader has the feeling there are too many *of*'s.

Images also become perfunctory at times. For example:

> And the moon walks,
> Hunting for hidden dolphins
> Behind the darkening combers
> Of the ground.

These lines really don't mean anything. At times Wright deludes himself into believing he has a poem when he really hasn't anything.

Another serious flaw in his work is his tendency to evade practical problems—that is, problems requiring action. The way he does it is by escalating them into terms appropriate to Armageddon or the Apocalypse. For example, throughout the second poem about Harding a question is constantly being asked: what is the American citizen to do about the fact that fools like Harding actually become president? The answer requires considerable cunning, and thought, but instead he simply ends the poem: "The hearts of men are merciless." This doesn't really help anyone. If the line is an answer to the question, "Why do all men sneer at Harding without trying to understand him?" it still doesn't really answer it, since Mr. Wright is himself a man. It appears to be an attempt to get to the grand statement without having earned it. James Dickey has the same fault.

The most general fault, then, is a tendency not to bite deeply enough into hard material, but to slide over it. Wright's powerful intelligence is always awake during the poem chewing on the problem of making a *poem*, but it does not always stay on the *subject*.

Finally, the psychic ground in his poems is not firm; there is a sense of a vague and shifting ego underneath.

This must be the end of a short journey through the poems of James Wright. Despite their faults, it is clear James Wright is an amazingly good poet. His lines are not stiff like sticks, but flexible like a living branch. Some emotion, rising very close to the surface, always seems to keep the words alive. In thought, his words, underneath, are in touch with something infinite. Another way of saying this is to say that his personality as a man drives forward, disregarding the consequences. Deep in his personality is the plower who does not look back. Everyone recognizes this in his work instinctively, and it is probably one reason for the great affection people have for his work. His instinct is to push everything to extremes, to twist away and go farther. It is obvious that out of devotion to poetry, he would leave any job in the world, with no notice, or live in any way. Men like Whittemore or Nemerov can never write anything new because they are on-the-other-hand men. If you say, "The Christian Church is corrupt," they would say, "On the other hand . . . ." If you say, "John Foster Dulles was as close to being crazy as most statesmen get," they would say, "On the other hand . . . ." Wright's tendency is the opposite—to follow an idea until it flies, or turns back into a fish. What he admires about the Chinese poets is their ability to get drunk without remorse, to write short poems for a whole lifetime without apology, to ride out of a gate into the desert without looking back.

His work shows an unusual intellectual enthusiasm. Behind the pleasant sense of something new in language lies a conscious and deliberate rejection of an entire structure of thought, which is very well understood. Behind the subtle language, which seems all emotion and fragrance, lies intellectual energy, in this case, extremely powerful intellectual energy.

He goes long distances when he starts, and gives the impression of someone obeying ancient instincts, like some animal who spends all summer with his herd, then migrates alone, traveling all night, drinking from old buffalo wallows.

I wrote this essay in 1965, and there are many sentences in it that I would change now. I especially dislike its insistence on polarizing: academic versus poetic, reason versus imagination, Nemerov versus Freud, past versus present. "At the Executed Murderer's Grave" is a much better poem than I thought it was, and most of the remarks in Part V amount to unrealized criticisms of my own poems. I still stand by the last three paragraphs.

The Continuity of
James Wright's Poems

WILLIAM MATTHEWS

BY NOW MOST EVERYONE who cares about American poetry knows the story about James Wright's *The Branch Will Not Break* (1963). But like the tale of Abner Doubleday and the invention of baseball, the story is more shapely than true, and its use has been primarily for polemicists. So because I think James Wright has already written a significant body of generous and beautiful poems, and because I think the story distracts us from noticing some of the more important things Wright has actually been doing in developing that body of poetry, I begin my essay-in-tribute by debunking it.

For Robert Bly, writing in *The Sixties* in 1966, *The Branch Will Not Break* signaled an escape. One kind of poetry, influenced by Eliot and Ransom, was a jail. The world is vast, various. "Yet the colleges still understand poetry as a climb into a walled garden."

Writing in *The Nation* in 1963, L. D. Rubin, Jr., had argued—embodying the tunnel vision that drove Bly to distraction—that Wright's book "is a kind of willful refusal to enter into the business of interpreting experience." Implicit in Rubin's diction is the idea of a poet as interpreter for hire. Perhaps the fatigue of writing criticism had so infused Rubin that he imagined in Wright a refusal that Rubin had not been able to make.

To other critics, technical differences were important. *The Green Wall* (1957) and *Saint Judas* (1959) contained primarily poems written in rhyme, metrically regular. *The Branch Will Not Break* did not. Neither did *Shall We Gather at the River* (1968), so that in *Alone with America* (1969), Richard Howard could contend that Wright "had written four volumes of poetry, two in verse and two (it is tempting to say) inversely." And in an interesting appreciative article in *The Georgia Review* in 1973, James Seay says that after Wright's second book, "the poems . . . became less formal."

But surely all poems are formal. They take shape. For them to take a shape relatively unlike the shape of other poems is not the same thing as it is to be informal or inverse.

Bly has written well of one important feature in Wright's early work. The themes for which Wright has been so widely praised since the presumed conversion marked by *The Branch Will Not Break* were present from the beginning. "He has more respect for those who break laws than those who keep them," Bly wrote during our war in Vietnam. Wright is drawn to the dead, the drunk, the defeated. He is interested "not in a poetic grief . . . but in an insupportable grief."

"The Seasonless" is a poem about the dispossessed from *The Green Wall*, written in octosyllabics in a recurring stanza (*ababcdeecd*). The truth is, many of Wright's early poems in traditional forms are not particularly well written. Here is the first stanza of "The Seasonless":

> When snows begin to fill the park,
> It is not hard to keep the eyes
> Secure against the flickering dark,
> Aware of summer ghosts that rise.
> The blistered trellis seems to move
> The memory toward root and rose,
> The empty fountain fills the air
> With spray that spangled women's hair;
> And men who walk this park in love
> May bide the time of falling snows.

This is not good writing. Adjectives like "flickering, summer, empty, falling," all seem predictable, both for their becalmed tone and to fill out the slack sail of the metrics. Throughout the stanza the emotional distance between the speaker and poem is considerable, as emphasized by the verbs "begin, seems, may." An indirect construction like "It is not hard" works similarly. Yet this emotional distance serves no purpose in the poem, which strives to be about the speaker's identification with these lonely men. Indeed, in the fourth stanza, "lonely underneath a heap / Of overcoat and crusted ice, / A man goes by, and looks for sleep." I think this man is the speaker of the poem. "Nothing about his face revives / A longing to evade the cold." Wright's distrust of consolation is one of the things I love most in his poems. But there is something too neat and summary about these two lines, as if they explained not something in the poem, but the poet's attitude toward the poem.

And after these two lines the poem closes with four more:

> The night returns to keep him old,
> And why should he, the lost and lulled,
> Pray for the night of vanished lives,
> The day of girls blown green and gold?

It is as if writing in a form that has been so well used by masters of English poetry makes it almost impossible for Wright not to load his lines with echoes, including those echoes of a general tone that produce a prettily blurred sound. "The night returns to keep him old" is noisily significant, but doesn't, actually, make sense. Can the night go away? Given that time goes on, can anyone be kept old or young? The specific echoes in the last line—of Housman, of Frost's "Nothing Gold Can Stay"—are so loud they constitute a failure of tact and proportion, and the line is difficult to read as anything but an echo.

I spend so much time on an early poem I don't like in order to suggest that Wright did not abandon, in a dramatic move similar to religious conversion, an early career as a glib poet in traditional forms. Like most young poets, he began in the currently accepted style. I think not only that he found it wanting, but also that it found him wanting. Comparing his early poems, let's say, to Richard Wilbur's, we see that Wright used traditional forms clumsily. To use a period style well, one has to fight its habits, which are often bad habits and are certainly bad in that they are the habits of others. And to find in a period style those elements that are genuinely and usefully traditional is a complex enterprise. I believe that Wright is a profoundly traditional poet, but that he discovered his personal uses for literary tradition through rhetorical forms, rather than through stanza forms or rhyming patterns.

Many of his rhetorical forms come from the King James Bible, both in its official and written form as Scripture, and in its unofficial and oral form as evangelists' spiels, florid persuasion. In these models the Word and the word are close. Another model is plain talk, which is direct, colloquial, confessional; here fancy language is a likely sign of insincerity, and Wright's declared use of E. A. Robinson and Frost as models makes sense as an attempt to reconcile his love and suspicion of rhetoric.

The poem "At the Executed Murderer's Grave," from *Saint Judas*, exhibits as well as any poem from this stage of Wright's career the war between rhetorical and stanza models. The poem is in iambic pentameter, and its metrical pressures cause some bad mangles. Here are the first four lines:

> My name is James A. Wright, and I was born
> Twenty-five miles from this infected grave,
> In Martins Ferry, Ohio, where one slave
> To Hazel-Atlas Glass became my father.

The first line is fine, and gives us the sense, typical in Wright, that to be born is to die in order to be born again. "Infected" strikes a prophet's note (Isaiah, I guess, would be the prophet Wright reads most avidly). But the inversion in lines three and four is ugly and metrically awkward. It is rough-hewn enough to be sincere, if sincerity is measured by a certain retraction from glossy skill. But paying attention to roughing up the lines, on the one hand, and to the measure by which we judge them rough or smooth, on the other, reveals a divided attention. And Wright's urge is to be whole.

> Earth is a door I cannot even face.
> Order be damned, I do not want to die,
> Even to keep Belaire, Ohio, safe.

In a later poem, I think, Wright would have written "a door I cannot face." The "even" is filler. But not "can't" for "cannot." And these lines bring the poem close to a central imaginative problem for Wright. The earth is lovely and it lives by death. What can we do with such knowledge?

To say that Wright's language grows at once simpler and more successfully formal is to go upstream against the implications of Bly, Rubin, Howard, and Seay. To talk of prose style in such terms would surprise nobody. Dialogue in Hemingway is both "simple" and "formal," and Nabokov's elaborately "formal" rendering of Lolita's simplicities is one of the glories of American fiction. But in reference to poetry, such terms are too often assumed to be contradictory. I don't understand why. To see a sonnet as more "formal" than a list in Whitman is to believe an ocelot more formal than a lizard. Neither am I interested to imagine which animal is more "organic."

The poems in *The Branch Will Not Break* and *Shall We Gather at the River*, and the poems in Wright's subsequent *Two Citizens* (1973), continue his characteristic themes. We see the faded, the defeated, the dead. And for everyone, a vast loneliness. In one poem Wright tells us that "the sea . . . once solved the whole loneliness / Of the midwest." For loneliness to be both whole and soluble is a paradox central to Wright's imagination.

But Wright's style had changed, becoming both more plain and more formal. It reminds me as much of Sherwood Anderson's prose as it does of any poet. Here is a passage from a letter Anderson wrote to a son who was a young painter.

> The object of art is not to make salable pictures. It is to save yourself.
>
> Any clearness I have in my own life is due to my feeling for words.
>
> The fools who write articles about me think that one morning I suddenly decided to write and began to produce masterpieces.
>
> There is no special trick about writing or painting either. I wrote constantly for fifteen years before I produced anything with solidity to it.
>
> For days, weeks, and months, now I can't do it.
>
> You saw me in Paris this winter. I was in a dead blank time. You have to live through such times all your life.
>
> The thing, of course, is to make yourself alive. Most people remain all of their lives in a stupor.
>
> The point of being an artist is that you may live.

I'm reminded of these lines from "She's Awake," in *Two Citizens*.

> For God's sake, wake up, how in hell am I going to die?

> It was easy.
> All I had to do was delete the words lonely and shadow,
> Dispose of the dactylic hexameters in amphibrachs
> Gather your lonely life into my life,
> And love your life.

Another poem in *Two Citizens*, "The Old WPA Swimming Pool in Martins Ferry, Ohio," ends:

> I have loved you all this time
> And didn't even know
> I am alive.

I think that for Wright the object of art *is* to save yourself, and the point of being an artist is that you may live.

The passage from Anderson also reminds me of Wright because it is in the plain style. Anderson can write a sentence like "I was in a dead blank time" only by deleting the words *lonely* and *shadow*. Wright has worked hard to make such deletions. Bly complained, justifiably, I think, that in *The Branch Will Not Break*, "even the ants are well-read." In that book we find lines like

> Mother of roots, you have not seeded
> The tall ashes of loneliness
> For me. Therefore,
> Now I go.

The same poem ("Goodbye to the Poetry of Calcium") ends:

> Look, I am nothing.
> I do not even have ashes to rub into my eyes.

In *Collected Poems* (1971), Wright included a selection of his translations (from Jimenez, Guillen, Neruda, Trakl, Vallejo, Salinas, and Goethe) between *Saint Judas* and *The Branch Will Not Break*. A translator can bring over into his own language the denotative level of a poem and its physical imagery. But tonal and textural peculiarities in the poem are in the language—we might almost say *of* the language—in which it was written. They can't be detached from it. The average translator stops here. Wright is a good translator, and invents for his English versions devices to produce an effect in the reader that feels something like the way the poem in the original felt to Wright. But even when a good translator is at work, his version is usually slightly less complicated, tonally and texturally, than the original poem. So that when Wright was working on these translations and producing English versions simpler than the poems in his own first two books, he may well have taken courage in his struggle for a plain style in his own poems. Certainly lines like

> Look: I am nothing.
> I do not even have ashes to rub into my eyes

are better, cleaner, and embody clearer emotions, than almost any lines from the first two books.

Translating can influence a poet in other ways. In English we indicate whether a genitive construction is subjective or objective by word order; in Romance languages this is done by inflection. So in a Romance language a genitive can sometimes be ambiguous, either subjective or objective. To translate the phrase into colloquial English would require resolving the ambiguity. It would either be the roots' mother or a mother made of roots. To preserve the ambiguity a translator says "mother of roots." Now, that phrase is Wright's own. But it was after he made many of his translations that he began to use the *of* construction frequently in his poems. Its effect is compression. The poem "Twilights" ends with a single line set off as a separate stanza:

> A red shadow of steel mills.

In that line the compression and ambiguity are effective. But in "mother of roots" and "tall ashes of loneliness," because the whole passage is not principally written to evoke a complicated mood or perception (as "a red shadow of steel mills" is), but in part to advance an argument, the ambiguity is an impediment.

There are passages in the translations included in *Collected Poems* that must have given Wright special excitement to translate, for they spoke, in their varying accents, in nearly the way he would come to speak in his own. Here's the end of Wright's version of Pedro Salinas's "Not in Marble Palaces":

> That's why our life
> doesn't appear to be lived:
> slippery, evasive,
> it left behind neither wakes
> nor footprints. If you want
> to remember it, don't look
> where you always look for traces
> and recollections.

> Don't look at your soul,
> your shadow or your lips.
> Look carefully into the palm
> of your hand, it's empty.

I greatly prefer these lines to George Trakl's "Sleep," in Wright's version:

> Not your dark poisions again,
> White sleep!
> This fantastically strange garden
> Of trees in deepening twilight
> Fills up with serpents, nightmoths,
> Spiders, bats.
> Approaching the stranger! Your abandoned shadow
> In the red of evening
> Is a dark pirate ship
> On the salty oceans of confusion.
> White birds from the outskirts of the night
> Flutter out over the shuddering cities
> Of steel.

Everything in the poem smells, to me, of shopworn poetic grief. The garden isn't so fantastically strange, after all; it is made from Halloween props. And the *of* constructions are telling. The "salty oceans of confusion" is paraphrastic, and "the outskirts of the night" portentously poetic. The emotional tone of the poem should be fragile, but everything is crude, black or white, in heavy outline.

Trakl's influence, in the story about *The Branch Will Not Break*, liberated in Wright an ability to use images to refer directly to intense emotions, indeed to create those emotions in the reader rather than refer the reader to those emotions. But Trakl's influence, or whatever combination of Wright's instincts the phrase "Trakl's influence" points to, also provided Wright with a new form for struggling against his taste for fancy writing.

Here is "The Jewel," from *The Branch Will Not Break*.

> There is this cave
> In the air behind my body
> That nobody is going to touch:
> A cloister, a silence
> Closing around a blossom of fire.

106

> When I stand upright in the wind,
> My bones turn to dark emeralds.

In an essay in *Field* in 1973, Wright says that while "the great poets write their books in secret, we discover their books openly." I think he might say, as well, that we live our lives in secret, whether we are great poets or not poets at all, and that if we are lucky and generous a few people love us openly. So the first three lines of "The Jewel" are wonderful to me. Lines 1 and 3 play off a kind of speech I heard and spoke as a boy in Ohio. I can hear a boy's mock-defiance in "That nobody is going to touch," and in the casual "There is this cave" I hear the offhanded beginning often used to introduce some important topic. The second line is strange. A cave is air shaped by walls, but this cave is shaped by air. This space, this solitude Wright speaks of, is palpable but immaterial.

But the last four lines of the poem are fancy writing. There is something heraldic about the cloister, the blossom of fire, and the bones turned to dark emeralds. One almost expects a unicorn.

I think the poem is about whether or not its speaker is worthy to be loved, and that the cave serves both as a space to which he may retreat if unworthy, and also as an impediment to those forms of love—probably the only valuable forms—in which it is crucial not to hedge your bets. The poem puts the issue starkly, and the fancy writing of the last four lines is a way to turn away from that starkness and its challenge.

In *Shall We Gather at the River* Wright has a remarkable poem, a prayer called "Speak."

> To speak in a flat voice
> Is all that I can do.
> I have gone every place
> Asking for you.
> Wondering where to turn
> And how the search would end
> And the last streetlight spin
> Above me blind.
>
> Then I returned rebuffed
> And saw under the sun

The race not to the swift
Nor the battle won.
Liston dives in the tank,
Lord, in Lewiston, Maine,
And Ernie Doty's drunk
In hell again.

And Jenny, oh my Jenny
Whom I love, rhyme be damned,
Has broken her spare beauty
In a whorehouse old.
She left her new baby
In a bus-station can,
And sprightly danced away
Through Jacksontown.

Which is a place I know,
One where I got picked up
A few shrunk years ago
By a good cop.
Believe it, Lord, or not.
Don't ask me who he was.
I speak of flat defeat
In a flat voice.

I have gone forward with
Some, a few lonely some.
They have fallen to death.
I die with them.
Lord, I have loved Thy cursed,
The beauty of Thy house:
Come down. Come down. Why dost
Thou hide thy face?

Wright here associates a flat voice with defeat. So that a round voice, or a fancy style, is for the lies a man may tell himself if he should hope for victory, or justification. It is the voice a man uses to cheer himself, to tell himself that there is earthly justice (the race to the swift). But in this poem there is no earthly justice, no consolation, and what fancy writing there is consists in taking on the accents and rhythms of religious dialogue, because the language of prayer and the language of the King James Bible are plain and formal.

The plain style also turns out to be the language for rejoicing. *Two Citizens* begins with a curse for America (just as *Shall We Gather at the River*, after a preface poem, begins with a curse for Minneapolis), and ends with ecstatic love poems. In the last of these Wright says,

> No, I ain't much.
> The one tongue I can write in
> Is my Ohioan.

And the book's epigraph—a primary example of plain speech in writing—is from Hemingway's "The Killers."

> "Well, bright boy," Max said, looking into the mirror, "why don't you say something?"
> "What's it all about?"
> "Hey, Al," Max called, "bright boy wants to know what it's all about."
> "Why don't you tell him?" Al's voice came from the kitchen.
> "What do you think it's all about?"
> "I don't know."
> "What do you think?"

In "A Poem of Towers" Wright says "Wise and foolish / Both are gone." The defeat in "Speak" has been by *Two Citizens* transformed into a cleared ground, a place to begin from, or just to walk around.

In Wright's earlier poems the Midwest is whole and lonely because every citizen is alone (thus whole, in that diminished sense), and with no links between citizens there can be no body politic, and no real citizenship. Everyone is atomic.

In *Two Citizens* Wright uses the word *alone* in a new way, to mean two lovers by themselves. "And me there alone at last with my only love, / Waiting to begin."

It's interesting to compare "The Young Good Man" from *Two Citizens* with "An Offering for Mr. Bluehart," one of the best poems in *Saint Judas*.

Mr. Bluehart owned an orchard from which the poem's speaker and some friends stole fruit; he had driven them away with gunfire.

> Sorry for him, or any man
> Who lost his labored wealth to thieves,

Today I mourn him, as I can,
By leaving in their golden leaves
Some luscious apples overhead.
Now may my abstinence restore
Peace to the orchard and the dead.
We shall not nag them anymore.

Two stanzas precede this final one, but it isn't until four lines from
the poem's end that we know what kind of fruit the boys stole. The
terms are economic ("restore," "lost his labored wealth to thieves")
and allegorical ("leaving in the golden leaves / Some luscious apples
overhead"). The prayer is to reverse a fall: "Now may my abstinence
restore / Peace to the orchard and the dead."

But in "The Young Good Man," a poem in three parts, whose second section I quote here, the speaker (Wright, himself, as the book
insists) has been warned by "everybody I knew, loved and respected"
that the wild crab apples "taste so bitter you pucker / Two days at
least."

I don't know why,
One evening in August something illuminated my body
And I got sick of laying my cold
Hands on myself.
I lied to my family I was going for a walk uptown.

When I got to that hill,
Which now, I hear, Bluehart has sold to the Hanna
Strip Mine Company, it was no trouble at all to me.
Within fifteen yards of that charged fence I found me
A wild crab apple.

I licked it all over.
You are going to believe this.
It tasted sweet.

I know what would have happened to my tongue
If I had bitten. The people who love me
Are sure as hell no fools.

Many of Wright's poems are about forgiveness, and many of his
early poems are haunted by the possibility that none of us deserves
love and we are therefore fools to love anyone. Throughout *Two Citizens* everyone is forgiven before the poems begin, even Wright him-

self. In a joyful passage from "The Streets Grow Young" he parodies the guilt-ridden man's willingness to seek crimes large enough to justify his guilt.

> Okay. I accept your forgiveness.
> I started the Reichstag fire.
>
> I invented the ball-point pen.
> I ate the British governor of Rhodesia.
>
> (But that was a long time ago,
> And I thought he was assorted fruits and chicken sauce.
> Still, all the same.)
>
> Okay now, hit the road, and leave me
> And my girl alone.

A similar exalted giddiness makes the book's love poems wonderfully believable and lighthearted.

> What have I got to do?
> The sky is shattering,
> The plain sky grows so blue.
> Some day I have to die,
> As everyone must do
> Alone, alone, alone,
> Peaceful as peaceful stone.
> You are the earth's body.
> I will die on the wing.
> To me you are everything
> That matters, chickadee.
> You live so much in me.
> Chickadees sing in the snow.
> I will die on the wing,
> I love you so.

Even Wright's long-running feud with the dead is behind him in this book.

And in his 1973 essay in *Field* Wright talks about his relationship to poetic tradition. Bothered by some bad polemical writing on free verse (perhaps he has been bothered, too, by some versions of the story about *The Branch Will Not Break*), he complains that "the theory of our current free verse involves a complete rejection of the past." Of course the practice of "free verse" does not, as Wright well knows.

I put "free verse" in quotes because I, too, am bothered by its similarity to a political slogan (Free Huey). Too much talk about poetics is really talk about politics in disguise. One bad polemic relishes William Carlos Williams's remark that the sonnet is a fascist form because it makes the words run on time. An opposite bad polemic equates traditional verse forms with established social, religious, and political orders. Such discussion seems to me both stupid and confusing.

Wright is speaking, in his essay in *Field*, out of what he knows about how a poet learns to write better. Slowly, as Sherwood Anderson was right to say. I think that we work hard to learn what little we learn, and that we learn almost all of it from the past.

Wright recognizes that it is a long and intricate enterprise to forge a personal relationship to literary tradition. The triumph of *Two Citizens* is that he has done so. The openness in that book and in the pieces he's published since has little to do, I'm sure, with open or closed forms, whatever they may be. It is a spiritual quality, which Wright learned to register in a language that is partly Ohioan, partly King James Bible and Billy Sunday, and partly a distillation from those poets in our literary tradition who mattered most personally to Wright.

Each of the books Wright has given us contains wonderful and memorable poems. We have no right to ask more of a poet, but our important poets ask more of themselves. It is such a vocation, such a calling, that I have tried to trace in these notes. I believe that Wright's great achievement so far has been to imagine the language in which he can make the simple assertions—though they are, since Wright is a religious poet, as basic as they are simple—of *Two Citizens*. It is as if, having made the language for himself, Wright wanted first to test it against the barest propositions: *I love you*, or *It is a beautiful day*. To expand the range and complexity of what he will say in his restored language will be, I expect, his next task, and it will be our privilege to watch him continue.

A World Immeasurably Alive and Good: A Look at James Wright's *Collected Poems*

JAMES SEAY

I AM SURE THAT before the appearance of James Wright's third collection of poems, *The Branch Will Not Break* (1963), I had read some of his previous poetry with appreciation—certainly the title poem from his second collection, *Saint Judas* (1959), and most probably "American Twilights, 1957," "At the Executed Murderer's Grave," and "An Offering for Mr. Bluehart"—but I cannot recall experiencing anything like that keen sense of discovery which I felt in reading *The Branch Will Not Break*. It was that sense of personal discovery which one knows is a result of antecedent discoveries that cost the poet more than fame or money or one's gratitude can ever repay and yet there are the poems in one's hands. What Wright offered in *The Branch Will Not Break*, as far as I could tell, was unlike anything being written in America at the time, and some five or six of the poems there seized upon my imagination like nothing I had read in a long time.

It was in that light that I was able to go back to the earlier work—*Saint Judas* and his first collection, *The Green Wall* (1957)—with a stronger appreciation, and it was with that certainty about Wright's work that I awaited more from him. His next book, *Shall We Gather at the River* (1968), was everything that it should have been: a natural and skillful extension of those lines of approach he discovered in preparing for and writing the poems of *The Branch Will Not Break* and a continued assimilation of the foreign influences that, in large part, made possible those discoveries. It should be mentioned here that after *Saint Judas* Wright had indicated that what he wrote from then on would be entirely different. The radical change that was evident in both *The Branch Will Not Break* and *Shall We Gather at the River* was for the most part a result of the strong influence of the work of foreign poets such as Neruda, Vallejo, Guillén, and the Austrian poet Georg Trakl, all of whom Wright had been reading and translating. (In fact, in the *Collected Poems* he places the section "Some Translations," containing his translations of these poets, between *Saint Judas* and *The Branch Will Not Break*.) Probably Wright felt that his earlier work, *The Green Wall* and *Saint Judas*, was too methodical in approach and lacked the visionary quality and sense of spontaneity that he wanted. Following the various examples of these foreign poets, he had in his own work begun concentrating on simplifying the individual line, sharpening the imagery within a given line, making it more obviously receptive to the irrational, and reducing exposition to a minimum. In this new spareness there was no room for rhetorical impulses. In general the imagery took on a more luminous nature and a dreamlike fluidity. As for the development of the total poem, he gave himself more freedom to depart from a strictly "logical" progression and introduce the unexpected, the unpredictable. The poems also became less formal, in the traditional sense. For example, only some half-dozen of the eighty poems in *The Branch Will Not Break* and *Shall We Gather at the River* employ rhyme, whereas almost all of the early work is rhymed.

What made *The Branch Will Not Break* and *Shall We Gather at the River* different from *The Green Wall* and *Saint Judas* was not a totally changed sensibility but a radically altered concept of what a poem should reveal about experience. It seems to me that after *Saint Judas* Wright became concerned with the question of how the poetic revelation in its unfolding could more closely approximate the actual sequentiality of images and ideas that led the poet to a given conclusion. That is, assuming some of the truths we arrive at are not the results of logical reasoning, how the unfolding of a poetic revelation could approximate the fluid process of its own realization more closely than in a strictly "logical" ordering of images and ideas after the fact of the discovery. The difference is perhaps one of effect; that is, the poet may well have gone back and rearranged the experiential sequence, may in fact have added to or deleted, but the difference is between that of asking the reader to come along as the poet actually follows the leads of both his logical instincts and his illogical impulses and that of saying to the reader "I have made a discovery and here is an analytical representation of how I arrived at it."

This difference can perhaps be demonstrated in the following examples. The first, from *The Branch Will Not Break*, is the poem
"Trying to Pray" quoted in its entirety:

> This time I have left my body behind me, crying
> In its dark thorns.
> Still,
> There are good things in this world.
> It is dusk.
> It is the good darkness
> Of women's hands that touch loaves.
> The spirit of a tree begins to move.
> I touch leaves.
> I close my eyes, and think of water.

Notice the seemingly random progression, which is accentuated
by the introduction of metaphors and images—"dark thorns" and
"good darkness / Of women's hands that touch loaves"—which one
would not ordinarily think to associate with this context. And yet I
am convinced of the rightness of both the images and the method of
development. The method suggests that the poet is more willing to
examine the irrational messages of his subconsciousness on the assumption that they may have been triggered by some psychic mech-
anism beyond his understanding and that they are connected with
what he is doing in a way he may not have realized if he had been
asked to bring the two elements together in a rational analysis. For
example, a phrase such as "touch loaves" in the above poem could
very easily have triggered in the subconsciousness the similar phrase
"touch leaves," or vice versa, and thus offered the poet a unique op-
tional direction. The idea is certainly not new, for it has long since
been central to any discussion of metaphor-making, and even of
rhyming. What I am saying is that in these poems by Wright the evidence of that process is brought into the poem more than we are ac-
customed to seeing, at least in American and English poetry—in any
effective or coherent way, that is. Note also in the above poem that
the conclusion is left open-ended, thus increasing its suggestibility.

In contrast to all of this is the basically logical progression and
conventional handling of images in a poem such as "The Cold Di-
vinities," from *Saint Judas*. I quote here only the concluding stanza.
The preceding five stanzas involve the poet's responses to his wife
and child as he watches them play along the seashore. He knows

that he should have been delighted at what he witnessed, but he is thwarted by the following realization:

> But slowly twilight gathered up the skiffs
> Into its long gray arms; and though the sea
> Grew kind as possible to wrack-splayed birds;
> And though the sea like woman vaguely wept;
> She could not hide her clear enduring face,
> Her cold divinities of death and change.

Nothing is left open-ended here; the poet wants to be fairly explicit about what he has discovered in the experience. In the sea, and in the woman, he has had a vision of mutability and mortality. All of the images are readily associated with the scene at hand, the movement of the entire poem follows a logical pattern, and the insistence of the iambic pentameter lines emphasizes the fact that the poet has worked to transform the event into a formal experience that bears the evidence of his analysis and craft.

None of what I have said, however, communicates the different ambience of Wright's poetry after *The Green Wall* and *Saint Judas*. Somehow he had found a way of conveying more while saying less, and the sense of intense feeling which has always been at the heart of his poetry was rendered all the more acute in the change.

With the publication of the *Collected Poems* (1971) it is clear in the thirty-three new poems that there has been no letup in Wright's development. One senses in the new poems the incipience of a voice that, in my opinion, Wright has been attempting to achieve since the time of the stylistic shift that marked *The Branch Will Not Break*. It is possible that in the following passage from the long new poem "Many of Our Waters: Variations on a Poem by a Black Child" Wright is, in part at least, expressing an intention to free himself from the foreign influences mentioned above to an even greater extent than he did in *Shall We Gather at the River*, where the assimilation of those influences, we can now see, was almost complete:

> All this time I've been slicking into my own words
> The beautiful language of my friends.
> I have to use my own, now.
> That's why this scattering poem sounds the way it does.

There is other evidence that Wright is modifying his style somewhat in the new poems. In at least one of them he shows a willingness even to accommodate tendencies that characterized the early style from which he departed so radically. Note the similarity of these passages, the first taken from *The Green Wall*, the second from *New Poems*:

> Be glad of the green wall
> You climbed across one day,
> When winter stung with ice
> That vacant paradise.
>> "A Fit against the Country"

> and [I] know the world
> Immeasurably alive and good,
> Though bare as rifted paradise.
>> "The Quest"

The paradoxical aspect of both passages is obvious, as is the thematic affinity. This kind of irony, generally speaking, has not been present in his work since *Saint Judas*, although irony was characteristic of both that book and *The Green Wall*, owing possibly to Ransom's influence at Kenyon where Wright was a student. (The influence cannot be attributed wholly to Ransom, of course, for the heavy use of irony was simply part of the way one wrote poetry in America during Wright's early writing career.)

What cannot be fully seen in the above passage are the results of the formal attention that Wright has given to the new poem, which as I mentioned earlier is another aspect that has not been conspicuous in his recent work, perhaps because when he has chosen to employ them, the conventional rhythms are more varied and subtle and the rhymes more approximate than exact, as well as being more random. None of this, however, is to suggest that Wright is returning to the formalities and ironic tendencies that typified his first two collections. It is rather to suggest that he has achieved a fullness of voice and vision which affords a wider range of choice than was available to him when he first started moving away from the modes of his early work.

Most of what I have said so far deals with technique. As for theme, there are several concerns which have been manifest in Wright's poetry from the start. Probably his most abiding concern has been loneliness. It is the one abstract word that recurs most frequently in his work. In a sense the theme of loneliness gives rise to, or is somehow connected with, most of Wright's other thematic concerns. Death, for instance, figures significantly in a great number of the poems, and Wright sees in the experience of death the ultimate loneliness. Easily a third of the poems in *The Green Wall* and *Saint Judas* touch on death in one way or another, and the concern is still present in work as recent as the new poems in *Collected Poems*: "Every body / I know and care for, / And every body / Else is going / To die in a loneliness / I can't imagine and a pain / I don't know" ("Northern Pike"). For the most part, though, the new poems in which death is a factor seem to be less doom-ridden than the earlier poems. In the above poem, for example, the poet goes on to affirm that despite the fact that everybody is going to die in loneliness, he and the other members of the poem "had / To go on living" and thus ate the fish they had caught as the culmination to a kind of ritualistic ceremony in which various phenomena of nature are recognized and allowed for. The fish is accepted finally as a sacrificial gift: "There must be something very beautiful in my body, / I am so happy." Seldom does Wright arrive at such an affirmative conclusion in a poem that opens on a note of loneliness and death.

Another related theme has to do with Wright's compassion for what Auden, in his foreword to the first edition of *The Green Wall*, called "social outsiders"—criminals, prostitutes, drunks, and social outcasts in general. In Wright's poems these people are almost always lonely and damned. Some of them have had a vision of the final loneliness and stark terror of their condition. In an early poem, " A Poem about George Doty in the Death House," the Ohio rapist and murderer is described as having seen, either at the time of his crime or his capture, "the blundered birth / Of daemons beyond sound," and now in the light of that awful knowledge of his helplessness before both the dark forces within himself and the death that awaits him, he sits in his cell and sees "in the shaving mirror / Pinned to the barren wall, / The uprooted ghost of all: / The simple, easy terror." What makes Wright's treatment of this character unusual is his total sympathy for him, seemingly to the exclusion of any concern for the murder victim: "But I mourn no soul but his, / Not even . . . the homely girl whose cry / Crumbled his pleading kiss." Some consider Wright's conclusion here insensitive to the girl's fate. In his defense, it should be noted that Wright is speaking of what *soul* he mourns, and it is undeniable that Doty's is the one to be pitied and mourned. It is not the poem's purpose to elegize the girl. (Philip Larkin does very much the same thing in his fine poem "Deceptions." The focus of the poem is finally on the rapist rather than the drugged girl and he is seen as the pitiable one when Larkin concludes the poem with the image of his bursting into "fulfilment's desolate attic.") Still and all, the implications and conclusion of Wright's poem are a problem, and perhaps the poet himself had second thoughts, for he returned to the subject in his next book, *Saint Judas*, in the poem "At the Executed Murderer's Grave." Whatever Wright's motivation, he makes it clear that Doty's crime is abhorrent to him—"Doty, you make me sick"—but he still emphatically conveys a sense of understanding, even of sharing, the executed man's condition: "Doty, killer, imbecile, and thief: / Dirt of my flesh, defeated, underground."

A similar empathy is found in Wright's poem dedicated to the criminal Caryl Chessman, "American Twilights, 1957," and again the subsuming vision is one of man's aloneness: "Have mercy on man who dreamed apart. / God, God have pity on man apart." It is as if Wright has taken it on himself to intervene for the lonely and damned, enter a plea for them, find some way of looking at their condition more mercifully. For Judas he recreates history in the poem "Saint Judas" and, for whatever redemption it is worth, offers him the opportunity of a selfless act before his suicide. On his way to hang himself, Judas is allowed to find a man who has been beaten, robbed, and left to suffer. In Judas' final expiatory act can be seen a metaphor for man's need to escape his loneliness and realize a love that extends beyond Self: "Flayed without hope, / I held the man for nothing in my arms." As for the other "social outsiders"—drunks, prostitutes, the misunderstood—Wright has throughout his work made the same attempt as with Judas, Caryl Chessman, and George Doty—to bring them within reach of human compassion.

In the new poems the focus of his attention in this particular thematic context has widened to include blacks and Indians. There is, however, a slight shift in his attitude in the new work. He seems less willing to give himself over so totally and subjectively to history's victims. "I had nothing to do with it. I was not here. / I was not born," he says in the opening of "A Centenary Ode: Inscribed to Little Crow, Leader of the Sioux Rebellion in Minnesota, 1862," but at the end of the opening section we see his tone is actually half-

ironic: "it was not my fathers / Who murdered you. / Not much."
His admission, "If only I knew where to mourn you, / I would surely
mourn," brings the tone of the poem closer to that of previous work,
but still there is a general distancing in this and in other new poems
that was not always evident in the past. This tonal variation is consistent with the overall extension of stylistic range which I noted
earlier in my discussion of the technical aspects of his new work. (In
fact, in the new poems Wright has even found room for humor,
which is a rarity in his work—one poem consists merely of the title
"In Memory of the Horse David, Who Ate One of My Poems" at the
top of a blank page. It reveals a quality one has always suspected in
Wright but never had proof of.)

Wright's sentiments in the entire thematic context of loneliness
and its related themes are perhaps best summed up in a passage from
the poem "Speak" in *Shall We Gather at the River*:

> I have gone forward with
> Some, a few lonely some.
> They have fallen to death.
> I die with them.
> Lord, I have loved Thy cursed,
> The beauty of Thy house:
> Come down. Come down. Why dost
> Thou hide thy face?

It would be a mistake, however, to conclude that because of loneliness and thoughts of death and despairing humanity Wright is incapable of experiencing and expressing joy. Clearly, if the evidence of
poems such as the widely anthologized "A Blessing" is to be trusted,
he is a poet with great capacity for joy. The sources of this joy are
found primarily in the spiritual beauty of people whom the poet
loves, especially women, and in experiences where there is a surrender of the Self to another living thing which the poet senses is in
closer touch with the mystical forces of nature. This latter, too, can
involve a woman, for women in several of Wright's poems possess
powers that put them beyond human bounds. One such, Wright
playfully admits, he would have married: "Think of that. Being alive
with a girl / Who could turn into a laurel tree / Whenever she felt
like it. / Think of that" ("A Secret Gratitude"). In another instance

the poet recalls getting drunk and embracing a tree that blocked his path: "You may not believe this, but / It turned into a slender woman. / Stop nagging me. I know / What I just said. / It turned into a slender woman" ("Blue Teal's Mother"). Note that in both of these instances the image of woman is of an intermediary between two states of being.

There has always been in Wright's work this strong desire to find a closer union with the natural world—even a desire to escape corporal limitations and merge with some spirit that encompasses all nature, not just the human realm. In addition to women, horses appear frequently as possible intermediaries. In "Arriving in the Country Again" the concluding image of a horse grazing in the poet's shadow suggests, on a figurative level, that the poet could experience this mystical state by allowing himself to be consumed by the horse. In "A Dream of Burial" it is implied that his means of gaining entry into another spiritual state after his burial will be a horse. "I listened for the Sea / To call me. / I knew that, somewhere outside, the horse / Stood saddled, browsing in grass, / Waiting for me." The horse image appears again in one of the new poems. "I have come a long way, to surrender my shadow / To the shadow of a horse," he concludes in "Sitting in a Small Screenhouse on a Summer Morning," after having had a vision of the possibility of becoming "a horse, a blue horse, dancing, / Down a road, alone."

All of these references to women and horses as spiritual mediums are, of course, to be taken figuratively. Wright is simply communicating in a stylized way his desire for transcendence into a more intensely felt state of nature, and these are the experiences in which a realization of that state seemed somehow possible. As I have said, these experiences usually involve a surrender of the Self to another living thing which the poet senses is in closer touch with the mystical forces of nature, a surrender that is motivated by the hope of sharing that state of being. Wright is not a mystic, however; his concern is finally with human activity at a level where most of us usually experience it—in our own bodies in or around places such as Wheeling, West Virginia; Fargo, North Dakota; New York City, or Nash's Grove, wherever that is, and with people such as Garnie Braxton, Lemoyne Crone, and Roberta Pugh (and the horse David) who possess the same capacities for joy and despair that we ourselves possess.

It is important to note, however, that up until the new poems most of the expressions of joy in Wright's work involved private experiences of communion with some nonhuman part of the natural world such as horses or trees or with nature in general. Rarely did these experiences center on another person. In the new work there are some notable exceptions to that pattern. Wright seems to have found a source of spirituality within the human realm—in a woman, to be exact—and there is an indication that this discovery has somewhat diminished, or at least made more bearable, the anguish that informs so much of his work. The best example of this discovery is the conclusion of "The Quest," which Wright has placed at the front of the *Collected Poems*, thus giving it more prominence and setting it off from the other new poems that are held until the end of the book. The object of the quest is, of course, never made explicit, but the poet, having moved through a landscape that is defined by images of barrenness and desolation—trees "lorn of all delicious apple," an empty house given over to "dust that filmed the deadened air," "the bonehouse of a rabbit," and stars that hung beyond his reach—comes finally to his love:

> So, as you sleep, I seek your bed
> And lay my careful, quiet ear
> Among the nestings of your hair,
> Against your tenuous, fragile head,
> And hear the birds beneath your eyes
> Stirring for birth, and know the world
> Immeasurably alive and good,
> Though bare as rifted paradise.

It is as Yeats said in a letter to Olivia Shakespeare, "We poets would die of loneliness but for women."

Given the preoccupation with death and despair that sometimes makes Wright's poetry burdensome, I find this recent suggestion of additional spiritual possibilities in his poetic life tremendously heartening. It is not that I require a neat kind of balance between, say, negative and positive in a writer's work, for I know the poet has to be honest to his vision, whether it tends to focus only on that which defeats us or whether it tends toward a more expansive view. I find the implications of some of his new poems heartening because I think Wright's poetry is very special and important to the changing

poetic temperament in America and, because of the promise his poetry holds, it is valuable to us when he finds new resources for extending the range of his poetic sensibility. What makes Wright's poetry special is not that he has any new philosophical insights into
the problems of existence but that he has the gift of using language
in a way that the human spirit is awakened and alerted to its own
possibilities—both the possibility of diminishment and the hope of
increase through participation in an existence outside its own.

The Rise and Fall of James Wright

EDWARD BUTSCHER

JAMES WRIGHT'S ARRIVAL on the American poetry scene was heralded rather quietly by the appearance of *Saint Judas* in 1959. It was actually his second collection, but an initial volume, *The Green Wall* (the Yale Younger Poet selection for 1957) had little to recommend it, except some pretty ballad stanzas, a few startling metaphors and a determined inclination to identify with and deify social outcasts. *Saint Judas* is also the work of a traditional-minded poet little given to experiment, one who is quite content to function within a well-established imagistic framework, to follow William Carlos Williams into "the thing itself," though Wright is often guilty of a fuzzy emotionalism Williams would have never tolerated. The poems are of a piece, tightly structured, heavily rhymed and usually metered (iambic), and, in thematic terms, they are dedicated to being lyrically discontented, becoming, in effect, parts of a single long lament. When hitched to a real and immediate grief, as in "Complaint," his sparse vulgate tongue serves Wright well. His tendency towards the melodramatic is held in check, and the poetic material itself, ordinary language heightened by a series of original metaphors, assumes an objective value all its own:

> Childbirth and midnight sassafras and rain.
> New snow against her face and hands she bore,
> And now lies down, who was my moon or more.

This is not true for other poems in *Saint Judas*. For example, "At the Executed Murderer's Grave," his George Doty elegy, and "American Twilights, 1957," which is concerned with another murderer, Caryl Chessman, exhibit a distressing absence of either deep thought or complex sensibility. Despite several successful lines, both poems cannot escape their simplistic moral cores. The title piece itself, which the author must wish to echo the book as a whole, offers the figure of Judas in an ironic ethical light: already doomed and damned, on his way to suicide's ultimate negation, but still quite capable of spontaneous compassion. Seeing a man being mugged in the street, he runs like a good Samaritan to aid and comfort him. The memory of his own recent treacherous act, however, destroys the value of his "Christian" action. To be sure, his sainthood is affirmed by Wright's narrative, but he himself does not participate in its saving grace. The poem's insistent, emphatic tone permits us to accept the persona as the poet, or at least as generic artist, who knows the true worth of "proper" coins, though he is destined to be betrayed by a world without sympathy for human deviations. Also, there lurks the possibility of empathetic emotions in constant conflict with basic common sense. Sainthood remains his, and Doty's, but so do criminality, alienation, a life sentence of painful isolation from the nurturing community.

As is evident in these two elegies, and in poems such as "My Grandmother's Ghost" and "A Poem about George Doty in the Death House" from *The Green Wall*, Wright envisions his creative role in dualistic terms of outcast and savior from the very beginning, familiar stances not too far removed from Pound's concept of the artist as hero in the *Cantos*.[1] This enables him to wander freely beyond society's pale in search of themes and characters, evoking compassion for the inarticulate victims of our inequitable, antihuman institutions, while indulging personal passion for the confessional voice, and the thematic freedom it entails. Like Diane Wakowski, a much better poet, he strives always to yoke private memory to surrealistic techniques.

Verging on the sentimental throughout, Wright usually manages to avoid complete capitulation in his next and best volume, *The Branch Will Not Break* (1963), only through a fierce neoclassical restraint, a restraint of style not substance or feeling. It is this willingness to confront the unsaid, to appreciate and utilize selective silences and great white spaces, which lets him maintain the required distance between self and subject matter. More important, perhaps, it helps him introduce another notion of romantic oases into contemporary poetry's bleak terrain, a mission he seemingly deems fundamental.

For Wright, redemption is found in the old-fashioned verities of our pastoral past and its poets' Wordsworthian traditions, in crickets, owls, horses, and wheat stalks, which are almost inevitably appealed

125

to in climactic stanzas as significant means of flight from the depressing emotional inscape already established by previous stanzas. Their existence alone—their unconscious beauty and the speaker's sudden awareness of that beauty—minimizes the ordinary disasters of a tragic, unbalanced world, such as political injustices, books of bad poetry, and the terrible realization that there is no divine order governing the affairs of men. Furthermore, their delightful gestures of being imply a cosmological harmony (with nature and themselves) which appears to guarantee human survival. The risk of sentimentality, unthinking sentimentality, remains, of course, and a poem like "A Blessing" can only recover from its soggy portrait of anthropomorphized horses through those perfect closing lines:

> And the light breeze moves me to caress her long ear
> That is delicate as the skin over a girl's wrist.
> Suddenly I realize
> That if I stepped out of my body I would break
> Into blossom.

The majority of poems in *The Branch Will Not Break* accomplish their moving (if modest) ends, and, in style and final poetic success, "Two Hangovers" can be viewed as a sort of prototype for the rest. The surface is confessional in its apparently personal, unheroic experience, or in its "deep subjective images," and in its valid attempt to see an analogue for that experience. Actually, there are two distinct experiences involved, two lyrical gestalts resulting from two different hangovers, which are consciously opposite in terminal mood and tone. Though both proceed from the ego dislocation engendered by a fierce physical discomfort, the first sinks into despondency, absolute disgust with creation, as the speaker concludes with a desire for the sparrow outside and the light bulb inside to be extinguished, while the second, not too subtly subtitled "I Try to Waken and Greet the World Once Again," returns to the pastoral relief sought earlier, to the pure joy transmitted by "a brilliant blue jay" leaping up and down on a slender limb, confident, as is the laughing poet, that "the branch will not break."

The pattern so prevalent in previous poems has again reasserted itself: despair and celebration, ritual damnation and ritual salvation, the agony of human existence miraculously made bearable by nature's endless eloquence. Although seemingly open to manifestations of the universe's mysterious design, Wright's poems are closed structures, circular staircases winding forever down towards a sensual basement paradise in which Darwinian rats are either ignored or explicitly refuted. Reminiscent, at times, of Emily Dickinson, he cannot or will not take his nature straight. It must always be transmuted into epistemological tableaus through the child's golden eye, with the observer's art becoming a primitive form of animism in the process, not in itself dangerous, but fraught with seductive potential for overstatements, as well as oversimplifications. The blue jay is confident of creation because the poet will have it no other way, which is his literary right, but the poetic configuration projected as artistic proof of that right lacks persuasive sophistication.

And yet, the poem does succeed, particularly in the second section, where Wright is operating inside the sparse anecdotal format he prefers. Its major flaws are all located in the first section, which is predicated upon favorite motifs of haunted recollections and blatant social protests, but Yeats's "cold eye" is notable by its absence. The ideas of the section extend—they do not evolve—from two perennial confrontations, with death and purposeless human suffering, respectively symbolized by the moon and the sun, and with the central dilemma of the modern artist who wants to achieve redemption through art, a primary task in secular twentieth-century poetry. Striving to maintain a conversational informality through the strict avoidance of artificial meters and rhymes, the initial section spirals like a shell along a series of key metamorphoses toward a singular rejection of everything already depicted, i.e., human misery, immutable nature, and the poet's relentless efforts to mediate between them. Lying in his bed of pain, both allegorical and real, the speaker begins to transform aspects of the winter landscape presumably visible through his streaked window into pathetic human beings. Locusts and poplars become "unmarried women / Sorting slate from anthracite / Between railroad ties." And winter is a figure left over from depression days, "yellow-bearded," counting bottle caps in a tarpaper shack "under the cold trees / Of my grave."

In these terse lines of the second stanza, the speaker pauses to reconfirm his own sorry condition, "half drunk," and to reconfirm as well the poem's negative ethos through a somewhat adolescent image of the old women outside the window "hunching toward the graveyard." Enough has become too much. The stanza could have been deleted without any loss of reader awareness and tends to slow down the poem's gathering momentum. Fortunately, the third and concluding stanza recovers lost ground, opening with the sun in the guise of a drunken Hungarian—personification is crucial—whose "big stupid face" pitches, appropriately, into the stove. The wounded "I" then draws attention back to himself by reference to a dream he had about "green butterflies searching for diamonds / In coal seams." This fine little image suffices as Wright's signet of the poet's difficult chore, to draw beauty from the hard black desolation of a tortured humanity; and it fits neatly into his growing obsession with the coal-mining town of his Ohio birth, which was a casualty of the 1930s, and with its lower-class laborers (foreign-born) and their desperate women, who have come to occupy an important place in his mythology.

The dream also included "children chasing each other for a game / Through the hills of fresh graves." The recurrent images of the depression, a depression in a historical *and* psychological context, are clearly meant to continue, with biographical force, toward winter's arid vista, which is going to be cast aside in the second section, along with death's death-grip. Its effectiveness, however, is diluted rather than strengthened by the constant harping upon graves and graveyards. There is no sense of a ballad's refrain here, no feeling of awful, compulsive reiteration. Nor is there the more sophisticated reinforcement and development found in a villanelle, which is, I think, what Wright is trying to duplicate. Instead, the funereal repetitions narrow the poem's range, turn its visual plateaus and valleys into a mountainous obsession, a childlike obsession at that, one which had stunted the growth of another American writer committed to the unsaid, Ernest Hemingway.[2] The persistent dwelling upon death, and in such clumsy metaphors, seems excessive to the point of morbidity, too shrill for poetic conviction.

The poem's first section reaches its pallid climax with the sun's inglorious return, drunk yet but now "from the sea," as a sparrow is heard singing dolefully "of the Hanna Coal Co. and the dead moon." Although too forced to impel belief, the specific details do propel the narrative forward by enlarging the reader's small pocket of information. Sense data and their poetic treatment supply a particular time and place for the speaker's pain-filled memory and suggest that the nagging concern with death, supposedly generated by alcoholic *disease*, has a definite locus in remembrances of childhood in a depression-ridden coal town. The bird serves to link mankind's two awesome oppressors: human mortality and his own exploitive economic establishments. Poet as bird is hardly a new concept,[3] but the last three lines use it efficaciously to convey the artist's elemental function, and its intrinsic limitations:

> The filaments of cold light bulbs tremble
> In music like delicate birds.
> Ah, turn it off.

These lines are even more clever than they appear and deserve admiration. The filaments reproduce the bare winter trees, and their trembling motions in the unseen wind are literal fact married to imagination, stimulated, perhaps, by Shakespeare's "bare ruined choirs / Where late the sweet birds sang." Regardless of literary references—and the poem is a nice conflation of Shakespearian and Whitmanesque values—the birds retain their value as symbols for the artist's essential manipulations of reality, emphasizing the irony behind the speaker's request that an unlit ("cold") bulb be turned off. The artist alone, of course, could make a dead light bulb waver in song, that being his special glory, but the final line expresses a weary disgust with this gift, denies, in fact, the entire poem up to this point, especially its stubborn attempts to bind past and present horrors into an organic aesthetic. Since it does not alter or lessen the agony involved, the pain of characters and author, including a younger self, such salvation deserves refutation. That is the mocking "message" of the first section, but, as noted, the compact last section will skillfully imply that the poet's role cannot be shed so easily. The drab sparrow will become a brilliant blue jay, restored in spirit and substance, imbued with a natural trust in creation's soundness.

Taken as a whole, the poem attains a high degree of lyric grace and manages to overcome Wright's almost innate sentimentality. A state of grace is what the poet is seeking, and his characters remain innocent in their miseries, as do nature's tokens of seasonal endurance. Religious or not, Wright has thus refused an irrational universe. The logical path chosen, from physical discomfit through terrible dreams and memories to the closing affirmation, presents an integrated world of balanced alternatives in which the state of grace, or innocent purgation, can forgive everyone everything. For all its coy simplicity, the artist's redemption does not strike false, though his descent into childish death images nearly upsets the coal cart. His art in "Two Hangovers" is a positive, healing act of will thrust upon a harsh reality.

Unhappily, with the publication of *Shall We Gather at the River* (1968), Wright's penchant for the sentimental finally overwhelmed his very real, if limited, talent. The book's title, a question without a question mark taken from the declarative line of a revival hymn, significantly indicates a preordained affirmation. It is this imposed affirmation, a religious one, which drags him and his frail aesthetic to earth. Without the probing doubt evident in his earlier volumes— despair remains, and, indeed, appears to increase, but it is more hysterical than true—his poetry loses its necessary tension. The ultimate benevolence of God's entire creation has become a secret conviction that allows his sentimental inclinations to loom unchecked. On the surface, he often gives the impression of operating within the same lyric confines present in previous work, within a relaxed, conversational style, but the patterns of neoclassical restraint are now mere trappings as sentimental distortions slop over their sides like pea soup. Always a strong point, his metaphors suffer the most, frequently disappearing altogether. He is too often content with unquickened, untransfigured pathos, the pathos of a stark situation, as in "I Am a Sioux Brave, He Said in Minneapolis" and "In Terror of Hospital Bills," which revolve around the plight of an American Indian trapped in a hostile culture. Even the collection's best piece, "A Christmas Greeting," which again utilizes Charlie, Wright's favorite representative for the downtrodden, stumbles, at the end, into inadequate soap opera:

> *Charlie, I don't know what to say to you*
> *Except Good Evening, Greetings, and Good Night,*
> *God Bless Us Everyone. Your grave is white.*
> *What are you doing here?*

Because it so overtly defines its "new" aesthetic, the poem that has to stand at the heart of *Shall We Gather at the River* is "Speak." Here, and in "To the Muse," Wright is again directly confronting his art, endeavoring to describe its precise motives and boundaries:

> To speak in a flat voice
> Is all that I can do.

> I have gone every place
> Asking for you.

Addressed to God, the work does achieve a flat voice, too flat, becoming prose, but it is a prosaic prose at best. After a brief description of his search for poetry and love in the first stanza, the speaker returns to Doty (his beloved murderer) in the second and yokes him to Sonny Liston taking a "dive" in his fight against Cassius Clay, equating both figures with defeat in "hell again." Jenny appears in the third stanza, a female Charlie, and breaks her spare beauty in "a whorehouse old" before leaving her baby at "a bus-station can." The stanza concludes with her dancing away through Jacksontown, which is identified in the fourth stanza as "a place I know," one in which the speaker was once arrested by a good cop, "Believe it, Lord, or not." The poet's determination to speak "of flat defeat / In a flat voice" is reiterated, then the last stanza has him stress past saintly attitudes, his St.-John-of-the-Cross consciousness of and identification with earth's countless sinners and outcasts, having gone forward with "a few lonely some" and dying with the rest. The final four lines belong to Job, again recalling the poet's heroic past and demanding divine intervention, if not reward:

> Lord, I have loved Thy cursed,
> The beauty of Thy house:
> Come down. Come down. Why dost
> Thou hide thy face?

The dramatic climax dons the mask of a complete, inconsolate doubter, with poor God reduced to a small *t* in the last line. Such a negative stance certainly complements the poem's general design, and the whole collection's questioning pose toward Christian revivalism, but it has a hollow ring. The melodramatic incidents, however *real*, the deliberate use of a hymn structure, the Spartan language and paucity of metaphors, the arrogant humility and sentimental stereotypes, all contribute an aura of insincerity. There is a smug heart inside the poem that vitiates its popular-ballad formula. As is clear from references in "The Minneapolis Poem" and "Inscription for the Tank," Wright has come to regard himself as another Walt Whitman, singer of the common man. Alas, he possesses neither Whitman's eloquence nor his gigantic soul, and his particular perception of America is as narrow as his limited characters'. The last stanza of the poem gathers its real power from echoes, and not from the author's added implications, as he imitates and steals (honest toil) to no avail. Complete capitulation still bespeaks an impossible art.

The decline into mawkishness continues into the *Collected Poems*, which won the 1972 Pulitzer Prize, reasserting that award's continued dedication to preserving mediocrity. Of the thirty-three new poems included, only two of them could be described as unqualified successes, and they, "To the August Fallen" and "Small Frogs Killed on the Highway," are substantially returns to the subjective-imagistic techniques of *The Branch Will Not Break*. Their modest rosaries of metaphors never preach or whine, are content to let their imaginative potentialities carry the burden of the poems to its logical summation. For instance, at the end of "Small Frogs Killed on the Highway," the image of tadpoles dancing "on the quarter thumbnail / Of the moon" precisely reflects the speaker's earlier desire to leap "Into the light." Similarly, in "To the August Fallen," Wright's lament for generations of dead strangers finds a beautiful echo in the fall of insects into a pond, which, in turn, leads to memories of Chinese Tartars (historical) and a cyclical climax that returns the speaker to his perch (literary) above death.

In spite of exceptional whole stanzas and individual lines, the rest of the new poems are almost embarrassing in their lack of sensitivity and basic poetic skill. Horror and despair are treated with such elementary sentimentality that they soon become grotesque. A typical, self-indulgent image from "A Secret Gratitude" will illustrate what I mean: "Man's heart is the rotten yolk of a blacksnake egg / Corroding, as it is just born, in a pile of dead / Horse dung." The feeling of profound disgust with human nature might be genuine, but the extreme metaphor tends to make the reader doubtful since no *Inferno* hellscape has been erected to frame its negative intensity. Its unidimensional excessiveness is better suited to propaganda than a lyric narrative intent upon finding and defining the *raison d'être* behind Edna St. Vincent Millay's art and life. Wright has obviously read Pablo Neruda, but he has been unable to penetrate or duplicate his surrealistic ethic, except at the most superficial level.[4]

Other tics have multiplied, become magnified. The word *lonely*, for instance, is used so often it loses all meaning, finally deteriorating into juvenile chants: "One afternoon I lonely found / Home when a lonely / Girl slipped her quick / Shelter down." And the few war protest poems included, such as "A Mad Fight Song for William S. Carpenter" and "Echo for the Promise of Georg Trakl's Life," further convince me that the Vietnam folly, besides destroying countless innocent lives and compromising America's honor, has ruined a large number of our contemporary poets. Being a deliberate craftsman, and a sincere one, Wright occasionally pauses to defend his new aesthetic, claiming his task as the restoration of "the pure clear word" to poetry. But instead of bold metaphors and diamond hardness, which this kind of vision should provide, he can only offer cute tricks, such as a blank page entitled "In Memory of the Horse David, Who Ate One of My Poems," or simplistic Hemingwayese, "The giant killer is / A dirty little bastard," which will reach an absurd zenith in a poem called "Northern Pike."

Whatever the grave faults (pun intended) of the new poems in the collected edition, and a whine is unappealing in any form, none of them can approach the disasters of Wright's most recent volume, *Two Citizens* (1973). Ironically, he has changed publishers from Wesleyan to the major house of Farrar, Straus and Giroux, at precisely that moment when his art is no longer viable. As has happened so often in the past of American literature, public success arrives too late, after the writer has begun his decline into mumbling repetitions and pathetic self-parody. From the standpoint of artistic achievement, *Two Citizens* is an almost total failure.

In the blurb, Wright describes the book as "an expression of my patriotism, of my love and discovery of my native place," which commences with a savage attack upon it and eventually takes "the shape of a beautiful woman who loved me and who led me through France and Italy," where he discovered *his* America. The whine is replaced by sobs of pleasure, and the woman, of course, is Annie, his new wife, who has rescued him from desolation—and in so doing has unconsciously contributed to his art's downfall. Without the despair and horror that pulsed in his earlier poems, Wright has nothing left to restrain his inordinate taste for sentimental resolutions of difficult problems. He has betrayed us and betrayed himself by refusing to accept the implications of his own gift, by insisting upon filtering all experience through the wringer of drunken emotions, regardless of their irrational narrowness.

Fittingly, the epigraph of *Two Citizens* is chosen from Hemingway's "The Killers," seeking midwestern roots, and its initial poem, "Ars Poetica: Some Recent Criticism," confronts its inheritance of the unsaid through imitation. Wright tries to use his Ohio recollections, a tale about Aunt Agnes and her good-hearted contrast to some boys who stoned a goat, to reiterate his contempt (pretended?) for America and to define the exact nature of his aesthetic. But ambition and accomplishment remain miles apart, and the sparse, tic-ridden language is an insult: "She stank. / Her house stank. / I went down to see Uncle Sherman / One evening. / I had a lonely furlough / Out of the army." Worse is yet to come as stereotypes of a native strain give way to foreign ones, as Aunt Agnes and Jennie and "even I swear to Christ" John Shunk are replaced by French and Italian counterparts, like the Parisian "retarded fat man" who "can't even beg" and the Florentine "organist waiting to begin."

There is little reason, and less joy, to continue. Wright has descended into a pit of his own making, the terrible depth of which can be measured by the vast distance between *The Branch Will Not Break* and *Two Citizens*. I am sure that there are critics, such as James Seay, who will find in the poet's new voice "no letup in Wright's developments."[5] I am equally sure that time and good taste will not bear them out.

NOTES

1. The persona at the heart of the *Cantos*, however, would never relinquish his aristocratic allegiance to the troubadors, such as Bertran de Born and other red-blooded figures from the Renaissance. Nor would he ever abandon "the hardness bred of reading Dante," even in the highly charged "Pisan Cantos."
2. This is especially true of the Nick Adams stories, but the theme of a personally malicious universe streaks through all of Hemingway's work, from *The Sun Also Rises* to *The Old Man and the Sea*, though sometimes with good effect.
3. I think Wright is deliberately seeking a connection here with Whitman's "Out of the Cradle Endlessly Rocking" as "Two Hangovers" is certainly, among other things, a poem about poetry.
4. In "I Come to Speak for Your Dead Mouths," *Poetry*, 112 (June 1968), 191–94, Wright expresses his deep admiration for the Spanish poet, for both his public life and poetic philosophy, discovering in Neruda a similar fascination with death.

5. See Seay's "A World Immeasurably Alive and Good: A Look at James Wright's *Collected Poems*," *Georgia Review*, 27 (1973), 71–81, for an intelligent contrary view and a sound discussion of Wright's major themes.

Open Secrets

STEPHEN YENSER

> "It is a ridiculous demand which England and America make, that you shall speak so that they can understand you. Neither men nor toadstools grow so . . . . I fear chiefly lest my expression may not be *extravagant* enough, may not wander far enough beyond the narrow limits of my daily experience, so as to be adequate to the truth of which I have been convinced."
>
> Thoreau, *Walden*

I

AT LEAST SINCE *The Branch Will Not Break* (1963) James Wright's poetry has been pulled in two directions—or in one uncertain direction by two sometimes opposing wishes. We might as well make these wishes horses, especially since, as he reaffirms in *Moments of the Italian Summer*, Wright considers horses perhaps "the most beautiful of God's creatures." One of them we could call David, after Robert Bly's swaybacked palomino who has appeared in several of Wright's poems. He is the older, the more reliable, the more steadily paced of the two—the likelier wheelhorse. He wants to keep the vehicle, if not in the ruts, at least on the road and headed toward home. On the other side there is Dewfall, also known as Nightrise and Basilica, all three of whose names, according to a riddling poem in *To a Blossoming Pear Tree*, were stolen by Napoleon from Spanish horses and later given to some heavenly swans. She is high-spirited and erratic. It is she who always sees something fascinating off to the side of the road and takes Wright out of his way. Sometimes she gets the bit between her teeth and tears off, and then neither David nor the driver can do much but go along until she winds herself.

136

Every writer knows some version of the situation, the tension between the impulses to give rein to "the imagination, that mysterious
and frightening thing," as Wright has called it in an interview, and to
keep the work in hand, moving constantly to some end that will
seem appointed.[1] Wright sets them in historical perspective in "The
Pretty Redhead," from the French of Apollinaire, where, addressing himself to the "long quarrel between tradition and imagination /
Between order and adventure," he sides with adventure:

> You whose mouth is made in the image of God's mouth
> Mouth which is order itself
> Judge kindly when you compare us
> With those who were the very perfection of order
> We who are seeking everywhere for adventure.[2]

The poem overlooks in the interest of polemic the fact that the two
impulses are complexly interdependent for the individual poet, but
its insistence on the "quarrel" suits a poetry distinguished by an
obvious restlessness, a sometimes dramatic movement, whether
among poems or within a given poem, back and forth between modes.

Wright's adventurousness, his extravagance, in the root sense resurrected by Thoreau, often declares itself in the "deep image" and in
what some have understandably called surrealism. In "The Pretty
Redhead" his party searches for "vast strange domains / Where mystery flowers into any hands that long for it" and where there are "A
thousand fantasies difficult to make sense out of." This search yields
much that is whimsical, cryptic, uncanny, or weirdly beautiful. It is
not always possible to decide which. To it we owe, for instance, this
sudden detour in a love poem in *Two Citizens*. Wright has been recalling a walk with his wife in the Yugoslavian countryside:

> The one thing that I most longed for to meet in the wildness
> Here was a spider. I already know
> My friends the spiders. They are mountains.
> Every spider in America is the shadow
> Of a beautiful woman.[3]

Making "here" instead of the expected "there" his occasion, and
slipping into the present tense, he swerves in a new direction, so
that the "wildness" is no longer the natural setting for the walk but
the very nature of the poem. We come around the bend of that first
line into a strange domain indeed, as though Wright meant to show

us how close to the neat, grammatical path the imagination, "that mysterious and frightening thing," is. For whatever dark purpose, the impulse to adventure asserts itself here in a characteristic manner.

Its steadier counterpart cannot be simply equated with Wright's "craft," or "the active employment of the intelligence," which he pairs with "imagination." The preceding lines have their own craftiness, the long first line that suspends and intensifies the longing itself, the shrewd positioning of "Here," the accentuation of the new, wry tone by the iambic meter in lines two and three, and the light rhyme, for example, testify to certain "patient pains," as Yeats called his complement to "passionate impulse." Carefully made as they are, however, those lines plunge off into inscrutability. The element in Wright's temperament that I have in mind not only resists such tangents but also urges him to speak as straightforwardly and plainly as possible. In addition to some dull or commonplace verse it fosters much taut, dramatic, moving poetry. (My examples would include "Autumn Begins in Martins Ferry, Ohio," "Two Hangovers," and "A Blessing" in *The Branch Will Not Break*; "Speak," "The Mourners," "Poems to a Brown Cricket," and "To the Muse" in *Shall We Gather at the River*; "A Mad Fight Song for William S. Carpenter, 1966," "Small Frogs Killed on the Highway," and "Northern Pike" in "New Poems" in *Collected Poems*.) When it exerts its influence in *Two Citizens* we get stanzas like these, which conclude "The Last Drunk":

> I sired a bitter son.
> I have no daughter.
> When I at last get done
> I will die by water.
>
> She, what she might have been,
> Her shoulder's secret gold,
> Thin as her mother is thin.
> I could have grown old!

Anyone who has read much Wright might sense the tug of adventure in the second line of the last stanza, but that would be partly because the word *secret* so often signals a veering into mystery in his work—and partly because the passage as a whole is so direct.

This is the side of Wright that demands clarity, immediacy, even simplicity, that convinces him that "To speak in a flat voice / Is all that I can do" ("Speak"), and that drives him to deny the applicability of the term "surrealism" to his work on the grounds that it is used to label passages in which his "attempt to be clear has failed."[4] If it is precisely his extravagance that comes to mind when he contrasts the practice of some other poets with his own object in "Many of Our Waters: Variations on a Poem by a Black Child" ("New Poems"), the well-known stanza itself avoids the incongruity:

> The kind of poetry I want to write is
>   The poetry of a grown man.
> The young poets of New York come to me with
> Their mangled figures of speech,
> But they have little pity
> For the pure clear word.

In effect, this stanza reprimands the speaker in "The Pretty Redhead," with his enthusiasm for the enigmatic and the *outré*; it might even remind us of a poet whose work Wright surely considers more ordered than adventurous. T. S. Eliot is glossing a remark in one of D. H. Lawrence's letters about the necessity of "stark directness" in modern poetry:

> This speaks to me of that at which I have long aimed, in writing poetry; to write poetry which should be essentially poetry, with nothing poetic about it, poetry standing naked in its bare bones, or poetry so transparent . . . that in reading it we are intent on what the poem *points at.* . . . To get *beyond poetry*, as Beethoven, in his later works, strove to get *beyond music.*[5]

Wright surprises himself with his own stark directness in "Inscription for the Tank" (*Shall We Gather at the River*): "My life was never so precious / To me as now. / I gape unbelieving at those two lines / Of my words, caught and frisked naked." By the time of "Many of Our Waters" the abashed surprise has become a rather defensive pride:

> This is not a poem.
> This is not an apology to the Muse.
> This is the cold-blooded plea of a homesick vampire
> To his brother and friend.

> If you do not care one way or another about
> The preceding lines,
> Please do not go on listening
> On any account of mine.

Of course Wright's specificity also reveals the difference between his aim and Eliot's. Eliot wants the poem to be a means of clarification whose art effaces itself. In the discursive sections of *Four Quartets* his transparency comes largely from delicate distinction, exactness of diction, an exquisite circumspection—all those virtues of discretion defined and exemplified at the beginning of "Little Gidding, V." Wright's clarity is closer to that of Catullus, whose ghost haunts *Moments of the Italian Summer* and *To a Blossoming Pear Tree*, the two most recent volumes. We begin to characterize it in terms of bluntness, idiomatic language, overstatement, reckless intensity. He wants the poem to be an emphatic statement whose passion seems to override its art.[6]

Its clarity notwithstanding, however, the preceding passage consorts oddly with "The poetry of a grown man." Simple clarity is not, after all, maturity, and the petulance of Wright's lines—whether gratuitous or strategic seems beside the point—embarrasses his explicit desire. Nor is "the pure clear word" the same as an unalloyed emotion, although Wright seems to identify those two as well. If his extravagance sometimes leads him into obscurity, his clarity courts sentimentality and simplism. Here is the conclusion of "Ohio Valley Swains" (*Two Citizens*), where he recalls some unspecified assault by a teenager on a girl he knew when he was a child:

> You thought that was funny, didn't you, to mock a girl?
> I loved her only in my dreams,
> But my dreams meant something
> And so did she,
> You son of a bitch,
> And if I ever see you again, so help me in the sight of God,
> I'll kill you.

Even if we can overlook its disconcerting egocentrism ("And so did she"), this stanza tries the patience. Either we must believe that the same James Wright who abhors capital punishment would kill a man who molested a girl some forty years ago, regardless of what has happened to him since; or we must suppose that the poem works up the simplest emotion for the sake of immediacy.

We might try to write these lines off as ironic bluster—in the vein of Wright's vow that *Two Citizens* was his last book: "God damn me if I ever write another."[7] But that seems as desperate a resort as wringing a pun from the first word of the title of "Lying in a Hammock at William Duffy's Farm in Pine Island, Minnesota" (*The Branch Will Not Break*) to justify that poem's famous conclusion: "I have wasted my life." That line, too, has always made me want to reverse Proust and say, *il est trop sincère d'être honnête*. What distinguishes it from the last sentence of Rilke's *"Archzïscher Torso Apollos,"* surely Wright's model, is precisely its passionate oversimplification. Rilke's *"Du musst dein Leben ändern"* summarizes the effect of the radiant sculptural fragment, which, like some transfiguring mirror, lets the poet see himself as though from a god's point of view and inspires in him an unspecific, perhaps undischargeable, but undeniable obligation: "You must change your life." Wright's poem fails as it were to gain the vantage of his floating hawk, collapses back into the deep well of the self, pronounces a melodramatic because impossibly harsh judgment, and therefore invites sympathetic correction. But that's not so, one wants to say— as indeed it was not. Rilke's poem crystallizes an insight while Wright's fans a flickering feeling.

Wright commits such excesses in the name of "the pure clear word"; they measure his desire for transparency, not to say confrontation. It is all the more remarkable, then, that he has so cherished his extravagance. A few lines after scorning those callow, "mangled figures of speech" he can say of the "grown man" that "The long body of his dream is the beginning of a dark / Hair under an illiterate / Girl's ear." One tries to imagine the expression on the face of the illiterate girl to whom these lines might be slowly read (with appropriate attention to *rejet*). Perhaps they demonstrate ironically the foregoing admission that he is "not yet a grown man"— but in context the metaphor looks less rueful than solemn. "The one tongue I can write in / Is my Ohioan," he proclaims in *Two Citizens*, yet the volume is fraught with exotic locutions like this: "Somewhere in me there is a crystal that I cannot find / Alone, the wing that I used to think was a poor / Blindness I had to live with with the dead." Evidently he means to have it both ways.

II

In *Moments of the Italian Summer* he does.[8] This is a splendid little book, a chain of "brilliants," to borrow one of Wright's charmed words. Its fourteen prose poems, introduced by a poem by Annie Wright, are as transparent as anything he has written, though they are shot through with whimsy. In fact, in the best of them, extravagance provides coherence and sophistication alike.

A note by Annie Wright, published earlier with some of these pieces in Michael Benedikt's anthology, *The Prose Poem*, confirms what one immediately suspects: they grew out of daily journal entries.[9] Reading through this book, surely everyone will recall certain inspired jottings—written in the diary while the setting sun turned ochre the old house across from the pensione or scrawled on a paper napkin stained with cappuccino while the promenaders streamed by—jottings that somehow never came to anything more. Wright's version of the prose poem, with its evident tolerance for loose ends, its appetite for digression, its fugitive unity, seems exactly the form to contain without warping them. But to think that mere acquaintance with this sequence would make the difference is of course an illusion. One might as well depend upon a visit to Athens to produce a maid to write about. These prose poems are no less personal and earned than Wright's best verse, their beguiling capriciousness and clarity no more inherent in the genre than Brunello di Montalcino is in the grape.

They often begin like postcards, with a designation of setting that flaunts its artlessness. "I am sitting contented and alone in a little park near the Palazzo Scaligere in Verona," Wright announces, or "It is a fresh morning of late August in Padova," or "I am sitting in an outdoor cafe across the street from the Colosseum." Then the warming up turns into something serious and exciting, as imagination and memory (if they are not the same thing) take over and the prose carries us on and on. A prose poem called "Young Don't Want to Be Born" in *To a Blossoming Pear Tree* puts into parable form what happens to the poet when "that mysterious and frightening thing" sweeps him away. The "you" is knocked off his feet by the riptide and comes up clinging to the tail of a giant stingray headed out to sea and destinations unknown. Something of that sort often occurs in these pieces, although the force that takes us out beyond our depth is gently suasive rather than overpowering. This passage, at the heart of "The City of Evenings," might serve as a model:

Streamers, motorboats, trash-scows are moving past in large numbers, and gondolas are going home. In a little while we too will meet the twilight and move through it on a vaporetto toward the Lido, the seaward island with its long beach and its immense hotel, its memories of Aschenbach and his harrowing vision of perfection, of Byron on horseback in the moonlight, and the muted shadows of old Venetians drifting as silently as possible in flight from the barbarians, drifting as far away as the island of Torcello, taking refuge as Ruskin said like the Israelites of old, a refuge from the sword in the paths of the sea.

One thing leads to another as the reader drifts on in the current of association, sensing but hardly noticing that, as easily as the historical flows into the fictional, the Giudecca Canal merges with another body of water and that one is moving among shades other than those of evening. Wright does it all "as silently as possible"; as the elegiac overtones dissolve back into the tourist's language you are not even sure you heard them—though the concluding reference to passing time probably suggests that the poet has: "Maybe Torcello was nothing much for the princes of the sea to find, but the old Venetians discovered the true shape of evening, and now it is almost evening." This piece almost describes itself, for Wright too, drawn out of his way (or so it seems), thereby discovers his real subject and its own "true shape."

Progression by means of digression, toward a transformation of the present "moment," structures most of these prose poems. In some cases the movement seems more desultory than in others, and one feels that the process is not a matter, as for Herrick's Julia, of contriving an alluring disorder, but rather of teasing a welter of material into a tenuous form. "A Lament for the Martyrs," set near the Colosseum, meanders from Mussolini to God, thence to Horace and President Nixon, the barbarians and the Barberinis, the crooked politicians of the Ohio River Valley during Prohibition, a childhood essay on Howells, and so on, to conclude with reflections on the Christian martyrs. It seems at first an example of the journal entry insufficiently chastened. But then it appears that the archaeologist's work ("a careful revelation" of subterranean passages thronged with shadows and ghosts) corresponds to Wright's disclosure of his past ("the antiquities of my childhood: the beautiful river, that black ditch of horror"), itself linked with the political history of the United States, and to his rediscovery of Roman history. If the "starved people" and the "hungry" lions blur together in the shadows along with beauty and atrocity, so do Roman and American, distant and recent history. For all its apparent waywardness, the prose poem digs its own "intricate and intelligent series of ditches" that parallel and intersect one another, and by its end it has become a compassionate indictment of history's "hateful grandeur," the inextricable "greatness and horror" that fascinated Lowell in his treatment of Rome and the United States in *Near the Ocean*.

The modus operandi is not new in Wright's work. In 1967 he remarked that "if any principle of structure can be disentangled from the poems that I have written in free verse, it is, I suppose, the principle of parallelism, a term which of course need not be limited to a strictly grammatical application." Eight years later he was thinking about the same method when he said that Georg Trakl had influenced him as much as anyone. Trakl, he said, "writes in parallelisms, only he leaves out the intermediary, rationalistic explanations of the relation between one image and another."¹⁰ Like "A Lament for the Martyrs," "The Legions of Caesar" might be viewed as a domestication of Trakl's mode. While he watches some men fish for piccolini, Wright muses on the cessation of bombing in Cambodia, Catullus, Caesar's invasions of Britain, and the poet and composer William Barnes. These elements recur in new combinations, like filaments of sunlight in the shallows weaving themselves anew each moment. At the conclusion some boys are chasing a piccolino that has wriggled out of the bag:

> They are serious, hurrying, before the little fish stops struggling back towards the water and turns to stone. I don't know what time it is in Cambodia. I wonder if there is ever any silence there. Where is it, hiding from the invaders? The sunlight once glinted off William Barnes's coffin. From a hill so far away it seemed the other side of the earth, his friend Thomas Hardy wrote down the sunlight as a signal. He knew his friend was opening a hand, saying goodbye.

The importance of the piccolini becomes apparent—perhaps too apparent—when he calls the boys invaders; otherwise the conclusion leaves us to draw our own.[11] Curiosity perhaps takes us back to Hardy's tough, touching poem, "The Last Signal." Before the lines that Wright's last two sentences paraphrase, Hardy wrote that he "knew what it meant— / The sudden shine sent from the livid east scene; / It meant the west mirrored by the coffin of my friend there." One does not need to compare the two pieces to gather that Wright means the more recent "livid east scene" in Cambodia to parallel the Roman invasions, but Hardy's provokes us to contemplate a different twilight in the west, and its elegaic nature makes Wright's more resonant. It is interesting that Hardy says nothing of his hill's being "so far away it seemed the other side of the earth." Wright invents that detail both to coax out a parallel between himself and Hardy and to acknowledge the irrevocable distance between himself and the Cambodian victims (in preparation for the subtle daring of the implied friendship between them). Maybe we also hear echoes, because Catullus has come up earlier, of the elegy ending *"ave atque vale,"* especially since the brother for whom he wrote it died in the east. In any case, the loose connections that make the surface so casual also allow Wright to shape a response to a political situation that defies frontal assaults. How different this quietly moving piece is from "Ohio Valley Swains."

In his wonderfully evocative "The Lambs on the Boulder" Wright begins by comparing Giotto, "the master of angels," with Mantegna, whose "dead Christ looks exactly like a skidroad bum fished by the cops out of the Mississippi," and then goes on to meditate on the story ("which so intensely ought to be real that it is real") of Cimabue's discovery of Giotto, a shepherd boy, patiently sketching his lambs on a boulder with a sharp rock. At the end Wright recalls a painting by Giotto in which, far back in "a huge choir of his unutterably beautiful angels . . . singing out of pure happiness the praises of God," one smaller angel has turned from the light and hidden his face. "I don't know why he is weeping," Wright says, "but I love him best." He concludes with a sentence whose last clause lifts this embroidered story into parable:

> I think he must be wondering how long it will take Giotto to remember him, give him a drink of water, and take him back home to the fold before it gets dark and shepherd and sheep alike lose their way in the darkness of the countryside.

The young Giotto and his frightened lamb, the mature Giotto and his weeping angel, Cimabue and the shepherd boy, the poet and the "befuddled drunkards" he has known, Mantegna and the dead Christ: by subtly commenting on one another, these parallels—or variations on the shepherd and the lost sheep—keep the prose poem from losing its way even as they enlarge and complicate its vision. In the end it tells us something about the survival of the artist's early feelings in his later work, the mingling in that work of joy and sorrow, fear and hope, and losses and gains and the memory and discipline that mediate between them.

As these pieces range out from the moments at their centers they tend also to forsake the literal. They are imaginative flights, forms of transcendence. The ascent is actual in the last part of "A Letter to Franz Wright," where the poet tells us how he and his companions "drove up, and up, and around, and up, and around, and up again" until they arrived late one evening at San Gimignano, where the next morning they incredulously found themselves "poised hundreds of feet in the air" and "felt . . . strange in that presence, that city glistening there in the lucid Tuscan morning, like a perfectly cut little brilliant sparkling on the pinnacle of a stalagmite." "Saying Dante Aloud," the central and shortest piece, takes such an uplifting of spirit as its subject. This is the whole of it, round as Giotto's O: "You can feel the muscles and veins rippling in widening and rising circles, like a bird in flight under your tongue." One can feel the imagination itself moving in widening and rising circles in "Under the Canals," in which an old man carrying a ladder and a net, probably a chimney sweep, becomes richer and stranger as Wright muses on the odd figure he cuts. First he notices "the green moon-slime on his shoes" and half believes that he has "just climbed up some of those odd stairs out of a nearby narrow canal"; and later the old man becomes a "sweeper of sea-stairs" who has left behind him "a chimney, swept free, till this hour passes, of all the webs they weave so stoutly down there, the dark green spiders under the water who have more than all the time they need." In "The Silent Angel," a man with something in his hand, standing in "the vast petals of rose shadows" cast by the arena in Verona, becomes first a musician with a baton and then an ambiguous angel: "The wings of the smiling musician are folded. . . . my musician, who meant me no harm and only wanted to wave me away as gently as possible out of the beautiful space he guarded. . . . He may be fallen, as I am. But from a greater height, unless I miss my guess."

What happens in such pieces is that the bud of the actual blossoms into the extravagant flower of vision. What is seen is seen through, and we are made aware of the uniqueness and power, the potential centrality of any given moment. "The service of philosophy . . . toward the human spirit, is to rouse, to startle it to a life of constant and eager observation. Every moment some form grows perfect . . . for that moment only. Not the fruit of experience, but the experience itself is the end." Would Wright have been rereading *The Renaissance* during this stay in Italy? "But I care more now for the poetry of the present moment," he admits in "Piccolini"; he entitles another piece "The Language of the Present Moment"; and in the concluding prose poem he celebrates not "the enduring fruits of five hundred years," the paintings in an exhibit in Padua, but "The Fruits of the Season." Pater exhorted us to "be present always at the focus where the greatest number of vital forces unite in their purest energy"—and here is the last paragraph of "A Small Grove," which begins with a description of the poet's wife standing in some trees:

> She stands among them in her flowered green clothes. Her skin is darker gold than the olives in the morning sun. Two hours ago we got up and bathed in the lake. It was like swimming in a vein. Everything that can blossom is blossoming around her now. She is the eye of the grove, the eye of mimosa and willow. The cypress behind her catches fire.

In her "flowered green clothes" Annie Wright is, for the moment, the focus, the absolute and radiant center of those vital forces. At that center, as the inspired choice of "eye" tells us, subject and object, sight and sight are one. Slight as it is, this piece, to my mind, would better bear comparison with Rilke's sonnet than "Lying in a Hammock . . . ."[12]

"A Small Grove" might be described either as a dilation of its central moment or as a penetration of it. The same is true of "The Secret of Light," which focuses on the possibility of bringing to light the secret of the perceived object and the closely related possibility of bringing to the surface the beauty, the hidden light of the loved one. I take the following delicately skewed sentence to be central. Wright sees a woman sitting on a park bench in front of him:

Her hair is as black as the inmost secret of light in a perfectly cut diamond, a perilous black, a secret light that must have been studied for many years before the anxious and disciplined craftsman could achieve the necessary balance between courage and skill to stroke the strange stone and take the one chance he would ever have to bring that secret to light.

"Secret of light . . . a secret light . . . that secret to light": even as Wright turns his subject around to study it first from one angle and then from another (the whole prose poem repeats certain words like some prose canzone), he strikes the blow he imagines. Unlike this "anxious and disciplined craftsman," the poet never has only "one chance"—except in the sense that Pater stresses and that Wright mentions later in this piece, that he has "only one life"—but like him Wright has found in these prose poems "a necessary balance." A balance, that is, between the courage to be extravagant and the skill to make that extravagance disclose the moment's essence. Moving out from each moment, Wright moves in on it in order to make it and himself (as he says of the Adige and himself) "both an open secret." The phrase applies not only because the prose poems seem to expose the operations of "that mysterious and frightening thing" but also because the craft that makes them transparent itself remains virtually hidden.

III

Seven of these prose poems also appear in *To a Blossoming Pear Tree*, where some of them are considerably and wisely pruned. Like several of the prose poems, some of the poems rely upon our intuition of unexplained parallelisms. Take "Redwings," the subject of which is the redwing blackbirds whose increase has made them pests. ("It turns out / You can kill them," Wright begins; "It turns out / You can make the earth absolutely clean.") Like so many of his poems, this one understands the world to be divided into two camps. On our side, tenuously connected with one another, are those who are on nature's: the redwings, nameless "solitaries," a "skinny girl" the poet once loved who now has five children (the prolific birds too "used to be willowy and thin"), a kindly derelict who slept by the river (either Wright has known more saintly bums than Kerouac or he has multiplied a few experiences like loaves), and of course the poet himself. On the other side, equally loosely associated, are the scientists who have figured out how to exterminate the redwings, the strip miner the skinny girl married (or at least his bosses), and those responsible for "the dead gorges / Of highway construction." (Wright long ago consigned earth gougers to one of the lower circles in Hell.) He manages all this unobtrusively enough, but the poem arrives in its next to last stanza when he impulsively identifies himself (and all of us—the scientists are in an airplane) with the birds:

> Together among the dead gorges
> Of highway construction, we flare
> Across highways and drive
> Motorists crazy, we fly
> Down home to the river.

The transitions into and from this stanza are also first-rate, but this is the crucial passage, with its simultaneous description and incorporation of the birds' startling movement and its equation of the dangerous with the threatened species—which gently implies that our wars on nature are wars on ourselves. Here again extravagance is directness. At this surprising juncture, the whole poem comes together.

Or almost the whole poem. Earlier, describing the Kokosing River from an airplane, Wright says it looks

> Secret, it looks like the open
> Scar turning gray on the small
> Of your spine.
>
> Can you hear me?

This is another sort of flaring across the highway, as the question seems to acknowledge. Whose spine is involved? Anyone's, as it were? But why then the particular specificity in "the small"? And what is an "open / Scar"—since a scar is a closed wound? Almost the only thing we can ascertain is that this passage is more "secret" than "open." I am concerned with it not because it especially damages a fine poem (it does not—it is at worst a small scar), but rather because it represents a return, after the pervasive inventions in the prose poems, to that peculiar local kinkiness of the earlier work. Curiously, such passages often incorporate the word "secret." Thus in "Neruda" Wright tells us puzzlingly that "The leaves of the little / Secret trees are fallen" after he has discovered "The little leaves / That are trees in secret." "One Last Look at the Adige: Verona in the Rain" begins and ends beautifully, but halfway through we find the poet

> Alive in the friendly city
> Of my body, my secret Verona,
> Milky and green,
> My moving jewel, the last
> Pure vein left to me.

Perhaps I misunderstand these mysterious lines if I take them to convey a loneliness so extreme that it dotes on itself—but I do not see how else they might be taken.[13]

Sometimes it is as though the impulse to adventure had been suppressed and were revenging itself—or as though Wright were determined to invoke certain enigmas as evidence of a rarefied sensibility. He seems to need to insinuate that a part of his experience is ineffable, that the best he can do is drop his depth charges into the reader's subconscious and hope that they jar loose something similar. He has put the case for the subjective correlative, to adapt a term used by James Merrill, explicitly and persuasively in "A Letter to Franz Wright," where he sends to his son "these fragments of words I picked up on the hither side of my limits. I am sending them to you, because you will love them. Consequently, you will know to piece them together into a vision of your own design. Your imagination is not mine. How could it be? Who would want it to be? I wouldn't. You wouldn't. But I love both, so I trust yours. Here are some fragments of my hammer that broke against a wall of jewels." Given the fact of publication, the "you" graciously extends itself, at least in part, to include any sympathetic reader. And what reader, in view of such trust and in the face of such a generous supposition of his uniqueness and sensitivity, could fail to reciprocate—to grant Wright his license? Wouldn't to do so be to confess one's own shallowness? But I do not want to quarrel with this passage. It says quite eloquently what we have all felt when confronted with something "so appallingly beyond accounting for" as San Gimignano was for Wright, and in any case he later evokes the beauty of the place in terms that are faceted rather than fragmented. In short, his warning serves not to justify his account but to put it in perspective. I suspect, however, that a form of the intense subjectivity embraced here at least justifies and perhaps necessitates the arcana that ornament his poems.

"What Does the Bobwhite Mean?" insists nearly belligerently on the essential secrecy of significant experiences. "I don't know / Yet," the poem answers the question, which was evidently put by the man to whom it is dedicated: "Only you know."

> As for me, as for mine,
> We have held each other's hands alone, each alone,
> And felt the green dew turn dark gold, brilliants
> In the darkness outside.
> A town called Fiesole.
> What can the name of Fiesole mean to you?
> What does the bobwhite mean?

And so on: "What will your loneliness mean to me? / What does the bobwhite mean?" Perhaps unintentionally, the recurrent question comes to seem a mocking refrain, and the poem ends with a curt dismissal: "You know. / Go, listen"—as though to say that we are all poets and therefore have nothing to say to one another. We are "each alone," like the "solitary armadillos" that appear at one point. Wright's telling sympathy for shelled creatures reappears in "With the Shell of a Hermit Crab." Composed of tetrameter quatrains, each self-contained and fragile as the shell itself, it belongs to the tradition that began with Catullus's poem on the death of Lesbia's sparrow, whose opening line gives Wright his epigraph. But instead of Catullus's outcry against all-devouring death and his attention to Lesbia we have Wright's lament for the crab's former "loneliness" and a nearly reproachful allusion to his own (for the "you" must refer to an absent person):

> Today, you happen to be gone,
> I sit here in the raging hell,
> The city of the dead, alone,
> Holding a little empty shell.

The relationship between the two hermits can hardly be ignored. Even in this mournful poem, however, one feels an undercurrent of grim satisfaction in the isolation. As he sits contemplating the empty shell the poet recalls some cinquecento St. Jerome, alone by choice in the desert, gazing into the eye sockets of a death's-head.

As for the purportedly lonely crab, during his brief life he moved "How delicately no one knows." That is his secret. And since no one knows, any degree of delicacy can be ascribed. Just as we know nothing of the crab's delicacy, so we are ignorant of "The snail's secret" in "By the Ruins of a Gun Emplacement: Saint-Benoît" (which alludes to "The Snail's Road" in *Two Citizens*):

> I met a snail on a stone at Fleury,
> Where, now, Max Jacob walks happily among the candles
> Of his brothers, but I still do not know
> The snail's secret.
> I do not even know
> What we shall do if the round moon comes down
> The river and strolls up
> Out of the Loire
> To take once more your startling face up
> Among his drowsed swans.

I do not even know for sure what the round moon might portend, although I suspect from its earlier appearances, the setting of the poem, and the allusion to Jacob (who was arrested at Saint-Benoît and died in a concentration camp at Drancy) that it is meant to be at once ominous and seductive, a softly luminous skull with which (the diction and rhythms suggest) the poet is half in love. But then I wonder, since Wright's imagination is not mine, whether I have not placed the eerily beautiful fragments together into a vision of my own design. I wonder too whether the mystery is not the essence of the poem, whether that is not the point of the lines on the snail, whether I am not being invited to go look at the moon and be sensitive myself.

Another poem that I want very much to admire goes out of its way to create a secret. "On a Phrase from Southern Ohio" recalls a childhood incident and reads for the most part like a sarcastic response to "Fern Hill": "it is not / Maiden and morning on the way up that cliff. / Not where I come from." Here the hill is a foothill, across the Ohio River from Steubenville, whose side has been jackhammered away and covered with concrete. Instead of princes of the apple towns,

Wright and his friends are punks who steal a skiff to get over to that "Smooth dead / Face" so that they can climb it. Once on top they find instead of an idyllic orchard "a garden of bloodroots, tangled there, a vicious secret / Of trilliums" and two black boys, whom they beat up and chase off. Instead of Adam in Eden this is Cain in Nod, and it is all done with a marvelous sense of the rawness and the sourness and the savagery of the summer life of boys growing up to become strip miners and jackhammer operators in a spoiled mid-American town. Then the poem ends:

> And still in my dreams I sway like one fainting strand
> Of spiderweb, glittering and vanishing and frail
> Above the river.
> What were those purple shadows doing
> Under the ear
> Of the woman who was weeping along the Ohio
> River the woman?
> Damned if you know;
> I don't.

The first sentence suggests memories of a light-headedness after the incident, but it is too portentous for that to be its sole purpose. In addition to his own "A Dream of Burial" (*The Branch Will Not Break*), Wright might want us to call up "A Noiseless Patient Spider" with its "gossamer thread" unanchored, so these lines might say something of his hopeless isolation. But the elegantly swaying sentence itself floats free of the poem and retains its mystery. Along with the odd personification and the superfluous question, it seems intended to bemuse, while the last sentence, which pugnaciously recasts the slang phrase in the second person, flatly dares us to make sense of any of this. One has the feeling that to do so would be somehow to demean the poem, to rob Wright of its experience. And then one remembers "The Jewel," back in *The Branch Will Not Break*, with its bristling, defensive warning:

> There is this cave
> In the air behind my body
> That nobody is going to touch:
> A cloister, a silence
> Closing around a blossom of fire.

Why, precisely: Wright's poems seem to embody, in respect to "the pure clear word," what the psychologists call an approach-avoidance conflict—he wants to be open and direct, yet he seems to fear that in doing so he will snuff out that "blossom of fire," lose his singular vision. Hence perhaps the withdrawals into shells, caves, and secrecy. The fainting strand of spiderweb, the moving jewel of the body, and so on—these images both prove his isolation and validate it.

It is true that in the absence of such vagaries Wright's poems can be breathtakingly plain. "What Does the King of the Jungle Truly Do?" is a prose poem in praise of leonine purity that ends "Small wonder Jesus wept at a human city," and one longs for the sentiment to be even thinly disguised. "Simon," which comes perilously close to "plain American which cats and dogs can read," is little more than a schmaltzy tribute to Robert Bly's "huge gross" Airedale ("We slobber all over each other's faces"). Yet how nicely the simplicity of this poem sets off the tiny gem of adjectival wit, which in turn dignifies the sentiment, in the poem's last stanza. One has only to know that Simon was always picking up cockleburs in his long coat:

> Simon,
> Where are you gone?
> Some shaggy burdocks in Minnesota
> Owe their lives to you,
> Somewhere.

The sensuous directness of "The First Days," to continue moving up the scale, leads up to a sudden, inspired allusion to Virgil. Wright remembers a morning in Italy when he saw "a huge golden bee ploughing / His burly right shoulder into the belly / Of a sleek yellow pear." The pear fell to the ground with the bee inside, and he knelt

> And sliced the pear gently
> A little more open.
> The bee shuddered, and returned.
> Maybe I should have left him alone there,
> Drowning in his own delight.
> The best days are the first
> To flee.

The last clause translates the poem's epigraph, *"Optima dies prima fugit,"* an abridged version of the *Georgics*, III, 66–67. Wright lends Virgil's words an ironic depth by virtue of his preceding, nearly obstetrical image, and at the same time he uses them to throw into relief his conclusion, with its glance at the utterly changed landscape:

> The best days are the first
> To flee, sang the lovely
> Musician born in this town
> So like my own.
> I let the bee go
> Among the gasworks at the edge of Mantua.[14]

By making his last line turn Virgil's lament for lost youth so discreetly into prophecy, Wright elegizes the world that produced the *Georgics* and yet avoids sentimental cliché. Such touches are small but perfect, and no less inventive than the fainting strand of spiderweb.

In "Hook" and "To a Blossoming Pear Tree," both of which seem to owe something to "In Terror of Hospital Bills" (*Shall We Gather at the River*), Wright comes as close to "the bare bones of poetry" as anyone would want. "Hook" conveys a desolate scene in language so stark that it spurns even realism as frivolous embellishment. It has the economy of dream. The poem recounts a meeting years past on a street corner in Minneapolis with a Sioux man. The young poet is "in trouble / With a woman," alone in the snow with hours to wait for a bus, when the Sioux looms out of the night. "What did they do / To your hand?" the poet asks when he sees the prosthetic hook— and it turns out that the Sioux also "had a bad time with a woman." Then he puts sixty-five cents into Wright's "freezing hand" (which, like the "they" who do not need to be identified, also implies a mutual predicament) and the poem ends: "I took it. / It wasn't the money I needed. / But I took it." Surely what he needed was a sign of understanding or of the possibility of coming through; and the coins are a sort of viaticum, an irreducible symbol of both the bond between the two men and their unalterable loneliness. Cavafy could hardly have done it more cleanly.

The counterpart of this incident occurs in the title poem, where Wright remembers an old man who appeared out of another snowy night in Minneapolis. The man, "willing to take / Any love he could get," rather like Wright in "Hook" (which must be the point of the juxtaposition of the poems), made an advance that the poet rejected. The conclusion makes what amends it can, as it addresses in its richest language the self-sufficient pear tree, as aloof from such humbling experiences as Keats's "Cold Pastoral," and affirms the necessity of *humanitas*:

> Young tree, unburdened
> By anything but your beautiful natural blossoms
> And dew, the dark
> Blood in my body drags me
> Down with my brother.

This testimony is everywhere borne out: by the increasing burden of the consonants, by the downward pull of the enjambment and the delayed verb, by the disposition of stresses in the last lines. Still, and in spite of the sharp division precisely at the middle of the central line between the natural and the human, this sentence has something of the simple, effortless beauty of the tree itself—and that is one reason that Wright is finally at least as proud as he is envious or wistful. Dragged down though he must be, because he must be dragged down, he has made a poem that will stand—and keep that tree standing so gracefully. "Perfect, beyond my reach," he says earlier of the blossoming tree, a "Little mist of fallen starlight." Yet it is even truer to say, as the last stanza does, that human imperfection is beyond the tree's reach. Absolutely clear and nonetheless as mature in attitude as in technique, this stanza seems to me as round an example as we could wish of "The poetry of a grown man."

But to talk so much about these lines is to fog with one's breath the glass we should just see through. The very directness of such a poem might be thought extravagant. And Wright's extravagance, whatever its sources and however it shows itself, makes him one of the most original and exciting poets we have. But that last is no secret at all.

NOTES

1. Peter Stitt (Interview with James Wright), "The Art of Poetry, XIX," *Paris Review*, no. 62 (Summer 1975), 58. Robert Hass, in "James Wright," *Iron-*

wood 10 (1977), 74–96, has a good deal to say about Wright's "lean, clear, plain language" and especially about his "mere sensitivity" or "will to be beautiful." I read Hass's stimulating, far-ranging essay in the course of writing an earlier version of this one and, looking back at his piece now, I realize how much it helped me shape my thoughts.

2. In "New Poems" in *Collected Poems* (Middletown, Conn.: Wesleyan University Press, 1971), p. 178. Quotations from Wright's other volumes before *Two Citizens* also come from *Collected Poems*.

3. "Afternoon and Evening at Ohrid," *Two Citizens* (New York: Farrar, Straus and Giroux, 1973), p. 12.

4. "Art of Poetry," p. 51.

5. Unpublished lecture delivered in 1933, quoted in F. O. Matthiessen, *The Achievement of T. S. Eliot*, 3rd ed. (New York: Oxford University Press, 1959), pp. 89–90.

6. One might also compare Wright's lines with Ortega's comments on aesthetic transparency. "By art," Ortega says, most people "understand a means through which they are brought into contact with interesting human affairs": "Take a garden seen through a window . . . . The purer the glass, the less we see it. But we can also deliberately disregard the garden and, withdrawing the ray of vision, detain it at the window. We then lose sight of the garden; what we still behold of it is a confused mass of color. . . . But not many people are capable of adjusting their perceptive apparatus to the pane and the transparency that is a work of art. Instead they look right through it and revel in the human reality with which the work deals." (José Ortega y Gasset, *The Dehumanization of Art*, trans. Willard A. Trask [Garden City, N.Y.: Doubleday, Anchor, 1956], pp. 9–10.) Wright sometimes seems less interested in cleaning the window than in kicking it out. That the attempt quoted above fails on the face of it, and perhaps ends in smudging the glass, alters nothing. (Nabokov treats transparency in terms remarkably similar to Ortega's, by the way, in Chapter One of his novel titled after *Roget's* category, *Transparent Things*.)

7. "Art of Poetry," p. 56.

8. *Moments of the Italian Summer* (Washington, D.C.: Dryad Press, 1976). Several of the prose poems have appeared in different versions. In addition to *Moments* and *To a Blossoming Pear Tree* (New York: Farrar, Straus and Giroux, 1977), see *American Poets in 1976*, ed. William Heyen (Indianapolis: Bobbs-Merrill, 1976); *The Prose Poem*, ed. Michael Benedikt (New York: Dell, 1976); and *The New Naked Poetry*, ed. Stephen Berg and Robert Mezey (Indianapolis: Bobbs-Merrill, 1976).

9. *Prose Poem*, p. 605.

10. *Naked Poetry*, ed. Stephen Berg and Robert Mezey (Indianapolis: Bobbs-Merrill, 1969), p. 287; and "Art of Poetry," p. 48.

11. The apparently earlier version in *American Poets in 1976* lacks the reference to the boys as "invaders" and simply notes that the little fish is "like so much else."

12. The version in *American Poets in 1976* does not have the now indispensable last sentence.

13. If I understand his point, this is the sort of passage that Robert Hass explains as evidence of both "Calvinist and solipsistic dotrine" and "decadence" in Wright's work. In Hass's view, Wright's urge to utter merely "beautiful things" from the sanctuary of his "isolated inner world" derives from an alienated and further alienating rejection of the "degraded social world."

14. "Mantova," the earlier version of this poem published in *New Naked Poetry*, ends with the translation from Virgil. Because of the absence of the "gasworks" and its implications, "Mantova" is a thinner poem.

The Tradition of Sadness and the American Metaphysic: An Interpretation of the Poetry of James Wright

LEONARD NATHAN

I

His Topics

> He is worthy, thus, of the name so often misapplied, of Poet—*i.e.* Maker. You see an original genius both in the beauties and faults of the work. Its language, so simply strong and daring in its homeliness, its free and energetic motion, its fresh fearless touch, its fidelity to nature and to life, the quick succession and sharp brief poignancy of its pictures, its absence of elaboration . . . all combine to prove that the author has an eye, an imagination, and a purpose quite peculiar to himself. He treats "the Grave" with as much originality as if he had been contemporary with the earliest sepulchre.

This is the Reverend George Gilfillan in 1854, commending Robert Blair, one of the so-called Graveyard School of eighteenth-century poets whose preoccupation was not just with interment but also with the mood of melancholy and all its lugubrious trappings. Tone down the Reverend's floridity a bit and James Wright might have been his subject. Though Wright does not much go in for Blair's gothic effects, he is surely preoccupied with melancholy and often visits the grave in his poetry, chiefly to define at its darkest edges what he finds to be a basic human condition, loneliness. Both Blair and Wright aim to arouse in their readers a sense of overwhelming pathos, though for Blair that condition is redeemed by Christian promise. For Wright redemption is too strong a word. There are moments of relief discovered in fellow feeling, but poems that celebrate this sentiment are infrequent. And one other difference, perhaps more apparent than real: Blair's topic in his poem "The Grave" is ostensibly the grave and its melancholy ambience. Wright's topic is very often Wright. His own feelings occupy stage center in much of his work, and many times his feelings about himself. For example, a whole poem, apparently concerned with nature, can lead to the simple statement:

> I have wasted my life.
>> "Lying in a Hammock at William Duffy's
>> Farm in Pine Island, Minnesota"

So all the preceding material is unexpectedly set into the background as a painful contrast to the poet's uppermost concern, his own state. In both his foregrounding of the poet's self as a poetic topic and the strong pathos that self elicits, Wright is a deeply traditional poet.

By tradition, it must be clear by now that I don't mean that James Wright sometimes alludes to dead poets or classical meter in his own poetry, or that his mature work owes anything to the formal characteristics of English and American poetry of earlier eras. It's true that he began as a formalist poet in the line of Auden, Frost, and Yeats. But after *Saint Judas* (1959), Wright "opens" his verse and composes in one mode of the contemporary free style. His expressive units are not shaped by regular meter, rhyme patterns, and symmetrical division of line and line-groups. The movement of the verse now emulates the movement of speech, heightened by intensification of cadence and shortening or extending lines to suit his tone.

What is traditional in Wright's work is his recurring subject and the character he projects in the poems, and has projected almost from the beginning, though that character is by no means simple or comfortably consistent. From a talent of Wright's scope, we would assume nothing less than a character full of possibility. But it is nonetheless identifiable from its various stances in the poems, one of which I'm now going to examine as a way of defining both that character and Wright's recurring topic in order to find their kinships in the tradition.

"The Idea of the Good"

I am bone lonely
Down on the black rock.
Now once again I take
My way, my own way,
Alone till the black
Rock opens into ground
And closes and I die.
Two hundred feet below me two deer fled past just now.
I want an owl to poise on my grave
Without sound, but
In this mean time
I want bone feet borne down
Cold on stone.
I dream of my poor Judas walking along and alone
And alone and alone and alone till his wound
Woke and his bowels
Broke.
Jenny, I gave you that unhappy
Book that nobody knows but you
And me, so give me
A little life back.
Or at least send me the owl's feather
Again, and I promise I will give it
To no one. How could I?
Nobody else will follow
This poem but you,
My precious secret, how
Could they know
You or me?
Patience.

The speaker—and you don't have to be a reader of Wright's to know that he and the poet are to be taken as one—establishes his state and locale in the first lines, and both are minimal conditions: Wright isolated to the bone, his place, bare lightless rock. What follows is a brief allegory of the speaker's life, ending when the rock opens for him. We are then pulled back to the present in a sort of scary surreal glimpse of deer fleeing far below. But the thought of death refuses to be dismissed, as if some part of him has already died, leaving him mere bones to brood on his own final grave. The owl he wants on it is a funeral prop, adding its conventional gloom to the scene. But (and we're not to miss the pun in "mean time") the speaker's more urgent need is "bone feet" to match the "bone loneliness." The man of bone is the minimal man, reduced to his own least self, a vital part of him dead in a dead world, isolated in his death, but still alive to his chill loneliness. To this point Wright's stance is a kind of harsh adjustment to what he perceives as his true condition: if the world is a cold black rock, then he must be a man of bone to match its barren hardness. This adjustment, were the poem to end here, would be the "idea of the good," but there is more, much more.

It is at this point he introduces the pathos of Judas, "walking alone and alone." Judas, as his readers know, is an important figure in Wright's poetry, canonized in the title of his second book and still a presence in his later work ("Son of Judas," *Two Citizens*, 1973). For Wright he signifies more than the betrayer of Jesus. He is the basic human who always betrays (in both senses) his faith. And he is justified if not redeemed by his capacity to commune with others equally damned, a capacity wrung out of the humanizing pathos of his isolated condition. Wright clearly identifies with Judas in this and other poems, but the identification is especially strong here because the thought of the lonely betrayer comes out of the condition Wright is experiencing up to now in the poem. He thinks of Judas because his own lonely wanderings are of the same sort, that of a man whose spirit has been mortally wounded by betrayal (what the speaker's betrayal is we don't know, so his grief has to be taken on faith so far).

It is at this point in a poem already only held together by a loose association, that Wright makes a stunning leap. Suddenly he turns to apostrophize a person who was surely not present up to now and proves later to be present only in his mind. In his turning to Jenny, he also changes his relation to his audience, which up to now could assume that it was being directly addressed or was, at least, eavesdropping on a monologue. Now, the audience is not just ignored. It is expelled, dismissed as "they," and relegated to the status of those who can never understand Wright and Jenny and what was between them. I want to return to this shift away from the audience in a moment. But now the question is: who is Jenny? Readers of *Shall We Gather At the River* (1968) will recognize her as the dedicatee of the book and the subject of "To the Muse," its last poem, in which

Wright describes the suffering of a real girl whom he early loved and who apparently committed suicide. It is perhaps unnecessary to know all this however, since it is obvious from ("The Idea of the Good" that Jenny, dead, is still his muse, receiving in silence "that unhappy / Book," *Shall We Gather at the River*, whose deepest meaning only the two of them could understand. As he closes, the poet more and more enters into private conversation with the dead girl, asking her, as he would a muse, for an exchange of gifts: as he has given her his book, so she is enjoined to give him "a little life back," or at least "the owl's feather / Again." This is the man reduced to bones, begging his lost love and muse either for some of the life that was lost in her dying (which carries with it the possibility of love) or some token of their shared experience. It is probably unwise to press the owl and its feather too hard, though the bird has been almost everywhere "a bird of witchcraft, death, and doom." (Edward A. Armstrong, *The Folklore of Birds*, New York, 1970, p. 113). It is enough to see the feather here as an emblem of a doomed relation, as therefore *some* kind of significance to an otherwise unbearably meaningless experience which he cannot communicate to others ("I will give it / To no one. How could I?"). The poem concludes with the most private of assurances that only the poet and Jenny can understand what was between them, in this instance the very poem we are reading, and he counsels her to be patient, presumably till he joins her in the final union of death.

Why the startling apostrophe to Jenny and the almost flaunting exclusion of the audience which, of course, Wright knows will go on reading his poem with some hope of understanding what it signifies? The point is complicated but these moves make sense enough if seen as rhetorical devices. For example, the very abruptness of the break indicates that Jenny has been on the poet's mind from the beginning, that the first part of the poem didn't merely establish the speaker's locale and state, but is itself the result of his agonizing preoccupation with Jenny, whose death has put him where he is, particularly if we take it to be a literal death that expands to a larger loss (perhaps some essential betrayal of innocence or even *by* innocence that inheres in the human condition). The apostrophe to Jenny then bursts out of the poet's painful contemplation of his present state. This state, a profound melancholy, evokes Wright's professed muse and what transpires between them becomes more and more private, as their relation was ultimately private, as all relations are private and all humans, in Wright's world, essentially alone. This is why Wright apparently dismisses his audience. He wants them to experience a privacy so incommunicable that he forces them to feel by this drastic strategy what it's like to be party to his utterly personal grief. That is, he is rendering the response of a man feeling through the anguished ineffable solitude of a relation, a "precious secret" too difficult for even poetry to articulate. We are supposed to experience his anguish and thereby, without knowing, feel it, feel the overpowering pathos of it. The idea of the good, then, is that feeling in the midst of bone loneliness and black rock, and perhaps the patience to suffer it as the irreducible condition of humanity. By Wright's grief we are, at most, to see the sorrow of our own condition, and, at least, the sorrow of the condition of someone who has come to the essential truth of the "mean time." The seeing may change nothing but may be in some way redeeming—thus, the idea of the good.

Has all this a resonance that suggests something out of the past? It does. The melancholy character, as such, first appears in English poetry in Milton's *Il Penseroso*. Here, the figure is not the poet, but an aspect of the poetic personality whose pleasure is in the solitude of gloomy haunts and gothic atmosphere, meditating on deep and occult mysteries and tragedy, and whose gift is prophecy. *Il Penseroso* is an exercise (a companion piece to balance Milton's *L'Allegro*), but in the eighteenth century, the figure of the melancholy poet becomes something of a fixture in English poetry, gathering to it the trappings of interment in the poets of the so-called Graveyard School, the best known of whom was Robert Blair, whose "The Grave" was a celebrated example of its kind, full of the gloom and pathos of its subject. But it wasn't until the romantics that the character of "il penseroso" ceased being a sort of literary contrivance to convey a special poetic mood and became the poet himself, since it was the romantics who first, at least in theory, aimed to merge man and poet, poet and speaker, and speaker and speaker's deepest feelings and make those feelings the subject of many of their poems. That these feelings were often deeply sad is no surprise if one understands the dialectic of romantic poetic: children have direct contact with nature (nature by now has become the key to understanding and appreciating other humans, the world, and God). But innocence is lost in growing up, in the corrupting artificiality of society. This loss leads to a paralyzing melancholy which can only be escaped by a restoration of the lost connection with nature, at which time, the poet achieves something like a religious joy and the power to bless. A record of this achievement is found in Wordsworth's "Lines Composed a Few Miles above Tintern Abbey" and a record of failure to achieve it is found in Coleridge's "Dejection: An Ode." Keats gives an ode to melancholy, treating it in a revealing way, not as "il penseroso," but as a goddess who presides over the temple of Delight. He sees melancholy as intimately connected with pleasure, and this is a brilliant perception. For in fact, already in Milton, melancholy is experienced as a pleasurable state. In the later tradition it becomes at best a pleasant savoring of sorrow, at worst, self-pitying indulgence, though its sinister kinship with madness could not be ignored. Johnson, I believe, called it "the black dog." Keats himself, though in the "Ode" he personified melancholy as a goddess, is perhaps as close to being "il penseroso" as a mortal can get, and in poems like "Ode to a Nightingale" and "On Seeing the Elgin Marbles," he luxuriates in the pathos of his state, though in the former there is a nearly tragic understanding that, for humans, complete return to or identification with nature means a loss of personal identity, the very ground for the sensitivity, the consciousness that makes the rich experience of joy and sorrow possible.

By the nineteenth century "il penseroso" has been transformed into the poet, caught up in his solitary contemplation of life's rich melancholy. Wordsworth, speaking for his contemporaries, says:

> We poets in our youth begin in gladness;
> But thereof come in the end despondency and madness.
>
> "Resolution and Independence," *The Prelude, Selected Poems and Sonnets*, New York, 1948, p. 88.

What we have then is no longer a personified convention for a mood or imagined condition, but something far more serious. It is a conventionalized figure of the poet himself, claiming to be more than a convention, the thing itself, the man *of* and *in* the poem. This claim, based on the conviction that poetry must be sincere, must speak directly the poet's deepest emotion, led to something like a revolution in the poetic tradition. In the romantics, that revolution is only to be found in an almost obsessive inwardness in poetic discourse, the avoidance of certain rhetorical devices, and a tendency to perceive poetic structure as a climactic pursuit of intensity (which would be obviously the most passionate state of the true emotions). But the revolution had to wait till our century for the next logical step: if the man merged with the poet and the poet was speaking with the utmost sincerity, then formal patterns like rhyme, traditional meter, symmetrical line and stanza, surely had to go, and go they did for many a poet. First we got *vers libre* and in our own time, the "open" or "naked" poem which attempts to represent, both in its diction and cadences, actual speech.

"The Idea of the Good" then belongs to the tradition that begins with Milton, deepens through the nineteenth century, and becomes in our day a major mode. Wright is the melancholy man and his subject is loss. It is no accident that he finds a simulacrum in Judas, for betrayal is loss, in Wright a loss of innocence equivalent to the loss of touch with nature in the earlier romantics. His only way back is through reestablishing some connection with the source of the old feeling of communion, in this instance, his early love and muse, Jenny. "The Idea of the Good" is a prayer, but one that expects no answer. And that is a major difference between Wright (and perhaps many contemporary poets) and the early romantics. For the latter, redemption was always possible, even for a murderer of innocence like the Ancient Mariner, though ecstatic joy was forever beyond him. For Wright, if there is redemption, it is so minimal, so private, so much a matter of an owl's feather, that it finds itself circumscribed by—to use Coleridge's phrase—"Reality's dark dream." While not all Wright's poems find so small a redemption, the character he projects in "The Idea of the Good" and the subject he treats there are found in many, if not most, of his poems, and this before he had changed styles.

II

His Styles

In his essay, "Reality in America," Lionel Trilling had this to say about what he called the "American metaphysic": in it, "reality is always material reality, hard, resistant, unformed, impenetrable, and unpleasant. And that mind is alone felt trustworthy which most resembles this reality by most nearly reproducing the sensations it affords." (*The Liberal Imagination*, New York, 1950, p. 13.) Now, this sense of reality seems to invest much of Wright's style from the sixties on. He had begun his career in the decade before as a traditional stylist with measured iambics, a full complement of rhymes and symmetrical stanzas. But after *Saint Judas* (1959), something drastic happened. While he didn't entirely drop traditional usages, from this time on he characteristically composed in a "free" or "open" vein without the regular cadence or the neat rhyme and stanzaic patterns. Gone too are the literary language of the earlier poems and their tight narrative organization. Now his work hangs together more loosely, often as a catalogue of details that leads to some general statement as in "Lying in a Hammock . . ." or to a last detail intensified by its suggestion of ominous portent as in "A Poem Written under an Archway in a Discontinued Railway Station, Fargo, North Dakota," which concludes:

> He smiles with the sinister grief
> Of old age.

Trilling's observation on the American metaphysic may help explain what Wright was about in making this change, though not why he made it. And it may also explain the same for that rather considerable group of traditionalist poets of Wright's generation whose style underwent a like transformation. When the transformation came about (first clearly visible in the sixties), it was from a style that was recognizably literary to one that was recognizably something more proximate to ordinary speech and its rhythms. The shift from "tight" to "open" must, in any case, have amused the longtime followers of Williams and Pound. Who now were the heretics from the true poetic tradition? Obviously, the recanting followers of Yeats and Auden.

It is hard to say what it was that occasioned this relinquishing of traditional forms in favor of a style reflecting the American metaphysic. Maybe for many, though not all, formalist poets, the time had come when they could no longer accept the assumptions underlying traditional poetic composition, above all, the belief that the conventions passed down from the English poetic tradition were virtually synonymous with poetry itself. What the mid-twentieth century offered up as reality could have made those conventions seem an irrelevant luxury, and art itself, in its old-fashioned sense, a distraction from truth. Louis Simpson in the early sixties calls for a poetry that can, sharklike, swallow the otherwise indigestible "new" reality:

> Whatever it is, it must have
> A stomach that can digest
> Rubber, coal, uranium, moons, poems.
>
> Like the shark, it contains a shoe.
> It must swim for miles through the desert
> Uttering cries that are almost human.
>
> "American Poetry," At the End
of the Open Road, p. 55.

However much they admitted the heterogeneous lumpiness of reality in their own statements about it, Yeats and Auden could no longer serve as stylistic models. Their conventions, from the vantage of the American metaphysic, invited followers to exclude too much, to spit up the shoe.

For some—Richard Wilbur comes first to mind—the conventions held their own powers. For most, I think, they didn't, even before the poets themselves became conscious of the extent of their disbelief. The sheer sense of control and mastery over language that traditional style can give its users can also blind them to the possibility that they are enjoying an exercise rather than writing poetry. When I opened *The Green Wall* in 1957, I was dazzled (and said so in a review). Now it seems far less affecting. I am persuaded to nothing so much as the talent itself. (The tools are surely there, but the emotions and ideas they work with seem derivative or self-consciously literary.) This is not the sense you get in Yeats or, at his best, in Auden. Wright's early poems don't so much generate a poetic experience as enact a literary one, and I can see why he might have felt that he had reached a stylistic dead end in *Saint Judas*, where from time to time he strains after something else.

This something else Wright seems to have found in his translations, and particularly where some other poets of his generation have found it—in the "freer" modern poets writing in Spanish, Neruda, Vallejo, and Jimenez, though Georg Trakl surely reinforced his taste for the funereal. So Wright, with the help of foreign models, found a language to match the American reality. The result is found in his next book, *The Branch Will Not Break* (1963). It is a considerable leap, if not in topic or tone, then in style from

Walking around to breathe, I kick aside
The soft brown feather and the brittle beak.
All flesh is fallen snow. The days deride
The wings of these deluded, once they break.

"Sparrows in a Hillside Drift"

to

But now,
All day long I have been walking among damp fields,
Trying to keep still, listening
To insects that move patiently.
Perhaps they are sampling the fresh dew that gathers slowly
In the empty snail shells
And in the secret shelters of sparrow feathers fallen on the
    earth.

"I Was Afraid of Dying"

And this latter is a rather tender example. Wright is often apt to get closer to the style of the American metaphysic:

She slaps her grease rags
Into a basket,
And slings it over her skinny forearm, crooked
With hatred, and stomps outside.

"How My Fever Left"

But the style here does more than reflect a reality "hard, resistant, unformed, impenetrable, and unpleasant." It also puts James Wright the poet much closer to James Wright the man (or the man projected in these poems), the James Wright who, as I said earlier, is a primary topic of his own poetry, or at least exhibit A in the case for universal loneliness and melancholy. And that desired closeness between poet and person is something Trilling's definition only implies. In its exaltation of physical reality, the American metaphysic finds the craft of poetic arts suspect, and so supports a leading psychological principle of romantic poets: that literature, and above all poetry, must be personal or lose authenticity. Of course, personal poetry goes back a long way in the western tradition—to Archilochus and Sappho. But in the traditional personal poem, formal conventions have almost always guaranteed a certain distance between real poets and their audiences. In late eighteenth-century England, these conventions, in

169

theory if not practice, were threatened by a new poetic conception of this relation. But it took many social and literary earthquakes to bring practice into line with, and even exceed, theory. Contemporary poetic style is very much a part of this attack on the old distancing conventions insofar as it aims to bring, or give the appearance of bringing, the poet as a private person into immediate relation with an audience.

In this view then, poetry must convincingly be that person speaking in his own voice, undistorted by intrusive formal devices and deceiving rhetorical eloquence. What comes through must reflect not just a man talking to men, but a man talking (or confessing) nakedly, with no concealing prettification, no practiced and therefore false inflections. The poem then is not, as it was conceived in the traditional view, the artful product of the poet's mind. It is the very working of consciousness (or, more radically, subconsciousness) itself as it unfolds its deepest truths, that is, its feelings and sensations. Or at least that is what the reader must believe. Implicit in this notion is a sort of new antiartistic poem, perhaps even an antipoem. In it, ideally, raw feeling utters itself for whoever has ears to hear. It is one step away from an id speaking to ids.

The great advantage of what might be called the new American metaphysical style is that, in the hands of its best practitioners, it can generate a sense of the actual texture of personal experience, whether of the outside world or of the poet's subjectivity. And yet, like traditional poetry (and despite some of the theoretical claims of its proponents), it too has its conventions—colloquial diction, speech cadences, and deliberate breaks in syntactic and narrative continuity, to name only the most important. With these conventions, the poet can give intense immediacy to the outer landscape, in the manner of Williams, or to the inner one, in the manner of Plath, or to both, depending on what is wanted. And this immediacy can be offered in a fairly flat language or a richer one, akin to the style of poets of modern Spanish. Wright uses both. He also looks outward and inward, but most often the outward serves to illuminate the inward. Like Plath, he tends to the confessional.

The advantages of this style (or these styles), as one might expect, exact a certain price. Because poetic conventions are narrowed to so personal a perspective, things can get lost, things the older tradition could include with no discomfort, for example, the social world of the narrative, and in the lyric, the common wisdom and lore that mediated between one person's private experiences and those of another. The radical personalism of the new style makes it hard to accept tradition-based connections and the poet can find himself isolated with his own feelings and sensations, which are at once the sources of his power and of a uniqueness which can isolate him from the understanding of others, bridges that are wide enough to bear larger than private meanings or cries of despairing isolation. Often Wright's own poems seem the record of failures to build such bridges, failures that lead him to the desolating pathos of freight yards, dying rivers, and the grave. When he does manage a span of sorts, it is narrow and shaky, built from the thin lines of tentative affection, desperately sudden affirmations, and momentary sympathy or nostalgia.

But it would be unjust to insist that Wright finds no alternative beyond solipsistic pathos and small momentary celebrations. Some of his strongest work is that in which he has succeeded in establishing a common lore to include a world that demands more than raw grief. In "Two Poems about President Harding," he reaches for something like the magnitude of the traditional ode, "celebrating" a figure whose ruin is one monument to the American way of life. Like Pindar, he enters his own poem as a witness to a kind of wonder, but not in the stylized role of public singer. True to his assumptions about the necessity of the personal in poetry, he presents himself as a solitary man, a private citizen, his credentials exactly the ones for a singer of ruin and desolation:

> I am drunk this evening in 1961,
> In a jag for my countryman.

That Wright cannot find tragedy, only pathos, in his subject is the result of the limits imposed on him by the American metaphysic. The heavy intractableness of reality renders the individual helpless before events. At the end of the second poem, he suddenly turns to his audience and denies his responsibility for what he has described:

> But don't look at me.
> By God. I didn't start this mess.

There is a note of incensed if impotent defensiveness in this. Already in *Saint Judas*, Wright exhibits anger and disgust, sometimes against himself or his own art.

> I add my easy grievance with the rest . . .
> . . . .
> I croon my tears at fifty cents per line.
> "At the Executed Murderer's Grave"

Yet in this sorrow and accusation there is occasionally more than a hint of self-justification. For example, the sanctification of Judas occasionally involves what seems to me a curious ambivalence between self-contempt and self-righteousness. Clearly, Wright identifies with the betrayer of Jesus, even as late as "The Son of Judas" in *Two Citizens*. Judas embodies many of the poet's preoccupations: he is a loser, outsider, hypocrite, ultimate traitor to faith, suicide, and, in Wright's canon, saint. Maybe the ultimate truth Wright strives to formulate is that only the children of Judas can know, by having lost it, what redemption is. That stance gives Wright, who counts himself among their number, a certain moral authority over others who lack his special knowledge.

In some instances, it is this moral authority that allows him to turn and address his audience directly, sometimes, as in the second Harding poem, with scolding impatience. But mostly this sort of move is an artful tactic based on Wright's view of poetry: that it must, whatever the cost, throw art and caution to the winds for the sake of truth, for in the American metaphysic art and truth are antithetical. In short, rude honesty is a convention of the new "open" poetry, particularly in its confessional mode. Poets turning to address their readers are nothing new. Even giving them a good blast has its precedent in Baudelaire's famous: "*—Hypocrite lecture,—mon semblable,—mon frere!*" And there is Rilke's equally famous imperative: "*Du musst dein Leben ändern.*" But these apostrophes were always more or less distanced by formal controls. In the new mode they can (or, for the contemporary reader they can) have the effect of spontaneous interruption, the poet breaking through the lines to encounter his reader face to face, no sanitized breathing room left between them.

I have mentioned some of the strengths and weaknesses of "open" poetry. One more of the latter needs noting: a tendency to occasional obscurity, the sort of thing that turns up more in Wright's later work, especially in *Two Citizens* (for example, section 3, "The Streets Grow Young"). If poetry is the operation of consciousness and consciousness dwells mostly in the privacy of its own experience, that experience rendered "literally" is apt sometimes to remain private, obscure. And this obscurity is not the tactical variety found in Eliot and Thomas, but a "natural one."

Yet the new mode, whatever its shortcomings, is a powerful tool, most powerful, I think, when it elicits pathos. Wright may have written sad poems no matter what his era, but his temperament and the "open" mode seem meant for each other.

III

The Experience of His Poems

The American metaphysical style leads so often to pathos for all the reasons I have been discussing, but chiefly the helplessness of the individual before an ugly intractable reality. This pathos is intensified by the romantic assumption that poets must speak nakedly to their audiences, without the mediation of literary form, must speak as truthful solitaries in a world where connections are often painful and always precarious.

Where is the audience in all this? In traditional poetry, the poet entered the poem as some stylized self—one of a number of conventional types: lover, teacher, mocker, visionary, precator, and so on. The poem itself was seen as a formal communication, however intense, a mediated utterance separating real author from real public. This formality gave poets a certain freedom to be more than their individual selves. So Ben Jonson could comfortably separate out the real poet and the role he must play in his poems:

> Let me be what I am, as Virgil cold;
> As Horace fat; or as Anacreon old;
> No Poets verses yet did ever move,
> Whose Readers did not thinke he was in love.

The public—Samuel Johnson's Common Readers—understood this and judged the poem as something more than the expression of its maker (even though its maker was wholly responsible for its virtues and deficiencies). The poem was understood as a communication about a shareable world beyond the private ones of parties to the poetic transaction. The romantics, in part responding to a breakdown in that shareable world, tried to restore what they felt was a lost authenticity to poetic discourse. Their way was to try to bring poets closer to their audiences. This meant the conflation of poem and poet and poems that were thus expressions of a "real" self.

Such a poetry demanded a new kind of audience response. If poetry was not so much communication as (self) expression, then an audience had not so much to respond to as to *identify* with the poet, with the individual experiencing the feelings expressed. For the first romantics, however, there was still a larger world for sharing. Wordsworth believed that individuals were still blessed with a divinely-given imagination that linked private self to the world and other selves. For us this faith is mostly nostalgia. What is left is the identification of poet and audience but without a larger order of experience to give the identification grounds and scope. It is a matter chiefly of feeling, of stance. This quality is the source of the intensity that has been traded for scope in much contemporary poetry.

The consequence of all this is a change of bases for aesthetic judgment. A radical shift—working by degrees over two centuries—has taken place in the way poems are (to be) read. The confessional or naked poem does not ask to be judged for its artfulness or even its "truth to nature" (an old-fashioned critical term that implied a general faithfulness to how people and things looked, felt, or behaved). It asks to be judged rather on how well it makes its audience experience the real presence of the poet as a real person. I recall a reviewer of I think it was *Saint Judas* rendering what has to be the ultimate praise of contemporary criticism in words something like the following: "I wish I knew how to make him happy." It is no bad thing, human sympathy, whether for sorrow or gladness, the sort of gladness that begins to shine through a little more frequently in *Moments of Italian Summer.*

James Wright is superb at eliciting human sympathy, that shared sense of another life lived intensely. He has made powerful art of seeming to speak without art or, at least, of seeming to interrupt his art with passionate personal assertion when the human need arises. Individual poems can be stunning. A whole collection can be overpowering and it is then that some readers might long for the relief of less directness and the scope lost in the search for intense relation, and might long also for a sense of reality less bound by the American metaphysic. But maybe such longings are for what is now beyond our capacity to reinvent. Meanwhile, if there is a master among the practitioners of the contemporary personal poem, surely James Wright is a leading contender for that title.

That Halting, Stammering Movement

DAVE SMITH

WILLIAM CARLOS WILLIAMS, the original "in the grain" American writer, was not a misguided provincial in his passion for a native language. He raged against Eliot's refusal to employ the sufficient and various strengths of American English because he believed the possibilities for an American poetry could not be achieved through an appropriated language. Williams believed in the poet who would "make it new" in spite of critics who would equate new with crude. James Wright is such a poet, especially in the final poems of *Collected Poems* and *Two Citizens*.[1] Wright proposes for us the simple, though in practice still radical, idea that there is a language and a poetry adequate to express the pathetic yearning of our age and a tenuous consolation based on moral values.

Wright's critics have been strident in their opposition to his newer poems.[2] Gerritt Henry thrashed *Two Citizens* for a language that was "painfully plain and undistinguished" and then lumped Wright into a complaint against American poets who would play Huck Finn, saying: "Like so many 'in the grain' American writers (the book is prefaced with a passage from Hemingway), Wright is afraid to completely commit himself one way or the other, or to (what is taken to be) European high style and artificing."[3]

The argument against an American naiveté which posits the alternatives of an acceptable primitivism or a continuity of the sophisticated European is not new. Noah Webster, Emerson, Whitman, Williams, and others have confronted it. Whether it is better to write (if not to *be*) something other than American is both a political and artistic question which was reinforced by Vietnam and the violent sixties. Our best and worst poets turned away from militarism, homegrown impurity, and American language. We looked for answers not where Williams counseled, but in the poetries of Europe, South America, and Asia.

James Wright and Robert Bly were among the first poets of the contemporary generation to translate and then write a poetry influenced directly by translation. Obviously affected by the German, the French, the Spanish, the Russian, and the Chinese, both poets (moved away from poetry as an artificial, nonconversational artifact and toward a poetry of lyrical speech characterized by naked epiphany) and political engagement. If the poetry they created was not Eliotic English, neither was it Main Street American. It retained a goodly degree of European high style and artificing. Their internationalizing effect on American poetry, difficult as that is to gauge, is widespread and positive. Yet it also enhances the superficial notion that the American language, if not the American, is inherently inferior. A great intelligence is never comfortable with superficiality and, in consequence, James Wright has turned back to a language "in the grain" whose one purpose is to cut through deadly mannerism. In "She's Awake" Wright says:

> It was easy.
> All I had to do was delete the words lonely and shadow,
> Dispose of the dactylic hexameters into amphibrachs

that is, to cut through language which prevents recovery of what is loved, such as Emerson Buchanan, an uncle who is "one half-hendecasyllabic, / And almost an amphibrach." To fail to find that plain language, as Wright says in "Emerson Buchanan," means: "I try and try to hear them, and all I get / Is a blind dial tone."

Wright knows that his citizens, all of us, can scarcely help being citizens of the world as well as of our root-place. But vital poetry begins and ends at home. Americans are an openly affirming people who have believed in making realities of absolute ideals, dreamers whose despairs are exaggerated by such initial optimism. Wright insists that the most fundamental nature of poetry is its affirmation of *possibility*, exactly the root characteristic of the American dream. His new poetry is an aggressive reaching for and embracing of that possibility. In *Two Citizens* poems begin in the embrace of France, Italy, Yugoslavia, Bach, Dante, Horace, and Lu Yu, but translate themselves into American language relentlessly seeking transparency. Ironically, Gerritt Henry suggests an accurate figure for Wright: at mid-career he is achieving equipoise by balancing extremes in painfully plain language whose fidelity is to the old dream.

What many have thought sudden in Wright's new poetry is an evolution. His early work is well known for its polish and predictability. Hayden Carruth has written: "Wright's early poems recall exactly those years of the late 1940s, the time when we had an ideal music running in our minds."[4] *The Green Wall* (1957) and *St. Judas* (1959) remain admirable examples of what Ransom called music and verse texture. Yet, in retrospect, we can see the nuclei for Wright's more innovative work: the flashing personal voice, the semisurreal imagery, the epiphany, the accruing myth of Christ-Everyman in the Hell of Ohio, and especially the plain idiomatic speech woven among tones of Frost, Eliot, and Robinson. This idiomatic speech dominates *Two Citizens* and is neither arbitrary nor revolutionary; it is a crafted language reflective of a people and a time suspicious of ideal musics and unwilling to yield to silence.

We badly understand Wright to take this language's blunt and garrulous simplicity as a lapse in poetic control or richness. Indeed it is a pendulum swing away from modernist impersonality as well as those fifties' codes of decorum. It is language undressed, apparently, stripped of stylizations, forms, metric and sonic mannerisms, a language trying to be so transparently healthy that it appears to have skidded beyond poetry to bald statement and blatant proselytizing. I think, however, that Wright's effects are deliberate and that we must engage in cautionary *seems*. Wright is no less an artificer than he ever was. He tells us much when he says, frequently, that his master is Horace, a poetic innovator. Another master, one Wright rarely alludes to, is that angel of narrative, Dickens, for whom the writer's task is to create literal worlds which both absorb and change a reader. Such masters insist that the *real* is attained only through the most realistic, the least artificial artifice.

It has often been said that Wright's middle books showed him breaking from his artificial early work, a partial truth. With *The Branch Will Not Break* (1963) he began to abandon English devices of the metaphysical. But a paradox, for example, is useful without Donne's clothing. It may be turned, as one turns a prism, until it provides contrast without logical rhetoric. Bly and the Chinese showed Wright this possibility. In the sixties Wright's poems became assertive, skeletal, exotic as they rejected his laboriously traditional voice. "Lying in a Hammock in William Duffy's Farm at Pine Island, Minnesota," a poem which catalogued a brilliant, peaceful landscape, ended with the controversial last line "I have wasted my life." It was not artificial or unearned. It did not entirely abdicate the ideal music of paradox and tension created by a net of counterstraining ironies and logics. The poem is a skeletal paradox built on irony. The last line nails one argument against the poem's other argument, resulting in a blunt, factual effect possible only through high artifice.

Both artifice and statement, however, mean to convince. The difference is in the force employed. Any poem of faith and assertion is a paradox. Wright's use of paradox is not historically important except as it shows a recognition of complexity, which is truth, not available to flat statement. The truth, we say, is multiple and absolutes are at best relative. Paradox recognizes the contrary and irrefutable truths of opposites. It is one way to search for moral absolutes, but its use need not be limited to a poem's internal mechanics. There is also the paradox of poems set in polar opposition so that a book becomes a self-reflexive process, as *Two Citizens* is. Here "A Poem of Towers" is paired against "To You, Out There (Mars? Jupiter?)" in order to achieve a full respect for truth's complexity. The first poem is a positive, lyrical, intuitively achieved vision of a singing world at momentary unity. Wright says:

> and my love
> Leans on my shoulder precise
> As the flute notes
> Of the snow, with songs

and the poem's movement leaps. The second poem despairs of disconnection from God in plodding, rational, and sarcastic language. It imagines the same "nobility of dreams" though people are now:

> Alone in the griped cold, hopelessly longing
> To pray to someone whose name
> Is Streisand.

This is a world of "pubes and inner arms" where "You will not find God." Both poems lean at absolutes but together approach the possibility of balance and complexity that is not emotional gush but the wage of intelligence. (It would be beneficial to think of all of Wright's books in such a relationship.)

A third way to approach the possibility of truth is to realize a transparent language. That is impossible but skilled use of artifice may come close. For Wright, artifice is only as important as the end it serves and that end is the poem of equipoise where the truth may be held in the moment, the poem that is made possible only by the simultaneous employment of poetic equipment from the past and a language of immediate human vitality. In this regard I believe Wright may be approached, if not explained, through his connection with a poet more recent and less suspected than Horace or Dickens or Robinson. In 1959 Wright reviewed Robert Penn Warren's remarkable *Promises* and wrote:

> In effect [Warren] has chosen, not to write his good poems over again but to break down his own rules, to shatter his words and try again to recreate them, to fight through and beyond his own craftsmanship in order to revitalize his language at the sources of tenderness and horror.[5]

If words, unlike glass, may not be wholly reblown, it is still Wright's task to recreate language so long as it remains less than transparent, so long as artifice has not escaped artificiality.

While it is untrue to suggest that Wright has imitated Warren and of only marginal importance to worry over poetic influences, what Wright praises in Warren coincides in time and development with Wright's own interests. From the early sixties to the present no subject more concerns Wright than language, the way in which we know and experience reality. In "The Offense," one of the last poems in *Collected Poems*, he writes:

> Hell to me was a girl whose lonely body
> Needed me, somewhere, to be lonely with her.
> Hell to you was the difficult, the dazzling
> Hendecasyllabic.

The insistence on Hell, that moral abstraction, as more than a linguistic trick lies at the heart of a poetry trying always to define reality with the force of revelation. Wright knows exactly what he wants and does not want to create:

> The kind of poetry I want to write is
> The poetry of a grown man.
> The young poets of New York come to me with
> Their mangled figures of speech
> But they have little pity
> For the pure clear word.

By *Two Citizens* Wright's insistence on that clarity has created a language that is, to casual attention, stripped of poetic device. It is *apparently* nothing but the emotional effusion of one incapable of restraint.

Yet Wright's language is neither happy accident nor chaos come again. Language in the twentieth century is severely suspect. If it makes reality, it also distorts reality. Villanelles, sestinas, sonnets render atomic violence as remote artifacts. Burning Asian children are not contained in alexandrines. Of the Polish poet, Janos Pilinszky, Ted Hughes has written, "It has often been said that words, for his generation, were given an abnormal testing. Their experience screwed up the price of such terms as 'truth' and 'reality' and 'understanding' beyond what common language seems able to pay."[6] All that language seems capable of doing is to state personal abjection for many who, like Pilinszky, would write, "I am alone, orphaned of everything." And everything is orphaned from everything. Hughes on Pilinszky might well be Hughes on Wright: "This loneliness is something more than a cosmic experience. It is a metaphysical state. It is intimately connected, in all Pilinszky's poetry, through sexual love, to the pathos of the created world, where trembling creatures still go uselessly through their motions, in a radiant emptiness. This loneliness is separated from the nearest other creature as the flesh is separated from any form of consolation. The real presence of that other creature, in fact, would be the presence of salvation."[7] Wright's long-evolving myth of the exiled, wandering alien who is the human analogue of Christ is also Pilinszky's pathos and invokes the same suspicions of language. But Wright has gone beyond Pilinszky. His two citizens, James and Annie Wright, have recreated love, which is to say salvation or consolation. Annie Wright is both sexual and spiritual presence, a presence which requires of James Wright a new language to leap across the metaphysical loneliness and the radiant emptiness. Such a language must reaccommodate the absolutes priced out of poetry, must return poetry to a witnessing of the truth beyond pathos.

Language, for Wright as for Warren, will make only superficial poetry if it is disengaged. It must not stand between and frustrate a possible connection between poet and audience. Therefore, Wright works to stimulate a conversational idiom which is, nevertheless, an illusion of greatly shortened distance. It remains a system of organized symbols on a page, inert and closely manipulated, but with an identifiable human voice speaking urgently of urgent matters. As Dickens had, Wright's language croons, curses, sings, whines, giggles, fawns, shouts, demands, coos, and drones as is strategic. Such blatant wrenching of poetry grates on many ears in our age of mono-toned lyrics and Wright considers that, too:

> If these lines get published, I will hear
> From some God damned deaf moron who knows
> Everything.
>
> "At the Grave"

But poetry as a parlor game, however skillful, will not suffice for Wright's intention, which is *a gathering* and *an embrace*. When language exists as poetry it is true, it witnesses and celebrates the right human condition, it affirms the nature of the Good. Language conceptualizes and expresses the Good, but it also mortifies and obscures and hides the Good. Language can be effective in evil ways. Such simple nouns as *nigger* or *dago* have an effect but the effect is usually dehumanizing and that is exactly what poetry opposes. An active poetry, therefore, may have to resort to wholesale recreation, including new words. Wright speaks of:

> . . . my love and me wandering silent in the breeze
> Of a strange language, at home with each other.
> Saying nothing, listening

> To a new word for mountain, to a new
> Word for cathedral, to a new word for
> Cheese, to a word beyond words for
> Cathedrals and homes.
>
> "I Wish I May Never Hear of the United States Again"

Language, as Wright implies, is both home and cathedral, a way and a place of belonging, thus of possibility. And in possibility lies the dreamed moral life. Wright's chosen speech forces the reader to confront the lack of transparency in his own language and thereby perhaps to know again what *poetry* means. If Williams was correct about the validity of the American language in poetry, then Wright has more than willful self-authority behind his saying "The one tongue I can write in / Is my Ohioan."

But what exactly is the "Ohioan" in which Wright's poems are grounded? Here again the link with Robert Penn Warren is especially helpful. In the review-essay of *Promises*, that collection which marked Warren's own turn to a radically different poetry, Wright speaks with close attention and clear admiration about a forcefully dislocated syntax, an orchestral suspension of phrasing, a direct and earthy colloquial idiom, and a fuguelike weaving of formal and informal. After *Saint Judas* Wright began to evidence the same characteristics. In his criticism of *Promises*, Wright did not engage in citing "beautiful" lines and felicitous phrases; he was little concerned with metric patterns, choosing instead to examine the way in which Warren's language architecture supported a poetry of human truth. Wright admits quickly that Warren's language is eccentric and accepts it, thus rejecting the poem as seamless artifact. He concludes that *Promises* is written in the poetry of a grown man who cannot flinch from the contemporary paralysis of will and spirit nor yet live with it. What is important in Wright's judgments is the clear and early recognition that his language, like Warren's, belied his sense of reality. Warren had had to grapple with an eccentric speech to express his own frustration and in that speech Wright saw possibility. This is not to say that Wright grew out of Warren, only to suggest what Wright was approaching and revealing as he read Warren. The poetry of a grown man did not have to be the honed abstraction which participates in a kind of international drone. It might, as it had for the Chinese, be a kind of powerful and direct statement, though such a statement would have to recognize the simultaneous beauty and horror which truth is. In Warren, Wright saw the possibility of a wrenched language which had accommodated the oppositions a grown man understands.

Wright wrote of *Promises*, "The poetic function of the distortion is to mediate between the two distinct modes of tenderness and horror." And this was an "extreme exaggeration of a very formal style." That is, it was high artifice pushing toward immediate reality. Wright, as well as Warren, had had his lessons in artifice from John Crowe Ransom and his poetics were well steeped in Latinate composition. He had, therefore, full knowledge of where Warren's poetry had been and a clear sense of where it was going:

I propose the hypothesis that one can hear in the poem two movements of language: a strong formal regularity, which can be identified with a little struggle, but which is driven so fiercely by the poet that one starts to hear beyond it the approach of an unpredictable and hence discomforting second movement, which can be identified as something chaotic, something very powerful but unorganized. It is the halting, stammering movement of an ordinarily articulate man who has been shocked. The order and chaos move side by side; and, as the poem proceeds, I get the feeling that each movement becomes a little stronger, and together they help to produce an echoing violence in the syntax. . . . It is the exaggerated formality with which a man faces and acknowledges the concrete and inescapable existence of an utterly innocent (and therefore utterly ruthless) reality which is quite capable not only of cursing him, but also of letting him linger contemplatively over the sound of his own bones breaking.[8]

Wright's poetry, like Warren's, has become of necessity a halting, stammering movement whose function is to mediate between horror and tenderness, whose distortions and polarities represent an exaggerated formality that is quite simply trying to reawaken the reader's moral consciousness. His language is designed to display but, also, like a Virgilian guide, to go beyond the Sartrian nightmare of pathos. "Ohio Valley Swains," a poem of hideous cruelty, suggests the language and the figure of the poet hugely shocked. The poem begins "The granddaddy longlegs did twilight / And light," an invocation of Virgil's *lacrimae rerum*, but obscure. The speaker is fumbling backward in memory to recover an ugly scene where a girl is violated by local thugs and the speaker is sent helplessly away:

> What are you doing here, boy,
> In cherry lane?
>
> Leave her alone. I love her.

But, the poet says, "They knocked me down." He is denied help at "That tent where the insane Jesus Jumpers / Spoke in their blind tongues" and the "railroad dick" responded to his plea by saying "you go on home, / And get out of this." Speaking in precise, almost hallucinatory fragments the poet works by immediate accretion. When he repeats "here comes Johnny Gumball" the effect is terror unmitigated by time and it is the present tense we notice in "Guido don't give a diddly damn."

What marks distortion in "Ohio Valley Swains" is the lack of clear time demarcation, the nightmare-memory, the savage irony, the direct address of the speaker to the rapists over time and distance, the immediacy of a long-concluded violence. The speech is brutal, blunt, filled with swearwords ("The bad bastards are fishing"), and so tautly truncated that narrative is remote. The girl is, in fact, never present. Having taken this tour of Hell, Wright does not become meditative but an angry defender of innocence with a language to match:

> You thought that was funny, didn't you, to mock a girl?
> I loved her only in my dreams,
> But my dreams meant something
> And so did she,
> You son of a bitch,
> And if I ever see you again, so help me in the sight of God,
> I'll kill you.

Such language as Wright has come to employ is distorted, however, only in comparison to an expected poetic. It is not far from a poetry of common speech and, as such, it is vulnerable to glibness.[9] Glibness is a form of sentimentality and sentimentality leads Wright to monotonous verbal tags such as *shadow, good, clear, lovely, secret,* and especially *lonely*. But is this sentimentality? What Wright has to say of "the pure clear word" suggests something else. Hughes's comment on Pilinszky's loneliness also leads elsewhere. No word seems more abused by Wright than *lonely*. But why did Wright, in a recent essay ostensibly about his craft, cite the following passage from a letter by the poet Bill Knott:

> I'm so lonely I can't stand it. Solitude is all right.
> It's not the same thing. Loneliness rots the soul.[10]

Perhaps, when Wright uses *lonely* he is not whining about personal misfortune, but is using a code word to trigger a reader's sense of the greater decay in the citizenry. Such code words inform Wright's personal and poetic vocabulary and are so employed that they do not always mean the same thing, nor even what we expect them to mean. They are an attempt to redeem language, to make it clear.

Such an attempt leads to a poetry of great risks and risks invite poetic disasters. Indeed, the attempt, while laudable per se, matters only in so far as it succeeds more than it fails—and Wright does fail in *Two Citizens*. "The Last Drunk" is tediously thin. "Love in a Warm Room" is a paradox without the tissue of mystery that often makes Wright's poems explode. The first stanza of an otherwise marvellous poem, "Prayer to the Good Poet," suggests how Wright's meaningful distortion may dissolve beyond control:

> QUINTUS HORATIUS FLACCUS, my good secret,
> Now my father, a good man in Ohio,
> Lies alone in pain and I scarcely
> Know where to turn now.

The breathlessness of "scarcely" and the repeated "now" mean to gain emotional intensity but are excessive. This excess combines with an impatience to produce gratuitous arm-twisting in "Emerson Buchanan." "On the Liberation of Women" and "Hotel Lenox" are both weakened by a gushy rapture. And for a poet of Wright's power, language can also go limp, as it does in "You and I Saw Hawks Exchanging the Prey":

> They are terrified. They touch.
> Life is too much.

If such complacent and inert language does appear in Wright's collection, it is nevertheless the exception and ought not to obscure the more characteristic and functional vigor of the better work.

Wright views language as an almost organically active moral agent. It will not infinitely suffer abuse and shameless manipulation. Our government described the human carnage of Vietnam in numerical terms that were indistinguishable from stock exchange reports; citizens slept through the drone. Yet, ultimately, the jargon of "body count" became the ugliness it truly was. Nixon convicted himself in his slurs against Blacks, Jews, and intellectuals. Wright believes that language eventually strikes back at its abuse because the moral offense grows too great for bearing. Nowhere is it more morally aggressive than in poetry and Wright's attempt to revitalize language hopes to make it cut sharply for the truth and the good.

Pilinszky's experience in Poland and our own in Asia suggest part of why contemporary man is suspicious of absolute terms. Ideological fervor has too often meant barbarous destruction. As citizens of pathos, we have no connection to a significant vision of possibility. Too often this means an abdication of art's venerable function, the affirmation of the anti-pathetic values which humans have ceaselessly recognized as necessary for emotional, individual, and communal health. This abdication yields up intelligent consciousness in art; art becomes the panderer of sensation, then sensationalism, which is to say either no vision or a vision of nothing. The danger of absolutes is in all or nothing. Is an imbalanced art really art? Pope's warning about "a little learning" keeps its edge.

Yet consciousness need not lead to cynicism or to Laputan sterility any more than absolutes must lead to rapture. Wright demonstrates that poetry must mediate between tenderness and horror, recognizing that both are true and real, as it makes its way toward morality. This is not a fortune cookie moralism tagged in the poem, but a working out of a comprehensive vision and a matching language. Wright, like Warren, understands that the will to change begins in confronting the self and turns to communion with and celebration of the Good in society. This Good, simplistic though it may sound, is Love, a love that despairs of its inability to comfort the hurt and the suffering.[11] To despair of achieving an ideal, say a moral existence, is not the same thing as the denial of its possibility. Wright believes in a possible consolation inherent in language and poetry which balances love and horror, mind and emotion, sophisticate and vulgar. The authority for such a vision is the love offered gratuitously to Wright by all of his muse-women, from the prostitute Jenny in all his books to his wife Annie, who radiates in all the poems of *Two Citizens*. Annie is Pilinszky's "real presence" who makes vision possible, who makes mediation a progress.

The absolute toward which Wright's vision continually leans is the moral dream of self and society in love. Wright defines it in "The Art of the Fugue: A Prayer":

> And me there alone at last with my only love,
> Waiting to begin.
>
> Whoever you are, ambling past my grave,
> My name worn thin as the shawl of the lovely hill town
> Fiesole, the radiance and silence of the sky,
> Listen to me:
>
> Though love can be scarcely imaginable Hell,
> By God, it is not a lie.

Here Bach and Dante are, by God, warrantors of love's truth and absolute value. In Wright's "Prayer to the Good Poet" Horace has the same function and Wright knows his poetry must try to achieve the solidity and clarity of these visionaries.

Wright has been called a dark poet, a poet of pessimism and disbelief. He is not. He is a religious celebrant who cannot avoid the darkness engulfing the human spirit but who, in the romantic tradition, always brings the quickening light of poetry to that darkness. *Two Citizens* is a denial of dark's permanence, an affirmation of the Good possible even for Judas, Jenny, Mary Magdalene, those sinners and sinned-against in one body. For Wright such figures are human paradigms and his continual effort is to afford them love and speech. To do so is to save himself from the nightmare of pathos. Wright's myth of creation and redemption from human cruelty is based on the single absolute which allows the self to grow toward recognition, acceptance, and consolation. Love is the only possibility for reconciling ourselves to ourselves and to the world.

Love and reconciliation actually construct the vision of *Two Citizens*. Wright's effort in these poems is always to draw together his ambitious dream of renewed possibility with a language that halts and stutters in a local passion. "Ars Poetica: Some Recent Criticism," the first poem in the book, is a kind of Genesis which not only forecasts the evolving progress of each poem but also provides a thematic point of origin. In its savage humor, the poem is a curse against America, that country which has subverted the Good. But America has also been the birthplace and residence of the great moral dream of possibility and liberty. In this way the poem is a love poem and a powerful lament. The final section of the poem reveals the poet's as yet unresolved ambivalence:

> When I was a boy
> I loved my country.
>
> *Ense petit placidam*
> *Sub libertate quietem.*
>
> Hell, I ain't got nothing.
> Ah, you bastards.
>
> How I hate you.

As children we love indiscriminately. With maturity we lose innocence. We gain frustration, bitterness, and hatred, which is a form of love. If we cannot reclaim love that alone leads to morality, then perhaps sword-rattling can help as a kind of electric shock therapy. Perhaps a blunt aggressive poetry can reveal our cruelty and ugliness.

"Ars Poetica" weaves a narrative spiced with the poet's terse comments on the nature of tenderness, horror, the blind self, poetry, and language. It tells the story of Wright's Uncle Sherman and Aunt Agnes, the woman he did not so much love as "he fell in with." Agnes, who went mad, was the source of all tenderness and knowledge in that country of Wright's youth. The two of them are prototypical Americans, metaphorical citizens analogous to the Wrights. If "Ars Poetica" is a love poem for the lost possibility of America, it is also a poem of love for Agnes, who becomes another of Wright's muse figures acting out a redemption:

> The goat ran down the alley,
> And many boys giggled
> While they tried to stone our fellow
> Goat to death.
> And my Aunt Agnes,
> Who stank and lied,
> Threw stones at the boys
> And gathered the goat,
> Nuts as she was,
> Into her sloppy arms.

Cruelty, violence, madness, and an ineradicable compassion are the facts of Agnes's American life. It is easy but fruitless to read this poem as a folktale of eccentricity in belligerent Ohio, for the event serves primarily as a base for Wright's reflections. Agnes, the citizen lost in Hell, participates helplessly in the violence yet maintains an ability to love. The scapegoat, which cannot escape, suggests Wright himself, torturously caught between tenderness and horror, and the "plot" is a searing parody of the American dream. But how is this a statement about the art of poetry or a response to "some recent criticism"? Perhaps Horace best answers, saying "It is not enough for a poem to be beautiful: / It must have something to get at the reader's mind,"[12] which is to say a proper poetry must engage matters of substance. The substantive matter for Wright is how not to be lost in pathos, or what to believe in. Agnes's story allows Wright to say what is missing as well as what makes the old dream hollow, the American lies:

> Reader,
> We had a lovely language,
> We would not listen.

> I don't believe in your God.
> I don't believe my Aunt Agnes is a saint.
> I don't believe the little boys
> Who stoned the poor
> Son of a bitch goat
> Are charming Tom Sawyers.
>
> I don't believe in the goat either.

If the old dream is only a sham of nightmarish and relativistic values which leave us nothing to believe in outside dogmatic and maddening absolutes, what possibility remains except the Hell of a perpetual hatred and hurt? Wright's answer is an immediate and very accessible poetry of love:

> I gather my Aunt Agnes
> Into my veins.
> I could tell you,
> If you have read this far,
> That the nut house in Cambridge
> Where Agnes is dying
> Is no more Harvard
> Than you could ever be.
> And I want to gather you back to my Ohio.

Here "Harvard" is a synecdoche for the kind of language which obscures the old dream that Ohio was. If the local and mythical reality of Ohio is now Hell, it was once love's reality and may be, in poetry, regathered. Possibility, as always, exists in the imagination driving forcefully toward recognition, acceptance, and consolation. In "She's Awake" Wright says:

> Lying myself awake,
> I imagine everything terrible in my own life,
> The hitchhiking drunk, the shame of knowing
> My self a fool.
> Bad friend to me.

Wright does not say he remembers, but that he *imagines*, for like Stevens and Williams, he is inventing what will suffice for love's renewal.

Indeed, the obsessive direction of Wright's poetry is toward a sense of communion between the deepest self and that exiled other which might bring the possibility of redemption. Love, Wright's poems discover, exists as the achievable consolation which can re-member, rather than dismember, the world's body. In the final poem of *Two Citizens*, "To the Creature of the Creation," he writes "You are the world's body." And in "Son of Judas," the poem which links this book with Wright's earliest work, he says, "I've discovered my body that was alive / After all." Wright's essential argument is, therefore, that though one cannot blink away the forces of dissolution and death one may oppose them in a healthy and angry imagination which can turn the oldest connections good. Consequently, the poet's function is more than discovery, it is a fathering of the moral community. In "Prayer to the Good Poet," Wright links himself, his father, and Horace in a continuity of poets struggling to know and understand love:

> More than love, my father knew how to bear love,
> One quick woman a dark river of labor.
> He led me and my two good brothers
> To gather and swim there.

Without ignoring the recurrent figure of the woman as the suffering source of love's birth, we see that Wright suggests the problem is not only to know that love exists but also to know what to do with it, a question that poetry must answer. Of Horace and his father, Wright says, "Some people think poetry is easy, / But you two didn't."

That the poetry of communion and possibility is not easy underlies Wright's demand for a pure, clear language and a constant gesture of embrace. Warren has said in "Caveat" that "every man / Is a sort of Jesus" and this has always been Wright's figurative stance. To be exiled is to live in the strange truth of an alien language that is all sound and to be driven back into the most basic language of one's self, to the most basic understanding of one's own reality. Thus, facing homeground in *Two Citizens*, Wright says in "I Wish I May Never Hear of the United States Again":

> In Yugoslavia I am learning the words
> For greeting and goodbye.
> Everything else is the language
> Of the silent woman who walks beside me.

The language of love begins in silence and in the simplest words, and it creates everything between beginning and end. To love implies the knowledge that love ends, because death is inevitable, and that suffering may not be escaped. Yet love and language have the power to deflect pain and, in art, to create imaginative consolation. The wait for such a consolation and the frustrating fear it might not exist, however, explain Wright's anger.

But anger is not what *Two Citizens* comes to. Again, Warren provides a touchstone in his poem "Waiting," which tells us "You will have to wait. Until it."[13] At the heart of Wright's poems is a plea for patience which is the prelude to possibility. After Wright tells us in "Prayer to the Good Poet" how Bennie Capaletti refused violent revenge for an insult and how his own father learned to outwait the ugliness that is "A bitter / Taste of one body," Wright pleads for the extension of this lesson:

> Easy, easy, I ask you, easy, easy.
> Early, evening, by Tiber, by Ohio
> Give the gift to each lovely other.

And in an elegy for his teacher, "In Memory of Charles Coffin," Wright says

> All right, you said: Ben Jonson said
> Give Salathiel Pavy one
> More chance, and give yourself one more.

Perhaps no poem in *Two Citizens* more tenderly and dramatically presents what Wright is after than "The Old WPA Swimming Pool in Martins Ferry, Ohio." Here, in a scene from America's Great Depression, the men of the Work Projects Administration have dug a swimming pool instead of the usual graves and it becomes a baptismal font:

> No, this hole was filled with water,
> And suddenly I flung myself into the water.
> All I had on was a jockstrap my brother stole
> From a miserable football team.
>
> Oh never mind, Jesus Christ, my father
> And my uncles dug a hole in the ground,

No grave for once. It is going to be hard
For you to believe; when I rose from that water,

A little girl who belonged to somebody else,
A face thin and haunted appeared
Over my left shoulder, and whispered, Take care now,
Be patient, and live.

I have loved you all this time,
And didn't even know
I am alive.

Assuming once again the role of sinner (theft) and innocent (Christ's bearing of man's sin), Wright establishes his connection with all men, those "uncles," and goes into the ground for them. But this time, as a second Christ, he ascends to accept the wisdom of the most living, a little girl whose love is lifesaving and absolute. "Be patient, and live" she tells him, and in that simple knowledge Wright sees the secret of what was always good about himself, his country, and the human. A poem as conversational as an anecdote, at times harsh and vulgar, one which begins in fear and anger and asks the question "What the hell is this?," turns to a prayer of celebration.

The circling movement in "The Old WPA Swimming Pool in Martins Ferry, Ohio" represents the largest movement of *Two Citizens*, the turn from despair to possibility, which is also the turn from Europe to America. This movement is countered by an internal movement whose rhythm is a pendulum swing between opposites, whose result is an orchestrated tension between the forces of destruction and the forces of affirmation. Wright's use of a distorted language, his code words, his blunt gouging at the reader, his rhetorical questions, his acrimonious petulance, his fusion of a Dantesque Hell with a local and industrial Ohio landscape, all operate in search of a poetry whose function is to release us from pathos and self-hatred. In "Names Scarred at the Entrance to Chartres," such a poetry is reduced to American names scrawled against Death "whose genius it is / to remember our death on the wet / roads of Chartres, America, and to forget / Our names." But even names, Doyle, Dolan, and Wright, are possibilities seeking the power to know an absolute which can contradict Death's absolute. And even in the complexly halting and surging rhythms of *Two Citizens*, a book of wandering, there is finally a moment of rest, a truth which shines through all darkness.

In "Bologna: A Poem about Gold" Wright offers another prayer, this time over "the heavy wine" and "the glass that so many have drunk from." Wright speaks of himself as having "come forth / Golden on the left corner / Of a cathedral's wing," which is a wonderful synthesis of an emerging butterfly and Christ's resurrection. Life in all ways begins with love and the golden wine of Bologna turns James and Annie Wright to celebrants at communion:

> White wine of Bologna,
> And the knowing golden shadows
> At the left corners of Mary Magdalene's eyes,
> While St. Cecilia stands
> Smirking in the center of a blank wall,
> The saint letting her silly pipes wilt down,
> Adoring
> Herself, while the lowly and richest of all women eyes
> Me the beholder, with a knowing sympathy, her love
> For the golden body of the earth, she knows me,
> Her halo faintly askew,
> And no despair in her gold
> That drags thrones down
> And then makes them pay for it.

To live in pathos and alienation is to indulge in the greatest horror, in what once was called the worst sin, but neither reason nor righteous saint nor any poetry remote from the humanness of a Mary Magdalene will answer despair. What is needed is "love / For the golden body of the earth" in which there is the possibility of a moral life where some things are not relative, but simply are. It is art's task to imagine and understand what these things may be in and out of artifice and the poet's task to find the inexhaustible secret of hope. As Wright says in his recent poem, "Cold Summer Sun, Be with Me Soon":

> And all I wanted to do was write something that you could
> Understand.
> Just as Dr. Williams said.
> For his own good.[14]

The great poets are always those who reconstruct our pain, who have become the mythical heroes of love descending into nether-worlds and returning with the good news of possibility and a language vigorous enough to shake us from lethargy and the abuse of our dreams. In his poem "Redwings" Wright tells us "It turns out / You can make the earth absolutely clean." It isn't easy, it may not be done without pain and shock, and there are no guarantees, but for his own good and the good of all of us this is what the poet must attempt. To live at all we must reclaim the old dream of possibility, the dream of love's reality which Wright insists on in his poem "The Art of the Fugue: A Prayer" and in the journey of *Two Citizens*:

> Whoever you are, ambling past my grave,
> My name worn thin as the shawl of the lovely hill town
> Fiesole, the radiance and silence of the sky,
> Listen to me:
>
> Though love can be scarcely imaginable Hell,
> By God, it is not a lie.

NOTES

1. All references in this paper are to the following editions: James Wright, *Two Citizens* (New York: Farrar, Straus and Giroux, 1973); James Wright, *Collected Poems* (Middletown, Conn.: Wesleyan University Press, 1971).

2. Because James Wright is a restless and innovative poet, he provokes controversial criticism. Paul Ramsey (in "American Poetry in 1973," *Sewanee Review*, 82 [Spring 1974], 394) says the book is "badly marred by personal indulgence and conversationality. He offers truculent assertions of blunt hostility and equally bare statements of affection, almost never poetically realized." And Edward Butscher claims: "From the standpoint of artistic achievement, *Two Citizens* is an almost total failure"; in "The Rise and Fall of James Wright," *Georgia Review*, 28 (1974), 267.

3. Gerritt Henry, "Starting from Scratch," *Poetry*, 124 (Aug. 1974), 294.

4. Hayden Carruth, "Poetry Chronicle," *Hudson Review*, 24 (Summer 1971), 331.

5. James Wright, "The Stiff Smile of Mr. Warren," *Kenyon Review*, 20 (Autumn 1958), 646. I am not alone in noticing Wright's connection with Warren and I refer the reader to Peter Stitt's essay, "The Poetry of James Wright," *Minnesota Review*, 12 (Winter 1972), 28, where Stitt says of Wright's *Shall We Gather at the River*: "What it resembles in its struc-

ture is a work like Robert Penn Warren's *Promises*, which is a collection of related lyrics, all of which aim at one goal. Warren, in his quest for some philosophy to leave for his children, also returns to the land of his youth, mining his childhood and its locale for materials."

6. Ted Hughes, "Janos Pilinszky," *Critical Quarterly*, 48 (Winter 1976), 80.

7. Hughes, p. 83.

8. Wright, "Stiff Smile," p. 650.

9. Peter Stitt (Interview with James Wright), "The Art of Poetry XIX: James Wright," *Paris Review*, no. 62 (Summer 1975), 54. Wright says that "my chief enemy in poetry is glibness. . . . I speak and write too easily . . . whatever else poetry is, it is a struggle, and the enemy, the deadly enemy of poetry is glibness. And that is why I have struggled to strip my poems down."

10. James Wright, "Letters from Europe, Two Notes from Venice, Remarks on Two Poems, and Other Occasional Prose," *American Poets in 1976*, ed. William Heyen (Indianapolis: Bobbs-Merrill, 1976), p. 442.

11. Stitt, "Art of Poetry," p. 50. Wright says: "I think that most of the people who are alive in the world right now are very unhappy. I don't want people to be unhappy, and I'm sorry that they are. I wish there were something I could do to help. And I think I've been trying to say that ever since I've started to write books. That's what my books are about."

12. Calvin Bedient, "Horace and Modernism," *Sewanee Review*, 85 (Spring 1977), 362.

13. Robert Penn Warren, "Waiting," *Atlantic Monthly*, 238 (Dec. 1976), 47.

14. James Wright, "Cold Summer Sun, Be with Me Soon," *Paris Review*, no. 62 (Summer 1975), 64.

James Wright

ROBERT HASS

> Young boys read verses to help them-
> selves express or know their feelings,
> as if the dim intuited features of love,
> heroism, or sensuality could only be
> clearly contemplated in a poem.
>
> Octavio Paz

> The kind of poetry I want to write is
> The poetry of a grown man.
>
> James Wright

I

I HAVE BEEN WORRYING the bone of this essay for days because, in an issue of *Ironwood* honoring James Wright, I want to say some things against his poems. The first of his books that I read was *The Branch Will Not Break*. It is supposed to have broken ground by translating the imagery of surrealist and expressionist poetics into American verse. That was not what I responded to. What mattered to me in those poems was that their lean, clear, plain language had the absolute freshness of sensibility. They made sensibility into something as lucid and alert as intelligence. We speak of animal intelligence, of the intelligence of the body, but my experience is that when we are most possessed by it, we are least aware of it, or least self-conscious about it. The part of the mind that needs to learn from it, to be able to reflect on it, is absorbed by it. And the only other way it is available to us is through art. Not all art, either, but the work of some few artists. It is rare enough, I think, and hard to talk about, but it involves a special kind of alertness. I can give you an example from *Shall We Gather at the River*:

Along the sprawled body of the derailed
  Great Northern freight car,

I strike a match slowly and lift it slowly.
No wind.

Beyond town, three heavy white horses
Wade all the way to their shoulders
In a silo shadow.

Suddenly the freight car lurches.
The door slams back, a man with a flashlight
Calls me good evening.
I nod as I write good evening, lonely
And sick for home.

Those last two lines are what I mean. They were not written by the poet who is lonely and sick for home, they were written by the man who noticed that the poet, sitting in his room alone, recalling a scene outside Fargo, North Dakota, nods when he writes down the greeting of his imagined yardman, and catches in that moment not the poet's loneliness but a gesture that reveals the aboriginal loneliness of being—of the being of the freight cars, silos, horses, shadows, matches, poets, flashlights. And that man, the man who wrote those lines, is not lonely. At least that is not quite the word for it. There is a poem by Basho that gets at this:

Not my human
sadness, cuckoo,
but your solitary cry.

The cuckoo, or hototogisu, is the nightingale of Japanese poetry. Its evening song has all the automatic associations with loneliness and beauty, and Basho is correcting that tradition. He is not, he says, talking about our plangent human loneliness but about the solitariness of being, of beings going about their business. The business of singing, if you are a bird, of feeling lonely, if you are a human. This is a distinction and it is the function of intelligence to make distinctions, but this one has been felt toward, with an absolute clarity of feeling, and that is what I mean by sensibility. It is a quality that flashes out from time to time in Wright's poems and it made *The Branch Will Not Break* an enormously important book for me. So I should probably rephrase my first sentence in the manner of *Two Citizens*: I want to say some things against James Wright's poems, which I love.

A brief might begin with what he has to say about "a grown man":

> The long body of his dream is the beginning of a dark
> Hair under an illiterate
> Girl's ear.

It's hard to know whether to complain first about the fabricated ingenuity of the image or the preciousness of the diction. Or about the fact that it is so sculpted as to be memorable anyway. Or the fact that Wright's characteristic tenderness almost redeems it. What bothers me, finally, is the familiar celebration of whatever is not mind, of everything unformed, unconscious, and suffused, therefore, with yearning. The important thing about the image is scale; it has the scale of body knowledge. It is as sharply focused as the body is in lovemaking or in pain. It is also predictable. The hair is dark, not light. The person is a girl, not a woman or a man. And just to make sure we are in the dark of sex or the dark of nature or the spirit's darkness, the girl is illiterate. This from a man who loves Goethe, for whom Horace is "a good secret," whose work has been an exemplary struggle with the difficult and specifically human possibilities of the lyric poem.

I think of Truffaut's severe and beautiful *Wild Child*, of the mixed feelings with which I watched, in grainy black and white, while the wolf boy of Aveyron struggled with language—which I wanted him to acquire, which I did not want him to have to acquire. In a very quiet way Truffaut makes us feel the cost of the struggle to perform those symbolic operations which turn body knowledge into symbol and make thought and feeling available to us, in the way that they are available to us. The best and hardest moment of the film occurs when the boy finally rebels and runs out of the house into the field where he sits in the high grass in the rain, rocking slowly back and forth in a state of mute, warm, fetal peace that shuts out his fear and confusion. The heart goes out to him completely and everything conspires against the heart, because so much of what moves us about the image belongs to culture, including the fact that it is an image: the French doors through which the boy is photographed, the espaliered trees in the background, the fact that the slanting rain looks like rain in Kurosawa, that the antic, melancholy music on the sound track is Mozart. So much light, so many centuries of the evolution of light, to render the pathos and beauty of that darkness.

Someone has calculated that the words *dark, darkness,* and *darkening* appear over forty times in the twenty-six pages *The Branch Will Not Break* occupies in the *Collected Poems. Green* must appear at least as often. And the book is full of those Wordsworthian words that no one is supposed to be able to get away with: *lovely, terrible, beautiful, body,* and *lonely* run like a threnody through all his books. I don't care how often James Wright uses any word, but I do care how he uses them and why. The early poems have helped me to think about this, particularly "On Minding One's Own Business" in *Saint Judas.* It's about a couple gliding on a lake after sundown:

> All evening fins have drowned.
> Back in the summer dark.
> Above us, up the bank,
> Obscure on lonely ground,
> A shack receives the night.

The speaker goes wide and quiet past the place. He is not going to interfere with whoever is inside, but he describes the kind of people who would, people who use "will," who have "force" and "weight":

> We will not land to bear
> Our will upon that house,
> Nor force on any place
> Our dull offensive weight.

This is an American poem and an American place, so the people who have will and force are puritans, the hard-sleepers, enviers of pleasure:

> Long may the lovers hide
> In viny shacks from those
> Who thrash among the trees,
> Who curse, who have no peace,
> Who pitch and moan all night
> For fear of someone's joys,
> Deploring the human face.

The poem ends, like many of Wright's poems, with a prayer:

> From prudes and muddying fools,
> Kind Aphrodite, spare

All hunted criminals,
Hoboes, and whip-poor-wills,
And girls with rumpled hair,
All, all of whom might hide
Within that darkening shack.
Lovers may live, and abide.

Maybe the worst thing about American puritanism is the position it forces its opponents into. If the puritan can't distinguish a hobo from a hunted criminal, a little nighthawk from a girl who does the sorts of things that rumple hair, the poet won't. Hunted criminal, in fact, equals hobo equals bird equals girl. The puritan can't tell one from another and knows they are all bad; the poet can't tell either, only he knows they belong to the dark and are good. When he agrees to disagree with the puritan on his own terms, he gives away will, force, power, weight because they are bad American qualities and he settles for passivity and darkness. This explains why the grown man's dream is the beginning of a dark hair under an illiterate girl's ear. It explains why another early poem is called "All the Beautiful Are Blameless."

It glosses these lines from the poem about President Harding:

"Warren lacks mentality," one of his friends said.
Yet he was beautiful, he was the snowfall
Turned to white stallions
Under dark elm trees.

And it is the only thing that can explain the puzzling and repellent lines that end one of the poems about the rapist, George Doty. Wright has been meditating on the execution of this man who "stopped his car and found / A girl on the darkening ground, / And killed her in the snow." He says this:

. . . I mourn no soul but his
Not even the bums who die
Nor the homely girl whose cry
Crumbled his pleading kiss.

Wright has often been praised, to use the curious language of *The Norton Anthology of Modern Poetry*, for his "compassionate interest in social outcasts." That has never seemed to me to be the way to say it. What has always been a remarkable, almost singular, fact about his poetry is the way in which the suffering of other people, particularly the lost and the derelict, is actually a part of his own emotional life. It is what he writes from, not what he writes about. He has a feeling in his own bones for what a cold and unforgiving place the social world is. More than that, he has a feeling, almost Calvinist, for how unforgiving the universe is, so that he can make poetry of Warren Harding who claimed "the secret right to be ashamed," of Judas "flayed without hope." He is fascinated by defeat the way some men are fascinated by money, as the intelligible currency of our lives. His poems return and return to this theme, to the unformed hopes growing in the warm dark and the cold dark to which they return, until loneliness and death seem like the price exacted for living.

In the poem about George Doty, he is thinking hard about these issues, however mindless and uncanny those last lines seem. The bums, for example, whom he doesn't mourn, appear in an earlier stanza:

> Beside his cell, I am told,
> Hardy perennial bums
> Complain till twilight comes
> For hunger and for cold.
>
> They hardly know of a day
> That saw their hunger pass.
> Bred to the dark, their flesh
> Peacefully withers away.

I don't believe this (and neither does Wright in "The Minneapolis Poem"), but it explains what the bums mean to him and why he doesn't mourn them. They live and die in the dark, more or less contented with complaining. It also explains why he does mourn George Doty:

> Sick of the dark, he rose
> For love, and now he goes
> Back to the broken ground.

There are things to doubt here, too. But if it is true that the man raped and murdered in a dark channel of the impulse to love, then it is not hard to see why he is a crucial figure. It still doesn't explain why Wright uses the conclusion of the poem to say so explicitly that he mourns the killer but not the victim. What I think is that he is trying to speak as intensely as he can the depth of his identification with the criminal and the criminal sin of rising.

Rise. Rise and *gather.* They must be the most important active verbs in Wright's work. A dream of transcendence and a dream of community. This theme of rising is echoed later and very richly in *Two Citizens*:

> The last time I tried to escape from my body,
> You threw me down into a tangle of roots.
> Out of them I clambered up into the elbows
> Of a sycamore tree . . .
>
> . . . .
>
> I rose out of my body so high into
> That sycamore tree that it became
> The only tree that ever loved me.

And again:

> There used to be a sycamore just
> Outside Martins Ferry,
> Where I used to go.
> I had no friends there.
> Maybe that tree was no woman
> But when I sat there, I gathered
> That branch into my arms.
> It was the first time I ever rose.

And again, in a daffy, ecstatic love poem:

> Oh tree.
> We climbed into the branches
> Of the lady's tree.
> We birds sang.

We might add to this, for the imagery of light and dark, sick and cold, his account of how, one summer, he came to steal crabapples:

> I don't know why,
> One evening in August something illuminated my body
> And I got sick of laying my cold
> Hands on myself.
> I lied to my family I was going for a walk uptown.

Having no language to explain rising, illumination, in the ordinary world, he invents.

I come back to that remark by Octavio Paz. All these lines by the older man remember the young man's discovery of his own inwardness, of his consciousness of himself, some passion in him akin to love and sexuality and prayer. In the early poem he is thinking about George Doty and the crime of rape and the crime, less intelligible, of state execution, but he is also thinking about himself and about poetry which is in himself and beautiful and lonely and some kind of sexual crime. So another early poem is a sonnet about a fugitive. It begins:

> The night you got away, I dreamed you rose
> Out of the earth to lean on a young tree.

The sestet owes something to Robinson and something to old Warner Brothers movies:

> Hurry, Maguire, hammer the body down,
> Crouch to the wall again, shackle the cold
> Machine guns and the sheriff and the cars;
> Divide the bright bars of the cornered bone,
> Strip, run for it, break the last law, unfold,
> Dart down the alley, race between the stars.

Hopeless, this melodramatic grandeur. You could not tell the qualities of the poet who wrote it except for that one phrase, "the cornered bone." It is what Wright knows and what makes his poems, so often, tense with the impulse to escape.

"We Americans," the older man writes, "loneliness of body, / Puritans sick at the beauty of the body." "Ugliness," he writes, "What is it? A bitter / Taste of one body."

Over and over again in American writing, this theme or discovery, that the inner life has no place, that it makes outlaws of us. Whether it is Huck deciding to go to hell or the hell of West's *Miss Lonelyhearts*, or Gatsby thinking the rich with their good teeth and fast cars can transform the ugly midwestern body of the world or poor Clyde Griffith, who rises from the squalor of his childhood when he glimpses velvet curtains in a Kansas City hotel, or Robinson's loyalty to Luke Havergal and the boozy moon, there is always this sense of a radical division between the inner and outer worlds and the hunger for a magic which will heal it, a sanctification or election. It gives a kind of drama to Wright's search for a style, but it also gives me the uneasy feeling that the way of posing the problem is the problem.

These themes persist through all the later work: a poetry that aims at beauty of feeling, a continuous bone-aching loneliness, a continuous return to and caressing of the dark, a terror of the cold dark, a compassion for whoever suffers it, a desire to escape from the body. The new manner of *The Branch Will Not Break* doesn't signal a change in theme, but a different rhetorical strategy. The more relaxed rhythms, with pauses at line end, feel like a man taking a deep breath:

> Po Chu-i, balding old politician,
> What's the use?

And the playfulness of the titles insists on the fact of imagination. So do the plain words from romantic poetry, *lovely, beautiful, terrible*, that don't describe anything but tell you that someone is feeling something. And the images let go of the known configurations so that they can look inward and try to name the agency of transformation:

> Tiller of waves or whatever, woman or man,
> Mother of roots or father of diamonds,
> Look: I am nothing.

This is the freshness of the book and it helps me to understand why I responded to it so deeply and why I end by gnashing my teeth over so many of the poems:

> . . . Only two boys
> Trailed by the shadow of rooted police,
> Turn aimlessly in the lashing elderberries.
> One cries for his father's death,
> And the other, the silent one,
> Listens into the hallway
> Of a dark leaf.

The means, this style that is to make transformation possible, keeps wanting to be the end, the transformation itself, the beauty by which we are justified. There is no ground in these lines between the violent outer world and the kid listening poetically down the hallway of a dark leaf. There must be a Yiddish joke somewhere or a story by

Peretz in which the poet appears before the recording angel who asks
him what he's done and he says I listened down the hallway of a
dark leaf or the long dream of my body was the beginning of a dark
hair, etc. And one of the angels, maybe Raphael whom Rilke called
the terrible one, says, this guy has got to be kidding.

Wright knows this most of the time, that the "one wing" of beauty
won't take him very far. But again and again in *The Branch Will Not
Break* he tries to see what can be made to happen by saying beautiful
things, by repeating his talismanic nouns and adjectives of the discovery of the inner world:

>   Two athletes
>   Are dancing in the cathedral
>   Of the wind
>
>   Small antelope
>   Fall asleep in the ashes
>   Of the moon
>
>   . . . I am lost in the beautiful white ruins
>   Of America
>
>   The sad bones of my hands descend into a valley
>   Of strange rocks
>
>   The secret shelters of sparrow feathers fallen
>   in the snow
>
>   . . . if I stepped out of my body I would break
>   Into blossom
>
>   At a touch of my hand
>   The air fills with delicate creatures
>   From another world
>
>   Only after nightfall
>   Little boys lie still, awake,
>   Wondering, wondering,
>   Delicate little boxes of dust.

This last is from a poem called "The Undermining of the Defense
Economy." Many of the poems make political reference and it was
very exciting to me to see a poetry that brought sensibility to political issues, that could confront the utilitarian spirit—which *is* a way

of feeling, an admiration for efficiency and coolness—with what is fuller and stronger and clearer in human feeling. But these lines don't do that. Against the active man who despises the world in the light, there is the passive man who loves it in the dark:

> I want to lie down under a tree.
> This is the only duty that is not death.

The poem is called "A Prayer to Escape from the Market Place." The fugitive again.

In 1963, the year in which *The Branch Will Not Break* appeared, Robert Bly printed in *Choice* a passionate, ragged, very contradictory and very important essay called "A Wrong Turning in American Poetry." He attacked the modernist movement, especially imagism, as a kind of pictorialism, mesmerized by things, frightened of the spirit, preoccupied with technique, a replica of American culture. A great deal of what Bly had to say is true. He wanted a poetry that was inward, fresh, alive to its own impulse. "When the senses die, the sense within us that delights in poetry dies." "In a poem, as in the human body, what is invisible makes all the difference." But much of it read like an evangelical tract. It distrusts the mind and it insists on the radical and permanent division between the inner and the outer, believing only in the election of inward illumination: "A man cannot turn his face at the same moment toward the inward world and the outer world: he cannot face both north and south." Imagination is the source of election and, as in Wright, the world is its enemy. "The imagination *out of its own resources* creates a poem as strong as the world which it faces." And, as in Wright, the world is a jail in which the soul is imprisoned. Bly translates Rilke's "die Befreiung der dicterish Figur" as "the releasing of the image from jail," and adds, "the poet is thinking of a poem in which the image is released from its imprisonment among objects." But what is an object? A horse? The round white stone on my desk? The old curled postcard of a still life by Georgia O'Keefe? It is when the imagination withdraws from things that they become objects, when it lets the world go. This is a Calvinist and solipsistic doctrine. No wonder that the poetry of the deep image is preoccupied with loneliness.

Here is Bly's account of the role intelligence plays in the life of imagination: "The intelligence knocks at the door, demanding some imagination to put between a flat statement and a piece of glass and rushes out with the gift. Then it hurries back to get a little more imagination to prevent two subway cars from rubbing together. The imagination is continually disturbed, torn away, bit by bit, consumed like a bin of corn eaten gradually by mice. The imagination does not want these constant knockings on the door. It prefers to remain in its chamber, undisturbed, until it can create the poem all of one substance—itself." This is polemical and funny and it gets at certain kinds of deadness in poetry. But it has to be fundamentally wrong about the relationship between imagination and intelligence because, as everyone knows, the imagination is luminously intelligent. Imagination cannot be without intelligence, any more than it can be without feeling. This description, which is contradicted anyway by Bly's best poems and by other, more plausible things he says in the same pages, is typical of the hatred of intelligence that pervades puritan culture. Regarding imagination as a kind of ruminative wombat denies that perceptive and apprehensive cooperation between ourselves and the world, between imagination and things, which makes the world a place to live in and makes poetry communicable, gives it its active force. It leaves the poet isolated and the world dead. "Great poets," he says, "are merely sensitive."

Galway Kinnell has said some of these things with less polemical distortion. "We have to feel our own evolutionary roots and to know that we belong to life in the same way that other animals do and the plants and the stones. . . . The real nature poem will not exclude man and deal only with animals and plants and stones, a connection deeper than personality, a connection that resembles the attachment one animal has for another." This seems to me to say many of the things that are valuable in Bly's essay without hauling in a Manichean dualism, if we add to it that the poem has to be made out of the whole being and not out of assent to the idea.

Wright is both a more literary and less theoretical poet than Bly or Kinnell. If Bly seems sometimes to apply his ideas about imagination to the activity of writing, Wright suffers the tenor of a style as if it were the temperament of a lover. He lives inside it, feels through it. That's why his poems reflect, with desperate force, the lameness of the isolated inner world, "the sight of my blind man," its mere sensitivity which issues so often in the same nouns and adjectives, the same verbal constructions, the same will to be beautiful. Against the defense economy, we place—as plea and touchstone—little boys wondering, wondering. Against Moloch, as Allen Ginsberg said in a moment of lovely impatience, the whole boatload of sensitive bullshit.

Aestheticism is what I am talking about, decadence. It's a cultural disease and it flourishes when the life of the spirit, especially the clear power of imagination and intelligence, retreats or is driven from public life, where it ought, naturally, to manifest itself. The artists of decadence turn away from a degraded social world and what they cling to, in their privacy, is beauty or pleasure. The pleasures are esoteric; the beauty is almost always gentle, melancholy, tinged with the erotic, tinged with self-pity. Pound and Eliot, Joyce and Lawrence grew up in a period of decadence in poetry. They did not put down the aesthetes who ought to have been their fathering generation; they honored them. Pound was especially alert to their courage and "Hugh Selwyn Mauberly," whatever else it is, is both a tribute to them and a measure of the trap.

The issue seems to me urgent and I want to say the whole thing against these poems, this tone, in Wright because his struggle with it belongs so much to our culture, to American ugliness, to every kid who wanders into every public library Carnegie built in every devastated American town and, glimpsing the dim intuited features of his own inwardness in some book of poems he has picked up, is, when he emerges into the sunlight of drug store, liquor store, gas station, an outcast and a fugitive. *The Branch Will Not Break* is a book vivid with inward alertness, but it also brings us up against the limitations behind the aesthetic that informs it.

Wright's subject, like Wordsworth's, is the discovery of his own inwardness and the problem of what it can mean, what form it can take in the world. A large part of Wordsworth's struggle had to do with the fact that, in his time, there was no coherent psychological or philosophical accounting for the intensity and reality of his own experience, so he labored in *The Prelude* both to make it visible and to find a form for it in thought. Wright's problem is different in crucial ways. For one thing, he was born a convicted sinner in southern Ohio. For another, his experience is closer to the erotic. For that reason, it seems to me, by some measure, truer because it is through the erotic that one body turns to another and social life, in which the intensity of human inwardness has to find a form, begins.

II

> As far as life, spontaneity, sorrow and
> darkness are concerned, I have
> enough of my own; it flows through
> my veins. I have enough with my own
> flesh and my bones and in the flame-
> less fire of my conscience. What I
> need now is clarity, a dawn above my
> life.
>
> Jose Ortega y Gasset

"Autumn Begins in Martins Ferry, Ohio" is about a form the inner
life takes in the world. Everyone knows the poem, but let me quote
it so we can have it here on the page:

> In the Shreve High football stadium,
> I think of Polacks nursing long beers in Tiltonsville,
> And grey faces of Negroes in the blast furnace at Benwood,
> And the ruptured nightwatchman of Wheeling Steel,
> Dreaming of heroes.
>
> All the proud fathers are ashamed to go home.
> Their wives cluck like starved pullets,
> Dying for love.
>
> Therefore,
> Their sons grow suicidally beautiful
> At the beginning of October
> And gallop terribly against each other's bodies.

In the first version of Blake's "London" the opening lines went
like this:

> I wander'd thro' each dirty street,
> Down where the dirty Thames does flow.

Raymond Williams in *The City and the Country* talks about the
kind of difference the revision made. *Dirty* is a protest; *charter'd* is a
seeing; it confronts not squalor but an order that men have made. It
meets power with power, the power of poetry to illuminate and clarify, to speak out of its whole being. Wright's poem does the same, I
think, but with important differences. These Friday night football
games are in one way a deeper order than either the political or the

economic systems of which Blake is thinking, because their necessity is entirely imaginative. This is a harvest festival and a ritual. Ritual form is allied to magic, as it is in every community, and magic is allied to the seasons and the sexual potency of the earth.

Because this festival is American and puritan, it is an efficient transmutation of lovelessness into stylized violence. "Gallop terribly": or changing chickens into horses. It is a way of describing and evoking the animal beauty in the violence of the dying year, the explosive beauty of boys who are heroes because they imagine they are heroes and whose cells know that it will be their turn to be ashamed to go home. Even the stanzaic structure of the poem participates in the ritual. The first two stanzas separate the bodies of the men from the bodies of the women and the third stanza gives us the boys pounding against each other, as if they could, out of their wills, effect a merging. Insofar as this is a political poem, it is not about the way that industrial capitalism keeps us apart, but the way it brings us together.

This is, in other words, the poem Wright has always been writing:

> Sick of the dark, he rose
> For love, and now he goes
> Back to the broken ground.

Everything about those fall nights is brought to bear here, even the harsh artificial light in which they occur and the cold and darkness that surround them. The poet knows—and tells us in "The Minneapolis Poem"—what happens when the season is over:

> The Chippewa young men
> Stab one another shrieking
> Jesus Christ.
> Split-lipped homosexuals limp in terror of assault.
> High school backfields search under benches
> Near the Post Office. Their faces are the rich
> Raw bacon without eyes.

Later again, in "A Mad Fight Song for William S. Carpenter," he will make the connection between this ritual and war—between the beauty of football and the beauty of war. Saying that, we are in the territory of *The Iliad* and the territory of tragedy. Beyond any social considerations, what the fall of the year tells us is that we are all going down to the dark, one way or another. It is Homer who describes battle as the winds of autumn sweeping the leaves, terribly, from the trees and it is Homer's Apollo who watches the battle and says, with a god's luminous contempt, "Men, they are like leaves, they flourish a little and grow warm with life, and feed on what the ground gives, and then they fade away." Suicidally beautiful: that adverb is not there to nudge us into feeling. It means what it says. It tries to describe what happens when the inner life can't find its way out of the dark and it also describes, illuminates that tendency in James Wright's art.

One of the things that has always moved me most about this poem is the situation of the speaker. There is an awful uprooting here. The man who sees this clearly is not any longer a part of the community he is seeing and it is unlikely that he could see so clearly if he had not been part of it. So, one of the things the poem records is a recognition; and another thing it records is an estrangement. The poet is alone, but not with the loneliness of the defeated fathers; present, but not with the immersion of the sons. If you ask whether this is a poem of the inner world or the outer world, the distinction seems meaningless. What there is here is an adult clarity which sees and feels with great affection and compassion and sees each thing as it is. I suppose that is why the completely plain opening lines have such resonance: *In the Shreve High football stadium, I think . . . .*

That is a distinction the poem does enforce, the one between *dreaming* and *I think*. This vision is not given to the defeated fathers or to the animal brilliance of the sons. Nor does it come from delicate boxes of dust wondering. And the words don't fall as they do when we are filling that emptiness in us that is starved for love. It is given to the man who thinks. That's why that *therefore* explodes on the page, though there are formal reasons for this as well. The poem does not at first feel as if it will have the force of a logical inference and a leap of imagination, because each of the first two stanzas ends with the hemistich of a Latin elegaic poem. Dreaming of heroes, dying for love; a liquid, quantitative dying fall so that you think melancholy grace and not the power of seeing is what the poem is about and then wham! something happens. The word *therefore* is what isolates the speaker, but it is also what gathers the people of Martins Ferry to the poet and his readers, makes them known and felt. The poet does not rise into suicidal light; he brings himself and them and all of us up into the different kind of light that poetry is so that, even though what he sees is tragic, that he sees is a consolation.

III

> Maybe Jehovah was drowsing, and Eros
> heard the prayer and figured that
> love after all was love, no matter
> what language a man sang it in, so
> what the hell.
>
> James Wright

Suicidally beautiful: the poems have suffered from that temptation and the poems from this point on, the best of them I think, reflect a determination to face "the black ditch of the Ohio" and not be killed by it. This is announced—in another place by another river—in "The Minneapolis Poem," the second poem in *Shall We Gather at the River*, that utterly painful book:

> I wonder how many old men last winter
> Hungry and frightened by namelessness prowled
> The Mississippi shore
> Lashed blind by the wind, dreaming
> Of suicide in the river.
> The police remove their cadavers by daybreak
> And turn them in somewhere.
> Where?
> How does the city keep lists of its fathers
> Who have no names?
> By Nicollet Island I gaze down at the dark water
> So beautifully slow.

His response to this suicidal beauty matters to me because it introduces that odd comic tone which will continue into some very desperate poems:

> And nobody would commit suicide, only
> To find beyond death
> Bridgeport, Ohio

and because what he places over against that death is the life of the imagination:

> . . . I could not bear
> To allow my poor brother the body to die
> In Minneapolis.
> The old man Walt Whitman our countryman

>Is now in America our country
>Dead.
>But he was not buried in Minneapolis
>At least.
>And no more may I be
>Please God.

The poem almost ends in a familiar pathos of yearning, but there is also some note of skepticism, of self-mockery in the explicit specifications of the last stanza which suggests Wright has begun to distrust that verbal magic:

>I want to be lifted up
>By some great white bird unknown to the police,
>And soar for a thousand miles and be carefully hidden
>Modest and golden as one last corn grain,
>Stored with the secrets of the wheat and the mysterious
>   lives
>Of the unnamed poor.

The poem doesn't take us to that place. It reminds us that the sentence is about wanting; and whatever the poet wants, what he does is turn back to Ohio. A strange thing, a wonderful and strange act of imagination occurs in *Shall We Gather at the River*. It is the appearance of Jenny. She is the secret inside the word *secret* which appears so often in the book: the discovery of his spirit and of the beauty of the body and of the desire for love which grew up in Ohio and was maimed there. She is probably also the young girl in the earlier poem "Beginning" who lifts up the lovely shadow of her face and disappears wholly in the air. *Shall We Gather at the River* is dedicated to her and, in the hells of that book, she is glimpsed first through the fractured ballad rhythms of Robinson:

>And Jenny, oh my Jenny
>Whom I love, rhyme be damned,
>Has broken her spare beauty
>In a whorehouse old.
>She left her new baby
>In a bus-station can,
>And sprightly danced away
>Through Jacksontown.

Her next appearance is an arrival and a remembering:

> I am home again.
> Yes: I lived here, and here, and my name
> That I carved young, with a girl's, is healed over, now,
> And lies sleeping beneath the inward sky
> Of a tree's skin, close to the quick.

And finally she appears in the last, desperate, lonely poem in the book where the title, "To the Muse," identifies her:

> It is all right. All they do
> Is go in by dividing
> One rib from another. I wouldn't
> Lie to you. It hurts
> Like nothing. I know. All they do
> Is burn their way in with a wire.
> It forks in and out like the tongue
> Of that frightened garter snake we caught
> At Cloverfield, you and me, Jenny,
> So long ago.
>
> I would lie to you
> If I could.
> But the only way I can get you to come up
> Out of that suckhole, the south face
> Of the Powhatan pit, is to tell you
> What you know.

That suckhole is the one in "The River Down Home":

> Under the enormous pier-shadow,
> Hobie Johnson drowned in a suckhole.
> I cannot even remember
> His obliterated face.
> Outside my window, now, Minneapolis
> Drowns, dark.
> It is dark.
> I have no life.

And it is the ghostly one in "Miners":

> The police are probing tonight for the bodies

Of children in the black waters
Of the suburbs.

It is probably even "the shifting hole where the slow swimmer fell aground" all the way back in "To a Defeated Savior" in *The Green Wall*. We come to a point in these later books where Wright's poetry is so compressed with self-reference, with recurrent meditation on these images and themes, that tracing them belongs to long reading and not the ten thumbs of criticism. But the whole body of Wright's work lies behind "To the Muse" and gives terrifying pathos to this struggle to get the soul up into the light, the soul that is also the poor flesh:

> Oh Jenny
> I wish to God I had made this world, this scurvy
> And disastrous place. I
> Didn't, I can't bear it
> Either.

This nightmare poem is everybody's hospital nightmare, the bad long dream of the body, of how it ends up, of the mechanical heart and the draining lung, of what work can do to you and life can do to you, and the three fates, the one who unwinds and the one who spins and the one who cuts the thread:

> Three lady doctors in Wheeling open
> Their offices at night.
> I don't have to call them, they are always there.
> But they only have to put the knife once
> Under your breast.
> Then they hang their contraption
> And you bear it.
>
> It's awkward a while. Still, it lets you
> Walk about on tiptoe if you don't
> Jiggle the needle.
> It might stab your heart, you see.
> The blade hangs in your lung and the tube
> Keeps it draining.
> That way they only have to stab you
> Once.

This is the least bearable of Wright's poems to me, as wrenching as anything in Sylvia Plath, worse in some ways because it glints with so many more tones, with the will to live. And when it ends, this book that began with the waters of the Mississippi ends:

> Come up to me, love,
> Out of the river, or I will
> Come down to you.

In the new poems at the end of the *Collected Poems*, Jenny is "The Idea of the Good," and as she emerges, her name echoing all those sentimental midwestern songs, Wright returns again and again to the terror of the river down home:

> The Ohio River
> Has flown by me twice, the dark jubilating
> Isiah of mill and smoke marrow. Blind son
> Of a meadow of huge horses, lover of drowned islands
> Above Steubenville, blind father
> Of my halt grey wing

and:

> That black ditch
> Of river

and:

> . . . into the
> Tar and chemical strangled tomb,
> The strange water, the
> Ohio River, that is no tomb to
> Rise from the dead
> From.

And, quoting the old poet H. Phelps Putnam:

> "That reeking slit, wide, soft and lecherous
> From which we bleed and into which we drown."

What emerges from this birth and death was not possible in the diction of the early poems or in the willful beauty of *The Branch Will Not Break*—the poems about Uncle Willie, Uncle Shortie, Emerson Buchanan, Aunt Agnes, Wright's teacher Charles Coffin, the poems of the people of Ohio, his own Winesburg. Much of this is in *Two Citizens*, where Jenny is identified as "the Jenny sycamore" who had been "the one wing, the only wing." But it isn't only Ohio that emerges in these poems. There is also a more open insistence by Wright on his art and the traditions of his art. And this has required him, once again, to find a new language, a style that can accommodate what he has learned and gather it to the spoken language of his childhood. The way he has achieved this is, I think, intensely artificial, even a little weird, and I think it is meant to be. At its best it's very funny and playful:

> The one tongue I can write in
> Is my Ohioan.

This is based, presumably, on the well-known Ohio habit of speaking in off-rhymed couplets; the lines come from a poem that moves in and out of a grave iambic trimeter, like that of Yeats, and contains some of the most powerful writing in the book:

> This poem frightens me
> So secretly, so much,
> It makes me hard to touch
> Your body's secret places.
> We are each other's faces

and:

> The sky is shattering.
> The plain sky grows so blue,
> Some day I have to die,
> As everyone must do,
> Alone, alone, alone,
> Peaceful as peaceful as stone.

At other times its artfulness consists in rendering peculiarities of diction exactly. The first poem is called "Ars Poetica" which sounds solemn enough. It begins:

> I loved my country
> When I was a little boy.
> Agnes is my aunt,
> And she doesn't even know

> If I love anything
> On this God's
> Green little apple.

The *even* is what delights me. And "God's green little apple" is full of guile: one of the best poems in the book is about licking the sweetness from very tart green apples and having the sense not to eat them.

Here and there in the artifice is something like boozy insistence, that strange pride that dares you to contradict:

> I was a good child,
> So I am
> A good man. Put that
> In your pipe.

It makes me feel vaguely like Raskolnikov being collared by Marmeladov in a bar: "Pardon me, sir, but may I inquire whether you have ever spent a night on a haybarge in the Neva?" And it's not clear who is being addressed, though one guesses Jehovah, since the passages tend, like this one, to call off original sin.

Sometimes the manner blusters through difficulty, but at their best these poems do make a wholeness. Especially "Prayer to the Good Poet" in which he links his own father to Horace, one of his fathers in poetry, and the poems to his Ohio teacher, and the unmannered fluidity and assurance (and amazed gratitude) of some of the love poems. And here, in the lines I have already quoted, Jenny becomes the sycamore, his first rising and discovery of poetry. That is why "October Ghosts" is the most crucial poem in the book, for me. It's a poem in which Wright makes a kind of peace with the terror and loneliness of "To the Muse":

> Jenny cold, Jenny darkness,
> They are coming back again.
> We came so early,
> But now we are shovelled
> Down the long slide.
> We carry a blackened crocus
> In either hand.

And then these lines in which Wright seems to have, at last, two wings. One of them is Jenny who is beauty, loneliness, death, the muse, the idea of the good, a sexual shadow, a whore, the grand-mother of the dead, the lecherous slit of the Ohio, an abandoner of her child, a "savage woman with two heads . . . the one / Face bro-ken and savage, the other, the face dead," the name carved under a tree in childhood close to the quick, a sycamore tree, a lover, the first time he ever rose. The other wing is his art, and with both of them he returns to his native place. The lines are a four-verse sum-mary of "The Heights of Macchu Picchu" and, because they gather—at the river—the whole struggle of James Wright's poetry, I think they are among the most beautiful and simple lines he has written:

> I will walk with you and Callimachus
> Into the gorges
> Of Ohio, where the miners
> Are dead with us.

This is the poem that ends, "Now I know nothing, I can die alone." Which is what has to be, and did not seem possible before.

IV

I had mostly finished writing these notes before I came upon the little book called *Moments of the Italian Summer*. I had thought I would end by saying that James Wright was writing the poetry of a grown man and that I expected it would be sometimes a poetry of light. And that I was grateful for it. But in this book of prose poems, he is saying a good deal of this for himself:

> It is all right with me to know that my life is only one life. I feel like the light of the river Adige.

Especially in "The Lambs on the Boulder," he says it. The poem deals with the legend of Giotto, that Cimabue found him a shepherd boy drawing lambs on a stone with a sharp rock and saw that he had genius and took him home and taught him to draw. It is a little like the story of the wild boy of Aveyron. Here is how he treats it:

> One of my idle wishes is to find the field where Cimabue stood in the shade and watched the boy Giotto scratching his stone with his pebble.
> I would not be so foolish as to prefer the faces of the boy's lambs to the faces of his angels. One has to act his age sooner or later.

Still, this little planet of rocks and grass is all we have to start with. How pretty it would be, the sweet faces of the boy Giotto's lambs gouged, with infinite and still uncertain and painful care, on the side of a boulder at the edge of a country field.

This is a poem about his own art. It ends this way:

In one of the mature Giotto's greatest glories, a huge choir of his unutterably beautiful angels are lifting their faces and are becoming the sons of the morning, singing out of pure happiness the praises of God.

Far back in the angelic choir, a slightly smaller angel has folded his wings. He has turned slightly away from the light and lifted hands. You cannot even see his face. I don't know why he is weeping but I love him best.

I think he must be wondering how long it will take Giotto to remember him, give him a drink of water, and take him back to the fold before it gets dark and shepherd and sheep alike lose their way in the darkness of the countryside.

I don't see how this could be any better. It has that stubborn preference for animals and angels, that wish to cut out the middleman, but it is about the mature artist Giotto who must, if anyone is going to, lead both the shepherd and the sheep out of the dark. That is what makes the poem feel intricate with thought. You could even say that James Wright has mentality.

And he is beautiful.

James Wright: Returning to the Heartland

BONNIE COSTELLO

JAMES WRIGHT WAS an elegaic poet of place. Place names echo through his lines as through deserted villages and wintry valleys, for Martins Ferry, Ohio; Fargo, North Dakota; Wheeling, West Virginia, are all dying. While he admired D. H. Lawrence's essay "The Spirit of Place" and tried to follow its guidelines, his own subject raised a special problem since it was the departure of spirit that he best portrayed. Wright tried repeatedly to call this spirit back, but his finest poems are those which catch it crossing the last hill crest or disappearing into the mist. One might argue that there is, indeed, a spirit in this place, one hopeless, ignorant, and long suffering, nonetheless beautiful and mysterious. This ghostly genius is the poet's invention, designed to fill the vacancy of home, something conjured in the half-lights of dream and memory, where soul and body, wishes and facts, inner and outer atmospheres bleed into one another.

This is, of course, a common characteristic of the literature of place. Joyce's Dublin is the land of the snow-covered dead. And as in the case of Joyce, the poetry of place is most often envisioned by expatriates, through a grid of ambivalence. Wright commented in an interview with Dave Smith: "My feeling about the Ohio Valley is . . . complicated. I sometimes feel a certain nostalgia about the place. At the same time I realize that . . . our problem when we were boys in Martins Ferry, Ohio in the industrial area enclosed by the foothills of the Appalachians on both sides, near the big river, was to get out." Poetry, the very means of escape, is ironically also the agent which brings the fugitive back. This sense of the fugitive or exile (or at least of the divided citizen) is a constant theme in Wright's poetry, but it also had a deep impact on his style, to good and bad effects. When he struggled with it he often produced a mysterious and intelligent lyricism. But sometimes his language caved in with despair, and sometimes his deep urge to affirm caused him to abjure intellect and embrace false simplicities. When he contrived a pose of wonder (as he did in the last two books) his language became prosaic rather than pure, though he aspired toward the latter just as one yearns for childhood or home. }

What makes "Autumn Begins in Martins Ferry, Ohio" one of Wright's better poems is its sense of grace and energy straining against a background of inevitable grays.

> In the Shreve High football stadium,
> I think of Polacks nursing long beers in Tiltonsville,
> And gray faces of Negroes in the blast furnace at Benwood,
> And the ruptured night watchman of Wheeling Steel,
> Dreaming of heroes.
>
> All the proud fathers are ashamed to go home.
> Their women cluck like starved pullets,
> Dying for love.
>
> Therefore,
> Their sons grow suicidally beautiful
> At the beginning of October,
> And gallop terribly against each other's bodies.

The communal spirit of the football game is dampened by the dirge of images. Wright achieves his best effects through such contrasts or shifts of tone. The technique can be overly theatrical at times, but here it is neatly integrated in emotionally complex images which work against the simple structure of the statement. Autumn is the harvest time, the beginning of the end, but also the beginning of the school year and a series of athletic triumphs. The contrast between the hopeless impotence of the fathers and the beautiful, futile strength of the sons is ironically locked in place by a conjunction of necessity ("therefore") as inviolable as the chain of generation. Here we understand both his nostalgia for home and his urge to escape. But too often Wright reduces his memories to black and white; irony gives way to sentimentality as the place becomes a source of wholesome, innocent love from which his own guilt has excluded him:

> Tonight Ohio, where I once
> Hounded and cursed my loneliness,
> Shows me my father, who broke stones,

Wrestled and mastered great machines,
And rests, shadowing his lovely face.

This Wordsworthian attitude, lacking Wordsworth's sublimity, tells us more about Wright's need to fill a void than it does about the simplicities of home.

Wright seems to have been aware of the dangers inherent in his search for the spirit of place, though he did not always heed his own warnings. In *Shall We Gather at the River* he sees, as Williams did, that "the pure products of America go crazy." The originals who once possessed the spirit of place are not so casually invoked:

I AM A SIOUX BRAVE, HE SAID IN MINNEAPOLIS
He is just plain drunk.
He knows no more than I do
What true waters to mourn for
Or what kind of words to sing
When he dies.

The tension this book confronts repeatedly is a romantic one: the yearning for unmediated experience against the obstructions of consciousness. But Wright's will to find a language of belief and belonging seems to have been stronger than the intelligence which denied it. In *Two Citizens* and *To a Blossoming Pear Tree* he tried to forge a rhetoric of sincerity and wonder that rings hollow every time. The same themes of human isolation and the elusive beauty of nature are repeated, but in a version which reaches no farther than it can grasp, which settles for the shallow satisfactions of familiar meanings and reassuring fictions.

Beautiful natural blossoms,
Pure delicate body,
You stand without trembling.
Little mist of fallen starlight,
Perfect, beyond my reach,
How I envy you.
For if you could only listen,
I would tell you something,
Something human.

The sentimentality of such poems contradicts their claims. The envy, the despair, the awe, were integrated into the vision of earlier books. Here the common, general adjectives "beautiful," "perfect" are not earned, as they are, astonishingly, in his best work. Wright obviously needed to settle with his homeland and with America, though his art was all in his uneasiness. The place of faith he constructed in the end was of the least durable materials: images of innocent generosity and fragile beauty framed in an easy rhetoric of the heart. Wright considered *To a Blossoming Pear Tree* his best work because the criterion of hope had overruled the criterion of depth. He was less convinced by the saving graces of *Two Citizens*, the book "of my patriotism, my love and my native place," but he ascribed its failure to the wrong causes. Rather than admit the ugliness that was still eroding through in that book, leaving a jagged surface, he let a kind of storybook wash color the earlier, more believable experiences described in *The Branch Will Not Break* and *Shall We Gather at the River*. The late poems are not without their dark moments and their acknowledgment of death, any more than the earlier poems are without their respites from loneliness. But when the old bitterness rises up in him he contains it in manageable frames and simple slogans so that it cannot poison his confidence. For every horror there is a kindness.

> Did you ever feel a man hold
> Sixty-five cents
> In a hook,
> And place it
> Gently
> In your freezing hand?

When America disappoints him in the late poems, it is "a shallow hell where evil is an easy joke." In the poems of the sixties, though, America is that place he crosses but never finds, which steals lives into its darkness until it is lost in an even greater darkness, as at the lovely end of the poem "Stages on a Journey Westward":

> America is over and done with.
> America,
> Plunged into the dark furrows
> Of the sea again.

When beauty is embattled and elusive, when it takes us by surprise, it has a more sublime and a more permanent kind of grace than the paltry beauty of his late work. "Blessing" borders on the self-conscious boyishness of later poems, but it holds back enough to give momentum to delight.

> Just off the highway to Rochester, Minnesota,
> Twilight bounds softly forth on the grass.
> And the eyes of those two Indian ponies
> Darken with kindness . . .
> Suddenly I realize
> That if I stepped out of my body I would break
> Into blossom.

His full heart remains occluded in this mystical communion. Words respect the wonder of such moments, for words can scare off the very things they invoke. They are not the grass he would like to lie down in. He has had to say "farewell to the poetry of calcium," to the pastoral dream of a heartland, in order to portray the true anemia of the Midwest. In the last books he tried to return to that optimistic, rooted wholesomeness. But he finds his patriotism in Europe, and such transplants do not really enrich an American soil.

The style of Wright's poetry changed as his attitude toward the landscape and people of the Midwest changed, and while critics have dismissed the differences as superficial, they do grow out of changing motivations and objectives. Wright designed *The Green Wall* (his first book), with its inverted word order, its extensive use of metonymy and periphrasis ("Suddenly on the eye / Feathers of morning fall"), its personifications ("the trees recall their greatness now"), its archaic words ("the day of girls blown green and gold") and conventional abstractions ("everlastingness"), its regular rhyme and meter, as an escape from home. While some poems contain local detail, notably "A Poem about George Doty in the Death House," they are removed, both in vision and diction, from their subject. Abstractions enchant the imagination that works through these poems, breathing the rarified atmosphere of "humanity," "time," "nature," "bondage," rather than the pungencies of Saturday morning, the Ohio River, Willy Lyons, the Hazel-Glass factory.

> The stone turns over slowly,
> Under the side one sees
> The pale flint covered wholly
> With whorls and prints of leaf.

> After the moss rubs off
> It gleams beneath the trees,
> Till all the birds lie down.
> Hand, you have held that stone.

But the hand hasn't really held anything; the stone exists in the mind. Even the lovely elegy "Arrangements with Earth for Three Dead Friends" grieves in a world of words. But as early as *Saint Judas* Wright is called back to the scenes and even the voices of the Ohio Valley. The style and attitude of the book recalls the *Lyrical Ballads*, for the diction and idiom are often colloquial while the verse retains a conspicuous artifice which sets it apart from the real language of men. "A Note Left in Jimmy Leonard's Shack" is typical:

> Near the dry river's water-mark we found
> > Your brother Minnegan,
> Flopped like a fish against the muddy ground.
> Beany, the kid whose yellow hair turns green,
> Told me to find you, even in the rain,
> > And tell you he was drowned.

His models during this time are Thomas Hardy, Robert Frost, Edward Arlington Robinson, all poets of place, but place reassembled on the well-manicured ground of verse.

In *The Branch Will Not Break* Wright abandoned rhyme and meter for "naked" poetry and replaced formal rhetoric with a blunt, processional, sometimes hypnotic utterance which depended more on inner shifts of tone, stirring combinations of images, or short lines and stanzas for its dramatic effects. "Lying in a Hammock at William Duffy's Farm in Pine Island, Minnesota" is an extreme example, enumerating without comment several natural details (all departing or ephemeral) and concluding in abrupt non sequitur "I have wasted my life." In this book we feel, as well, the influence of Oriental poetry, not so much in Wright's juxtapositions of images (which are more like the psychic dissociations of surrealism) as in his surprising conjunctions of highly specified titles with the open-ended poems which follow them. This book marks Wright's first attempt to involve his art with the facts of his surroundings. An inner voice and vision go out to meet the landscape, and the landscape moves in to shape the private world—"a butterfly lights on the branch / Of your green voice." Such surreal conjunctions become formulaic in this book, but they mark an effort to engage the imagination in the local, and to discover the boundaries of both.

Shall We Gather at the River deepens and integrates many of the new techniques begun in the previous book. The surrealistic shifts and animations are far more refined; they seem to arise from the scenes rather than from the poet's will.

> Outside the great clanging cathedrals of rust and smoke,
> The locomotives browse on sidings.
> They pause, exhausted by the silence of the prairies.
> Sometimes they leap and cry out, skitterish.

Shall We Gather at the River represents Wright's most honest attempt to find a language which can express both the particulars of place and his imaginative freedom from them. The forms range from poem to poem, even within individual poems, and include the most rigid metric structures as well as the most open, conversational ones. Wright expresses his dual citizenship here by combining the high lyricism of his earlier work with a more direct, colloquial manner. One style pulls against the other to express his deep ambivalence, his sympathy with the place and his need to lean away from it.

> The old man Walt Whitman our countryman
> Is now in America our country
> Dead.
> But he was not buried in Minneapolis
> At least.
> And no more may I be
> Please God.
>
> I want to be lifted up
> By some great white bird unknown to the police,
> And soar for a thousand miles and be carefully hidden
> Modest and golden as one last corn grain,
> Stored with the secrets of the wheat and the mysterious
>   lives
> Of the unnamed poor.

The beauty of Wright's middle books is indeed in their effort to present a direct speech of the heart without lapsing into mere pathos. But they avoid that pathos precisely through a constant struggle in the line between competing kinds of language. This tension is

also the subject of great uneasiness in the book. Wright is looking for
a unified voice which will hit against something solid, echo back the
spirit of place. "Speak" in part concerns such a search. Wright embodies his idea of the failing heartland in a muse named Jenny, a
beautiful casualty of the love-starved land. "To speak in a flat voice /
Is all that I can do. / I have gone everyplace / Asking for you." The
poem tries out many voices, veering from simple melody to bitter
outcry, mocking its own attempts to count losses in the measure of
art. The volume is dedicated to "Jenny" and invokes her again in the
final poem. But Jenny is absent by nature; like the earth itself, she
resides outside of language and his words can only mark the place of
her mute rest.

> Oh Jenny,
> I wish to God I had made this world, this scurvy
> And disastrous place. I
> Didn't, I can't bear it
> Either, I don't blame you, sleeping down there
> Face down in the unbelievable silk of spring

When he tries to resurrect Jenny in later volumes, in the guise of a
redeeming nature and a personal beloved, Annie, as though she were
fresh and innocent beside him and all his, the words are less persuasive. "On the Liberation of Women" lapses into pathos because there
is no friction in the open voice, no striving.

> In the middle of my age I walked down
> Toward a cold bloom.
> I don't give a damn if you care,
> But it half-rhymes with blossom.
> And no body was ever so kind to me
> As one woman, and begins spring
> In the secret of winter, and that is why
>
> I love you best.

The spacing forces a triumph of voice which we can't really recognize. These are the poems of middle-aged love, but without any of
the self-consciousness we want from middle age.

There are two authorities competing for Jenny's voice in *Two Citizens*: Hemingway, whose story "The Killers" is quoted as the epigraph, and Horace, to whom a poem is dedicated. These two models

are not necessarily at odds, of course, but they do pose a conflict for Wright, between the raw simplicity of the will and the refined simplicity of the intellect. He might eventually have made this conflict work for him, but here it does not. There is nothing prosaic in the hard-edged Horatian way of speaking. Wright obviously admired Horace's clarity and directness, but the classicist's formality is not really suited to his own disposition for the unmediated speech of the heart. Unfortunately, Wright did not so much succeed in banishing rhetoric from his verse as in contriving a very conspicuous and unconvincing rhetoric of sincerity. The example of Hemingway and other prose writers comes to the rescue here, guiding Wright toward a greater precision of observation and a greater tangibility. The prose pieces in *To a Blossoming Pear Tree* are generally superior to the poetry, not only because their bluntness seems more acceptable in prose, but because the greater objectivity of the prose retrieved some of the emotional complexity of Wright's vision. He had banished this complexity from lyric in favor of a coy, pseudo-Frostian charm: "What does the bobwhite mean? . . . You know, / Go, listen." The prose poem "The Moorhen and her Eight Young" invokes some of the old enchantment with the secrets of nature, but through an externalized, accessible language that satisfies Wright's aim to reach the reader directly.

> They are little balls of charcoal-gray mallow among drifting lily stems, as though the flower had escaped from the garden of the waters behind the hangman's cottage and chosen to blossom at night. Yet here they drift in the daylight behind their mother. Herself so dark, she almost threatens to blaze into another color entirely. She stays in whatever leaf shadow she can find. Only her beak reveals her sometimes. It is red as valerian rising from a night lily.

The particular is concrete but intrinsically mysterious. It requires no added questions or exclamations. The prose pieces are very uneven, but in general do not sink into bathos as the poems do at their worst. It is cheering to think that in prose Wright might have rediscovered some of the rigor and depth which make his best lyrics last.

Wright will be most remembered for his ghostly images. In part their haunting quality, especially in *The Branch Will Not Break* and *Shall We Gather at the River*, derives from their surrealistic disjunction, animation, and isolation. Such techniques are well suited to his elegaic moods, as in "Twilight" where images of human life recede into an inanimate landscape. "My grandmother's face is a small maple leaf / Pressed in a secret box . . . Far off, the shopping centers empty and darken. / A red shadow of steel mills." Wright moves freely between psychic and natural landscapes ("Locusts are climbing down into the dark green crevices / of my childhood") in order to render the subjective experience of place in a primary way. If these images depart from nature, they nevertheless begin there. Wright's mysteries arise from the domestic. These images are haunting also because the human scene is shrunken and barren. In "Gambling in Stateline, Nevada" for instance, the natural and the mechanical hold out a cold muteness which diminishes and isolates the human.

> The great cracked shadow of the Sierra Nevada
> Hoods over the last road. . . .
> Here, across from the keno board,
> An old woman
> Has been beating a strange machine
> In its face all day.

Out of the lifeless repetition of the lives he imagines, and the vast horizontal of the Midwest, Wright creates a vertical, ritual impression, building up a symbolic vocabulary of moons, rivers, snow, from a descriptive pretext. The Ohio or Minneapolis rivers recall the River Styx, George Doty becomes a figuration of Saint Judas, three dead swans are clipped Phoenixes. Without Eliot's erudition and didacticism, Wright's heartland is another waste land, inhabited by ravaged beauties, betrayed faiths, empty gestures. The deepest pathos consists in the denials of redemptive myth. Like the Rhine maidens of Eliot's poem, the dead swans suffocate in a "tar and chemical strangled tomb, / The strange water, the / Ohio river, that is no tomb to / Rise from the dead / From." "In Response to a Rumor that the Oldest Whorehouse in Wheeling, West Virginia, Has Been Condemned" puts Hell on both sides of the river.

> I will grieve alone,
> As I strolled alone, years ago, down along
> The Ohio Shore
> I hid in the hobo jungle weeds

Upstream from the sewer main,
Pondering, gazing.

I saw, down river,
At Twenty-third and Water Streets
By the vinegar works,
The doors open in early evening.
Swinging their purses, the women
Poured down the long street to the river
And into the river.

I do not know how it was
They could drown every evening.
What time near dawn did they climb up the other shore,
Drying their wings?

For the river at Wheeling, West Virginia,
Has only two shores:
The one in hell, the other
In Bridgeport, Ohio.

And nobody would commit suicide, only
To find beyond death
Bridgeport, Ohio.

This is not only the River Styx, but also the river in which Diana bathed with her nymphs, making the poet an Acteon, admiring and guilty. Such images leave more questions than answers as they blend past and present, living and dead. Something in the heartland always remains obscure. The river is dark, as the grave is. Wright relies too heavily, perhaps, on an elegiac vision, on the "one last night nurse shining in one last window," on abandoned railroad arches and dismantled fairgrounds. The "last picture show" perspective can become maudlin and self-pitying ("It is dark. I have no life."). But in the better poems the grays mix with strange reds and purples to yield more mystery than dreariness. Sounds are just out of hearing range, gestures just beyond recognition ("A widow on a front porch puckers her lips / And whispers."). Details float out of familiar settings. And behind and around the wreckage of life, an inhuman world touches him with its cold glamor. "The moon is out hunting, everywhere, / Delivering fire, / And walking down hallways / Of a diamond."

Wright's six volumes record an imagination evading but finally straining to rediscover American life. But these are also poems about the life within, and his efforts to escape, rediscover, and transcend himself.

The careful impersonality of the early volumes is abruptly broken in a section of *Saint Judas* called "The Part Nearest Home." He bursts out, as if inwardly compelled to confess:

> My name is James A. Wright, and I was born
> Twenty-five miles from this infected grave,
> In Martins Ferry, Ohio, where one slave
> To Hazel-Atlas Glass became my father.
> He tried to teach me kindness. I return
> Only in memory now, aloof, unhurried.
> To dead Ohio, where I might lie buried,
> Had I not run away before my time.

This gesture is the beginning of many, but Wright discovers later in the poem and in subsequent volumes the difficulty of such a return. The expatriate has become an exile. The place sifts through his imagination like dusk, and the bleak vision of *The Branch Will Not Break* and *Shall We Gather at the River* undermines the optimism of their titles. Wright discovers that the loneliness and vacancy of the landscape comes from within; that he himself is Hell.

> How many scrawny children
> Lie dead and half-hidden among frozen ruts
> In my body, along my dark roads.
> Lean coyotes pass among clouds
> On mountain trails, and smile,
> And pass on in snow.

Wright's gift was for such ambiguous passage between the inner and outer life. But just as the outer world has its delights, so the inner world, if a dark cave, is sometimes luminous.

> There is this cave
> In the air behind my body
> That nobody is going to touch:
> A cloister, a silence
> Closing around a blossom of fire.

> When I stand upright in the wind,
> My bones turn to dark emeralds.

In the central books loneliness is a pervasive but complex word for Wright. It loses its complexity in the end as he brings the inner life too close to the surface and tries to overcome loneliness by his "face to face" encounters with feebleminded relatives and sloppy dogs. Wright's emotional conversion within personal, domestic, love cannot bear the burden of new patriotism. Nor can "plain speaking" compensate for shallow vision. We can hardly blame Wright for inventing a wholesome image of soul and body. One gets tired of visionary dreariness. At the end of *Shall We Gather at the River* he promised to silence his complaints: "It is the old loneliness / . . . And it is the last time." What remained when the old loneliness vanished was an artificial flower, nothing so lovely as the fragile "trillium of darkness" that bloomed before. Wanting to call the world by a new, brighter name, Wright squints and makes a wish.

> I know what we call it
> Most of the time.
> But I have my own song for it,
> And sometimes, even today,
> I call it beauty.

Call it what he will, it is the old world just the same. Sometime after *Shall We Gather at the River* James Wright wrote that "The kind of poetry I want to write is / The poetry of a grown man." He had obviously grown a little weary of his *angst*. And indeed there is something immature about even the best poems of the middle period. But the kinds of resolutions Wright proposes in the last volume cannot sustain the life of a grown man; they try to forge a new innocence where everything conspires to deny it.

James Wright, His Poems:
A Kind of Overview, in Appreciation

MILLER WILLIAMS

> Though love can be scarcely imagin-
> able Hell,
> By God, it is not a lie.
>> "The Art of the Fugue"
>
> By God I want to live, and so do you.
>> "On the Liberation of Women"
>
> . . . the dark
> Blood in my body drags me
> Down.
>> "To a Blossoming Pear Tree"

WHEN A WRITING POET is among us, we think—partly in def-
erence to the poet, partly by critical convention—mostly of the current work. It's what matters, or so we have all decided; it's where a
developing poet (even if the poet is quite old) has come to. Earlier
work is not given much attention. A critic or anthologist may be accused of bad form for bringing it up.

When a poet dies, it all becomes simultaneous. All of a sudden, we
find ourselves reading from a body of work as we read from the work
of Donne or Dickinson or Whitman. When we read poetry for the
pleasure of reading poetry, and not to see what someone is doing
now, there aren't any periods.

There is—has been—so much talk of the earlier and the later
poems when Wright's work is discussed that it would seem unseemly not to look at it from that view at least briefly in so early a
retrospective. This will be the last time, I think, that I'll pay attention to such distinctions.

Nothing I have to say here is designed to prove or disprove anything, and this is not the sum of it; the work of any good poet adds up in a different way for each generation, and to some degree also for each person who reads it. Another reader in fifty years or in one may have very different things to say, out of a different perspective. This is what my perspective brings me to say. For now.

Almost all of James Wright's poems, whether they are tribal, addresses to strangers, political homilies, contemplations on (usually melancholy) events or on the desolation he saw around us and within us, or the rare love poem, are more often than not words out of his own darkness telling us about violence, loss, and death.

If, as I have maintained elsewhere, the poet's only subjects are sex, death, religion, and ambition (or, if you will, love, loss, awe, and the will to power), then Wright joins the houses of Hardy and Ransom as reigning authority for his time over a fourth of what poems are about. He is—was always—the poet of loss.

That loss comes usually—but not only—as death, and again like his two most admired teachers, he set about debunking the sentimentality surrounding death. Also like them, he was in increasing danger of creating his own.

Part of the problem lay in the unresolvable dilemma, the inability to accept either of the only two options a young man has:

> Order be damned, I do not want to die.
> "At the Executed Murderer's Grave"

> I'm afraid to die. It hurts to die.
> "A Christmas Greeting"

But just as much he didn't want the "sinister grief of old age" ("A Poem Written under an Archway in a Discontinued Railroad Station, Fargo, North Dakota," *Shall We Gather at the River*).

In great part, Wright's poems are informed by such dilemmas: he celebrated his humanity and wanted not to be a human being; he loved America and its midwest and hated them both; he had the vision of a romantic and the aesthetics of a classicist.

In the last of these collisions lies the explanation for much of what took place in the unfolding of Wright's career as a poet.

If a romantic is one who believes that modern urban civilization may damn us, that we may find some kind of redemption in nature, that intuition is to be trusted over reason and that there is an organic wholeness that makes the various single, then Wright was always a romantic. But he kept returning to poems of simple reportage, instead of the necessarily prophetic poems of the true romantic; he kept assuming a world that never changed much, and in which humankind was never likely to find its apotheosis, to the gods of hell or heaven either, and never quite had faith in the sine qua non of romanticism—a belief in the perfectibility of the species. And he appears at times to return to nature not—as the good romantic must—to redeem his humanity but to escape it.

That is to say, among other things, that James Wright was not converted to a way of poetry or of thinking that was not already within him; he may have been convinced to let his already romantic spirit take charge, but he never stopped going behind the barn to make his poems of formal patterns and reportage.

He had pretended for a while that he was not a romantic, then he pretended that he was.

Next to loss, he wrote poems of praise: praise of women, of friendship, of life itself, of the damned and the outsider, of the natural state and the beasts who are its citizens. Unlike Hardy and Ransom, Wright was also a poet of pure celebration, of awe.

The poems in praise of the unpraised—the killer, the whore, and others among the lost and losers—are among his strongest (and sometimes strangest) poems, but they stop after *Saint Judas*, except for the excellent lines of "In Response to a Rumor That the Oldest Whorehouse in Wheeling, West Virginia, Has Been Condemned," a poem of considerable distinction apart from this context: we see Wright as a comic poet here as we do nowhere else.

If he stops writing poems to the forces of pain and death—

> But I mourn no soul but his,
> Not even the bums who die,
> Nor the homely girl whose cry
> Crumbled his pleading kiss.
>> "A Poem about George Doty in the Death House"

—he stays far from reconciled to the rest of humanity, or to himself as part of it:

> Man's heart is the rotten yolk of a black snake egg
> Corroding, as it is just born, in a pile of dead
> Horse dung.

I have no use for the human creature.

"A Secret Gratitude"

He does, of course, and we know it. He did. We know that he lived
and wrote in the same dilemma. We turn with him, as we read, to
the only place there is to turn: to the plane of the animals, where—
in his poems as in other nursery tales and parables—the creatures
act out small scenes by which we may come to understand ourselves:

The black caterpillar
Crawls out, what with one thing
And another, across
The wet road.
How lonely the dead must be.

"I Am a Sioux Brave, He Said in Minneapolis"

The horse—once or twice the cow—is the means through which
humans may rediscover their natural beginnings, the point of
contact:

Yet earth contains
The horse as a remembrance of wild
Arenas we avoid.

"The Horse"

I let those horses in to steal
On principles, because I feel
Like half a horse myself.

"Two Horses Playing in the Orchard"

. . . the courteous face of the old horse David
Appears at our window.
To snuffle and cough gently.
He, too, believes we may long for
One more dream of slow canters across the prairie
Before we come home to our strange bodies
And rise from the dead.

"Poems to a Brown Cricket"

There is myth and fact aplenty, of course, to show it is meet that
horse and human join together, and the horse is the only domestic
animal that fares so well. Almost all of Wright's creatures are wild,
and only one of these is above the horse in Wright's hierarchy of

beasts: the bird—some twenty species of which fly through the lines of the poems—represented for him the freedom of spirit for which he longed: the lightness of soul, release from limited perceptions, dark visions, aging, and death—or at least from the awareness of aging and death.

A white bird suggests the most perfect of the perfect states, not of purity in the traditional sense of common morality, but of total innocence from the curse of knowledge, of civilization, of ourselves:

> I want to be lifted up
> By some great white bird unknown to the police.
>
> "The Minneapolis Poem"

This is as mythic as it sounds; the freedom he means has existed—for humans—nowhere except in myth.

The bestiary of James Wright would not be shamed by the Garden of Eden or the Ark. Besides the birds—who in frequency of appearance dominate the poems—there are all the domestic animals, even to the rat and the housefly, and no fewer than thirty species of wilder mammals, reptiles, fish, and insects and spiders.

There is little in Wright's poetry that doesn't have its own life. We see an occasional chair or table, but almost everything walks, crawls, swims, or flies. He was, for all his dark vision, for all his obsession— through most of his work—with desolation and death, our major poet of life, of the celebration of being. He is, after all, the great yea-sayer.

These creatures, it ought to be said, are in the poems on their own terms, for the most part. They don't wear heavy symbolic garb, excepting the bird, which almost completely disappears into its symbolic meaning and becomes by synecdoche only a wing, and then only a feather.

By the *New Poems*, in fact, Wright was not much concerned with the literal fact even of the wing, only the symbolic import mattered now, as in "I love most the soft / wing of the vein" ("To Harvey, Who Traced the Circulation").

Again, from *Two Citizens*:

> Somewhere in me there is a crystal that I cannot find
> Alone, the wing that I used to think was a poor
> Blindness I had to live with with the dead.
>
> "Voices between Waking and Sleeping in the Mountains"

The symbolic role for bird—or the synecdoches for bird—especially bird in general, when no species is given—is consistent throughout the poems, as when the speaker ("Listening to the Mourners"), who has "the voice of a scarecrow . . . stands up and suddenly turns into a bird." A full reading of the passage calls not only for a glance at Yeats's old man, "a tattered coat upon a stick," and to Ovid surely (there are a lot of metamorphoses in Wright's poems!), but to what we come to understand the bird to mean for Wright; the scarecrow takes flight as a bird not for Yeats's kingdom where art and artifact are supreme, but to a state of eternal organic existence, youth, love, and natural joy—eternal, at least, until we get all we need of them.

But for this one instance, and the small role of the horse, nothing living or not carries much in the way of symbolic meaning—any more, that is, than all of us and all of our objects do. Wright was not at heart a symbolist poet.

Leaping, as a kind of associative move has come to be called, requires a symbolic approach to a poem, and so does the deep image, which is simply the sensory end of a leap; both assume that a thing has an aura of significance beyond its physical fact, or no less important than the fact. It is by these auras that the kinship between things is recognized and the leap from one to another seen as right. We could not go from "mother" to "knife" if neither mother nor knife had meanings beyond their objective definitions. But Wright resisted those auras; he liked the furniture and population of this world for their own sakes.

And I suspect that he left the leaping alone, on the whole, after *Saint Judas*, because it so easily begins to parody itself.

Or maybe because he didn't want to do what he wasn't best at, and he must have known that others—Greg Orr, especially—did it better.

For whatever reason, he didn't leap for long about the symbolizing subconscious, nor forward us many images from there.

Still, one of my clearest pictures of James Wright is as a witch doctor, a shaman, wearing his bird-mask and raising his feathered scepter, delivering the kind and painful truth to his believers.

Well. So. Dilemma and paradox.

Still, it's a serviceable picture, for it's in the ritual act, I think—the rituals of language and of fellowship and love and a kind of worship—that Wright found the shape and direction we call sanity. It is in the statement through all the work:

> Standing alone before your grave, I read
> The name, the season, every decent praise
> A chisel might devise—
> Deliberate scrawls to guard us from the dead.
>
> "Devotions"

> I stand alone by an elder tree, I dare not breathe
> Or move.
> I listen.
> The wheat leans back toward its own darkness,
> And I lean toward mine.
>
> "Beginning"

> The spirit of a tree begins to move.
> I touch leaves.
> I close my eyes, and think of water.
>
> "Trying to Pray"

> I kneel down naked and ask forgiveness.
>
> "A Prayer to the Ramakrishna"

But the ritual which is art is found not only, not mainly, in what is said. Wright was not able to stay comfortably or for long away from the patterns by which poetry knows its rites.

The fact is that when he wrote free verse he was a good poet; sometimes he was very good. When he wrote his formal lines he was also very good, but he was sometimes superb. He was sometimes one of the best poets writing in English.

There are many who can write an impressive free-form poem; very few are world-class prosodists. One can understand the moves Wright decided to make in his career, but to celebrate his turn from the prosodic ritual to free verse is not far from suggesting that Baryshnikov turn to modern dance.

His foot reversals are elegant prosodic maneuvers, fine-edged examples of the way form and content can work together by working against one another.

From "Two Horses Playing in the Orchard":

> He turns, lost in a dream of trees

and:

> A few, trembling on boughs so low
> A horse can reach them, small and sweet.

From "A Girl in a Window," one of the best of Wright's poems in the four-foot line (and he was the master of that line):

> Let us return her now, my friends,
> Her love, her body to the grave
> Fancy of dreams where love depends.
> She gave, and did not know she gave.

The reversal on "fancy" emphasizes the double duty of both "grave" and "fancy" itself, and gives us the reassuring firmness of count we need after the near-glissando of "body to the grave."

From the next poem in *The Green Wall*, "On the Skeleton of a Hound":

> But I will turn my face away from this
> Ruin of summer, collapse of fur and bone.

Ah!

Probably to his credit today, Wright rarely made metaphors; most of the poems are compelling upon the reader's imagination because they are monuments to insight and style, but he knew how to make a metaphor as well as any, and better than some who make hobbies of them. Small boys lying awake are "delicate little boxes of dust" ("The Undermining of the Defense Economy," *The Branch Will Not Break*); a grandmother's face is a "small maple leaf" ("Twilights," *The Branch Will Not Break*); a pear tree in bloom is a "little mist of fallen starlight" (Title poem, *To a Blossoming Pear Tree*); a white rose is "the grave in blossom" ("The Life," *Shall We Gather at the River*), a startling and wholly convincing metaphor that barely begins to leap out of itself.

On those occasions when Wright did construct a metaphor, he meant it to carry its part of the poem and not to hang there as a decoration.

His submerged metaphors were made with no less attention and skill, and they glisten below their surfaces. We are not likely to forget or disbelieve when he tells us:

Suddenly I realize
that if I stepped out of my body I would break
Into blossom.

"A Blessing"

So what fault is there to find? Honesty asks the question, and so does James Wright. We find faults, of course, but not where we expect them to be.

A first book is nearly always an anthology of influences; *The Green Wall* is most remarkable not for the quality of the poems, which is high, but for the almost total absence of other poets' voices.

There are quotes of a kind scattered through all the work, clearly deliberate runs from other artists' repertoires, after the fashion of jazz musicians, to have some fun and to pay homage.

He did it mostly in the resolutions.

Here is Eliot, closing "The Seasonless" (*The Green Wall*):

The days of girls blown green and gold.

Here is Hardy, ending "Two Poems about President Harding" (*The Branch Will Not Break*) and closing the first stanza of "But Only Mine" (*Saint Judas*):

Whatever moon and rain may be,
The hearts of men are merciless.

Somewhere above me boughs were burning gold,
And women's frocks were loose, and men grew old.

Here is Nicanor Parra—a fine mask of Parra—resolving "The Poor Washed up by Chicago Winter":

I can remember the evening.
I can remember the morning.
I am too young
To live in the sea alone without
Any company.
I can either move into the McCormick Theological
    Seminary
And get a good night's sleep,
Or else get hauled back to Minneapolis.

These are fun for sure, and homage, but there was a question, and it ought to be responded to.

So, here: yes. There are failures, certainly. Some of them come from trying good moves and falling short, but not all. Some, like "In Shame and Humiliation" (*Saint Judas*), are irritatingly prolix; some, like "Little Marble Boy" (*To a Blossoming Pear Tree*), are precious.

If there are indeed poems that look like prose, then some, like "The Old WPA Swimming Pool in Martins Ferry, Ohio" (*Two Citizens*), are surely prose pieces that look like poems. This is not something that could happen often in Wright's work; no poet has had greater respect for the line as the unit of structure and function in a poem. I have a suspicion that when he began to be interested in the prose-poem, in carrying elements of poetry into the paragraph, he would inadvertently leave some of them there and bring back into his poems a sense of prose instead, so that the sentence and not the line became the unit he built the poem around.

Several poems in *To a Blossoming Pear Tree* ("By the Ruins of a Gun Emplacement: Saint-Benoît," for instance, and "Neruda," to name only two) seem to have been composed in a casual manner out of phrases lying easily at hand.

Some, like "Gambling in Stateline, Nevada" (*Shall We Gather at the River*), have a weariness in their lines, as if the author had grown tired of writing.

A couple of poems from *Shall We Gather at the River* ("The Minneapolis Poem," "Living by the Red River") keep striking me as having been not influenced by but written by another, as if Wright had been temporarily possessed.

On his own, though, he could sometimes stumble into an easy metonymy like "the good darkness / of women's hands that touch loaves."

There are some uncertain moments in the young poems, naturally, for being that, but there are remarkably few of them. When we are told, in "A Girl in a Window," that

> Behind us, where we sit by trees,
> Blundering autos lurch and swerve
> On gravel, crawling on their knees
> Around the unfamiliar curve,

we have no idea why the curve should be unfamiliar to all those drivers, or what it matters to the poem. When we are told, in "On the Skeleton of a Hound," how the speaker knows that

> . . . the mole will heave a shinbone over,

> The earthworm snuggle for a nap on paws,
> The honest bees build honey in the head

we may accept that earthworms must take a kind of nap, but we have to ask in what way bees are more honest than worms or moles, and what it matters to the poem.

To a Blossoming Pear Tree has a number of problems in the resolutions of the poems, a strange thing for a poet whose way with closing lines was always part of his mark.

We can read a long time in the poems of James Wright before we come upon plain triteness, but I wonder if "greener than grass" ("For the Marsh's Birthday," *Shall We Gather at the River*) is any more serviceable than "green as grass."

These are the turns that have bothered my reading sometimes. They don't come to much, and when one considers that we have before us some two hundred and fifty poems by a relatively young man who wrote with a passion to equal his considerable intellect and skill, it might be fair to ask why the hell we need to make any point of a few imperfect moves—if, in fact, I have read them right, and they are wrong, not I.

The reason is that no one was more contemptuous of a soft reading than James Wright, who knew perfectly well that all our works are graded on the curve, and that praise means nothing when everything is praised. He was too good a poet for us to dishonor by the sham kindness of condescension. He was an honest man; he would have seen—did see, I'm sure—more problems with his poems than I have seen. What James Wright abandoned in despair lends despair an unaccustomed luster.

What it seems to me must be called for, after an attempt to tell the underside of truth, is a run at the luminous moments, the hands-down victories. Of all the poems I have known by James Wright, these are the ones I go back to continually, the ones I turn to at times when it's two in the morning, there's amber in the glass, and everyone else is asleep. Some are the same poems mentioned before for their problems. So be it.

From *The Green Wall*—"A Girl in a Window"; the fine seventeenth-century poem, "On the Skeleton of a Hound"; "Mutterings over the Crib of a Deaf Child."

From *Saint Judas*—"On Minding One's Own Business"; "A Prayer in My Sickness."

From *The Branch Will Not Break*—"Lying in a Hammock at William Duffy's Farm in Pine Island, Minnesota"; "Arriving in the Country Again"; the simplest of catalogs, "Today I Was So Happy, So I Made This Poem"; "A Blessing" (!).

From *Shall We Gather at the River*—"In Response to a Rumor that the Oldest Whorehouse in Wheeling, West Virginia, Has Been Condemned."

From *New Poems*—"Written in a Copy of Swift's Poems, for Wayne Burns"; "Northern Pike."

From *Two Citizens*—"Love in a Warm Room in Winter," maybe Wright's most playful and plainly delightful poem; "Well, What Are You Going to Do?"

From *To a Blossoming Pear Tree*—"With the Shell of a Hermit Crab"; "Beautiful Ohio."

The list says more about my own head than about anything else, but that's as it should be; a reader ought to know the predilections of anyone who stands up to say anything about other people's poems.

I have just turned to count, and see that there are sixteen poems that I don't want to do without; there are many others I read with pleasure. I wonder how many I would have listed from the work of Auden, Stevens.

It's a damn good list.

Passion and vision and knowledge and intelligence. No poet of our time has insisted more fervently on the role of good sense in the making of poems, and there surely has been no time when the insistence was so much to the point. In conversation and in print he told us his dislike for poems that were not put into hard shape by the brain at its best.

A dilemma: having fallen among the new romantics after *Saint Judas*, Wright came to believe—or to write as if he believed—that the rational powers were suspect, and that only intuition and the leaps it guided could bring the poet, the poem, to a good end. The romantic in him said that this was so; the classicist said no.

Here are some notes from the classicist, from *Field # 8* (Spring 1973):

Poetry is the enemy of twitch. Every poetry has a theory, whether the bad poets know it or not. The theory of our current free verse involves a complete rejection of the past. . . . A rejection of the past is a rejection of intelligence. . . . What makes the new poetry so bad is its failure to realize that there is no sound poetry without intelligence.

Line! Line! Friends, let us all stop twitching and pay attention once more to the letters of John Keats.

If he had said no more to us than this, we would remember him with honor and gratitude.

We turn back to the letters of Keats.

"The difference in high sensations with and without knowledge appears to me this—in the latter case we are falling continually ten thousand fathoms deep and blown up again without wings and with all the horror of a bare-shouldered creature."

"An artist must serve mammon."

"I must be quaint and free of tropes and figures."

"I have not the least contempt for my species."

"Death must come at last; man must die."

But James Wright was not John Keats; he was James Wright, and he was with us:

Though love can be scarcely imaginable Hell,
By God it is not a lie.

and:

By God, I want to live and so do you.

and:

. . . the dark
Blood in my body drags me
Down.

This is what James Wright tells us, and it's enough. It's more than we have been able to deal with so far.

It's much to his credit that he had so many good ways to say what he wanted to say, so that we have wanted to hear. Or heard, whether we wanted to or not.

And one more, from "The Accusation," from *Saint Judas*:

Only the truth is kind.

We share the vision, and the passion, the sweet intelligence and the terrible knowledge, of one of our best. Death took away only what Death can understand; that was a great deal, but not everything.

Selected Bibliography

I. WORKS BY JAMES WRIGHT

A. Poetry:

The Green Wall. New Haven, Conn.: Yale University Press, 1957.
Saint Judas. Middletown, Conn.: Wesleyan University Press, 1959.
The Branch Will Not Break. Middletown, Conn.: Wesleyan University Press, 1963.
Shall We Gather at the River. Middletown, Conn.: Wesleyan University Press, 1968.
Collected Poems. Middletown, Conn.: Wesleyan University Press, 1971.
Two Citizens. New York: Farrar, Straus and Giroux, 1973.
Moments of the Italian Summer. Washington, D.C.: Dryad Press, 1976.
To a Blossoming Pear Tree. New York: Farrar, Straus and Giroux, 1977.
The Summers of James and Annie Wright. New York: Sheep Meadow Press, 1981.

B. Translations:

Hypnos Waking. By Rene Char. Selected and translated by Jackson Matthews with the collaboration of Barbara Howes, W. S. Merwin, William Jay Smith, Richard Wilbur, William Carlos Williams, and James A. Wright. New York: Random House, 1956.
Twenty Poems of Georg Trakl. With Robert Bly. Madison, Minn.: Sixties Press, 1961.
Twenty Poems of Cesar Vallejo. With Robert Bly and John Knoepfle. Madison, Minn.: Sixties Press, 1963.
Rider on the White Horse. By Theodor Storm. New York: Signet Books, 1964.
Cantico: A Selection. By Jorge Guillén. Norman Thomas di Giovanni, ed. Boston: Little, Brown and Company, 1965.
Twenty Poems of Pablo Neruda. With Robert Bly. Madison, Minn.: Sixties Press, 1967.
Poems. By Herman Hesse. New York: Farrar, Straus and Giroux, 1970.
Wanderings. By Herman Hesse. New York: Farrar, Straus and Giroux, 1972.

C. Prose:

"The Stiff Smile of Mr. Warren," *Kenyon Review*, 20 (Autumn 1958), 645–55.

"Delicacies, Horse-laughs, and Sorrows," *Yale Review*, 48 (Summer 1958), 608–13.

"Four New Volumes," *Poetry*, 93 (Oct. 1958), 46–50.

"Some Recent Poetry," *Sewanee Review*, 66 (Autumn 1958), 657–68.

"Poetry Chronicle," *Poetry*, 95 (Mar. 1960), 373–78.

"The Terrible Threshold," *Sewanee Review*, 67 (Spring 1959), 330–36.

"The Few Poets of England and America," *Minnesota Review*, 1 (Winter 1961), 248–56.

"Explorations, Astonishments," *Fresco*, 1 (Spring 1961), 153–54.

"A Shelf of New Poets," *Poetry*, 99 (Dec. 1961), 178–83.

"Gravity and Incantation," *Minnesota Review*, 2 (Spring 1962), 424–28.

"A Plain Brave Music," *Chelsea*, 12 (Sept. 1962), 135–39.

"Son of *New Poets*," *Minnesota Review*, 3 (Fall 1962), 133–36.

"The Delicacy of Walt Whitman," R. W. B. Lewis, ed., *The Presence of Walt Whitman*, pp. 164–88. New York: Columbia University Press, 1962.

Sobiloff, Hy. *Breathing of First Things*. New York: Dial Press, 1963. Introduction by James Wright.

"Frost's 'Stopping by Woods on a Snowy Evening,'" Oscar Williams, ed., *Master Poems*, pp. 920–25. New York: Washington Square Press, 1967.

"I Come to Speak for Your Dead Mouths," *Poetry*, 112 (June 1968), 191–94.

"Two Responses to 'The Working Line,'" *Field*, 8 (Spring 1973), 61–65.

"The Art of Poetry XIX," *Paris Review*, no. 62 (Summer 1975), 34–61. Interview by Peter Stitt.

"Letters from Europe, Two Notes from Venice, Remarks on Two Poems, and Other Occasional Prose," *American Poets in 1976*, ed. William Heyen, pp. 426–27. Indianapolis: Bobbs-Merrill, 1976.

"Hugo: Secrets of the Inner Landscape," *American Poetry Review*, 2, no. 3 (1973), 13.

Letter, *American Poetry Review* 3, no. 3 (1974), 69.

D. Uncollected Poetry:

"Villanelle for the New Soldiers," *Western Review*, 17 (1952), 40.

"The Garden of Paradise," *Interim*, 4 (1954), 64.

"Resurrected," *Poetry*, 84 (July 1954), 207.

"Sappho's Child," *Poetry*, 86 (Sept. 1955), 347–52.

"To a Friend Condemned to Prison," *Paris Review*, no. 10 (Fall 1955), 82.

"Sea Prayer for Friedrich Holderline; Waiting for Cleopatra," *New Orleans Poetry Journal*, 2 (Dec. 1955), 14–16.

"Vain Advice at the Year's End," *New Yorker*, Dec. 31, 1955, p. 22.

"A Love Poem with Mallards and Garlands; The Fourth Echo," *Quarterly Review of Literature*, 8 (1956), 298–304.

"To Heinrich Schlussnus," *New Orleans Poetry Journal*, 2 (Apr. 1956), 4.

"For Her Who Carried My Child; Where the Plump Spider Sways to Rest," *Poetry*, 88 (Apr. 1956), 1–6.

"Rites for a Dead Magician; To a Girl Heavy with Child," *New Orleans Poetry Journal*, 2 (July 1956), 7–9.

"David," *Yale Review*, 46 (Dec. 1956), 222–23.

"Surrender; The Fire; In Despair of Elegies," *New Orleans Poetry Journal*, 3 (Jan. 1957), 1–3.

"Mercy; Soft Sonata; To One Who Lived in Fear," *Poetry Broadside*, 1 (Apr. 1957), 4.

"A Prayer against Spring; A Silent Visit," *New Orleans Poetry Journal*, 3 (May 1957), 14–15.

"To the Ghost of a Kite; The Game of Chasing Shadows," *Western Review*, 21 (1957), 236–38.

"Aubade at Zarma Replacement Depot; Directions out of a Dream," *Poetry*, 89 (Mar. 1957), 353–56.

"Murderer," *Harper's*, 215 (July 1957), 64.

"Nightpiece," *Poetry*, 90 (Sept. 1957), 363–64.

"Under a Streetlight in Skid Row," *New Orleans Poetry Journal*, 3 (Sept. 1957), 5.

"The Revelation; A Balm for Easy Tears; Merlin Buried in Moonlight," *Hudson Review*, 10 (1957), 386–89.

"To L. Asleep," *Paris Review*, no. 18 (Spring 1958), 93.

"Lancelot Grown Old," *Quarterly Review of Literature*, 9 (1958), 184–86.

"For My Older Brother; Farmer," *Poetry*, 90 (Aug. 1958), 277–82.

"The Thieves," *Audience*, 5 (Autumn 1958), 62–63.

"Safety; With the Gift of a Feather," *Kenyon Review*, 20 (Autumn 1958), 594–96.

"To a Gnat in My Ear; A Voice Behind Me; To a Shy Girl," *New Orleans Poetry Journal*, 4 (1958), 12–15.

"What a Man Can Bear; The Animals," *Fresco*, 9 (Winter 1958), 14–16.

"Private Meeting Place," *New Yorker*, Jan. 3, 1959, p. 28.

"To a Young Girl on a Premature Spring Day," *New Yorker*, Mar. 14, 1959, p. 48.

"An Empty House and a Great Stone," *Poetry Northwest*, 1 (June 1959), 17.

"A Man in the North; Nu bin ich erwachet," *Audience*, 4 (Autumn 1959), 59–60.

"The Dream of the American Frontier," *The Fifties*, no. 3 (Fall 1959), 2.

"A Whisper to the Ghost Who Woke Me," *Big Table*, 1 (1959), 83–84.

"To a Salesgirl, Weary of Artificial Holiday Trees," *New Yorker*, Dec. 19, 1959, p. 40.

"A Young One in a Garden; Snow Storm in the Midwest," *Big Table*, 1 (1960), 73–74.

"By a Lake in Minnesota," *New Yorker*, Sept. 17, 1960, p. 168.

"To Some Uncertain Birds," *Harper's*, 221 (Oct. 1960), 94.

"Year Changes in the City," *Harper's*, 222 (Jan. 1961), 37.

"Near Mansfield, Ohio; Lazy Poem on a Saturday Evening; Miners," *Poetry*, 97 (Mar. 1961), 343–46.

"Late Afternoon in Western Minnesota," *The Nation*, Apr. 1, 1961, p. 287.

"Prayers under Stone," *Choice*, no. 1 (1961), 43–44.

"On the Foreclosure of a Mortgage in the Suburbs; To My Teacher, After Three Years; I Regret I Am Unable to Attend," *Minnesota Review*, 1 (Winter 1961), 146–49.

"Some Places in America Are Anonymous; Sickness; Poem on a Trip to Ohio; The Doors; Prayer for Several Kinds of Women; Travelling Home to Ohio with my Son, 1960; A Reply to the Post Office; The First Glimpse of Death," *Quarterly Review of Literature*, 11 (1961), 127–30.

"Saturday Morning," *New Yorker*, May 5, 1962, p. 136.

"Ohioan Pastoral; Written during Illness," *Minnesota Review*, 2 (Spring 1962), 277–82.

"Theodor Storm, 1962," *Choice*, no. 3 (1963), 108.

"Two Sides of the Sky; Facing the Sun with Closed Eyelids," *Minnesota Review*, 4 (Fall 1963), 30–31.

"Heritage," *Paris Review*, no. 31 (Winter–Spring 1964), 68.

"Micromutations," *New Yorker*, June 26, 1965, p. 97.

"Epithalamium," *Chicago Review*, 18, nos. 3–4 (1965), 18.

"Ohioan Pastoral," *Ohio Review*, 18 (Spring–Summer 1977), 40–43.

"A Poem of Powers," *Rapport*, 1, nos. 2, 3 (1972), 52.

"The Beginning of Autumn; Redemption," *American Poetry Review*, 2, no. 4 (1973), 35.

"Epistle to Roland Flint; On Ancient and Modern Modes; The Lambs on the Boulder," *Ohio Review*, 16 (Fall 1974), 72–77.

"To Horace; Breakfast; What Is Truth; The Divine Mario; An Announcement to People Who Sometimes Get Angry with Me; Cold Summer Sun, Be with Me Soon; The Last Day in Paris; Heraclitus; To Carolee Combs-Stacy, Who Set My Verses to Music; Dawn Prayer in Cold Darkness to My Secret Ghost," *Paris Review*, no. 62 (Summer 1975), 34–61.

"Lonely Poet; Art of the Bayonet," *Partisan Review*, 42, no. 1 (1975), 61–65.

"Small Wild Crabs Delighting on Black Sand," *New Yorker*, Feb. 20, 1978, p. 44.

"Lightning Bugs Asleep in the Afternoon," *New Yorker*, Aug. 20, 1979, p. 26.

"To the Cicada," *Georgia Review*, 32 (1978), 755–57.

"Above San Fermo," *Montana Review*, 1 (1979), 86.

"Leaving the Temple in Nîmes," *Montana Review*, 1 (1979), 87–88.

"Coming Home to Maui," *Ohio Review*, 20 (Spring–Summer 1979), 8–9.

"The Ice House," *Ohio Review*, 20 (Spring–Summer 1979), 10.

"Young Women at Chartres," *Georgia Review*, 33 (1979), 326–27.

"With the Gift of an Alabaster Tortoise," *New Yorker*, Dec. 10, 1979, p. 46.

"Apollo," *Ironwood 14* (1979), 19.

"In Gallipoli," *Ironwood 14* (1979), 20.

"The Limpet in Otranto," *Ironwood 14* (1979), 21.

"Entering the Temple in Nîmes," *New Yorker*, Jan. 14, 1980, p. 30.

"The Journey," *New Yorker*, Feb. 25, 1980, p. 46.

"At the End of Sirmione," *Antaeus*, 36 (1980), 37.

"In Memory of the Ottomans," *Antaeus*, 36 (1980), 38.

"Taranto," *Antaeus*, 36 (1980), 39.

"The Turtle Overnight," *Antaeus*, 36 (1980), 40.

"Regret for a Spider Web," *Antaeus*, 36 (1980), 41.

"A Mouse Taking a Nap," *Antaeus*, 36 (1980), 42.

"Time," *Antaeus*, 36 (1980), 42.

"Jerome in Solitude," *Antaeus*, 36 (1980), 43.
"Reading a 1979 Inscription on Belli's Monument," *Hudson Review*, 33 (1980), 177.
"Rain on the Spanish Steps," *Hudson Review*, 33 (1980), 178.
"A Dark Moor Bird," *Hudson Review*, 33 (1980), 178–79.
"Wherever Home Is," *Hudson Review*, 33 (1980), 179.
"The Vestal in the Forum," *Hudson Review*, 33 (1980), 180.
"A Farewell: To the Toulouse," *Hudson Review*, 33 (1980), 180–81.
"Milkweed," *Georgia Review*, 34 (1980), 246.

E. Uncollected Translations:

Vallejo, Cesar. "Three Poems from Trilce," *Chelsea*, 7 (May 1960), 51–52.
García Lorca, Federico. "Gacela of the Remembrance of Love," *Poetry*, 96 (June 1960), 151.
Neruda, Pablo. "Sexual Water," *Poetry*, 96 (June 1960), 151.
García Lorca, Federico. "Afternoon, August," *The Sixties*, no. 4 (Fall 1960), 16–27.
Vallejo, Cesar. "Distant Footsteps," *The Nation*, Mar. 11, 1961, p. 218.
DeNerval, Gerard. "Coming Awake on a Bus," *The Sixties*, no. 5 (Fall 1961), 3.
Rilke, Rainer Maria. "Orpheus, Eurydike, Hermes," *Fresco*, 1 (Winter 1961). With Franz Schneider.
Neruda, Pablo. "Sixth Poem; United Fruit Co.; Nothing but Death," *The Sixties*, no. 7 (Winter 1964), 2–17.
Storm, Theodor. "Women's Ritornelle," *The Sixties*, no. 8 (Spring 1966), 19.

II. Critical Sources

A. Articles:

Anonymous. "Beside the Styx," *Times Literary Supplement*, Oct. 17, 1968, p. 1172.
Anonymous. "From Literature and from Life," *Times Literary Supplement*, Nov. 28, 1963, p. 995.
André, Michael. "An Interview with James Wright," *Unmuzzled Ox*, 1, no. 2, 3–18.
Atlas, James. "Yelping and Hooting: Some Developments in Contemporary American Poetry," *London Magazine*, Apr. 1974, pp. 15–32.
Auden, W. H. Foreword, *The Green Wall*, by James Wright. New Haven, Conn.: Yale University Press, 1957.
Benedict, Estelle. *Library Journal*, Sept. 15, 1968, p. 3145.
Berg, Stephen, and Robert Mezey, eds. *Naked Poetry*. Indianapolis: Bobbs-Merrill, 1969.
Bly, Carol. "James Wright's Visits to Odin House," *Ironwood* 10 (1977), 33–37.
Bly, Robert. "James Wright," *Cafe Solo*, 2 (1970), 69.
———. "A Note on James Wright," *Ironwood* 10 (1977), 64–65.

―――. *Talking All Morning.* Ann Arbor: University of Michigan Press, 1980.

Browne, Michael Dennis. "Drawing a Bead on Louis Gallo from Minneapolis, Minnesota," *Carleton Miscellany,* 17 (Winter 1977), 33–37.

Butscher, Edward. "The Rise and Fall of James Wright," *Georgia Review,* 28 (1974), 257–68.

Cambon, Glauco. *The Inclusive Flame: Studies in Modern American Poetry.* Bloomington: Indiana University Press, 1965.

―――. *Recent American Poetry.* Minneapolis: University of Minnesota Press, 1962.

Carroll, Paul. *The Poem in Its Skin.* Chicago: Follett Publishing Company, 1968.

Coles, Robert. "James Wright: One of Those Messengers," *American Poetry Review,* 2, no. 4 (1973), 36–37.

Costello, Bonnie. "James Wright: Returning to the Heartland," *New Boston Review,* 5 (Aug.–Sept. 1980), 12–14.

Crunk [pseud. of Robert Bly]. "The Work of James Wright," *The Sixties,* no. 8 (1966), 52–78.

DeFrees, Madeline. "James Wright's Early Poems: A Study in 'Convulsive' Form," *Modern Poetry Studies,* 2 (1972), 241–51.

―――. "That Vacant Paradise," *Ironwood* 10 (1977), 13–20.

Dickey, James. *Babel to Byzantium: Poets and Poetry Now.* New York: Farrar, Straus and Giroux, 1967.

―――. "In the Presence of Anthologies," *Sewanee Review,* 66 (Spring 1958), 294–314.

―――. *Spinning the Crystal Ball: Some Guesses at the Future of American Poetry.* Washington, D.C.: Library of Congress, 1967.

Foster, Richard. "Debauch by Craft: Problems of the Younger Poets," *Perspective,* 12, no. 1 (1960), 3–17.

Friedman, Norman. "The Wesleyan Poets: The Formal Poets," *Chicago Review,* 18, nos. 3–4 (1965), 53–73.

―――. "The Wesleyan Poets II: The Formal Poets," *Chicago Review,* 19, no. 1 (1965), 55–73.

―――. "The Wesleyan Poets III: The Experimental Poets," *Chicago Review,* 19, no. 2 (1966), 52–73.

Gallo, Louis. "Thoughts on Recent American Poetry," *Carleton Miscellany,* 17 (Winter 1977), 12–27.

Goldstein, Laurence. Untitled Review of *Collected Poems. Michigan Quarterly Review,* 40 (Summer 1972), 214–17.

Hass, Robert. "James Wright," *Ironwood* 10 (1977), 74–96.

Hendricksen, B. "Wright's 'Lying in a Hammock at William Duffy's Farm, Pine Island, Minnesota,'" *Explicator,* 32 (Jan. 1974), 40.

Heyen, William, ed. *American Poets in 1976.* Indianapolis: Bobbs-Merrill, 1976.

Howard, Richard. *Alone with America.* New York: Atheneum, 1969.

―――. "My Home, My Native Country: James Wright," *Ironwood* 10 (1977), 101–10.

Ignatow, David. "What I Feel at the Moment Is Always True," *Ironwood 10* (1977), 45–46.

Jackson, Richard. "The Time of the Other: James Wright's Poetry of Attachments," *Chowder Review*, 10–11 (1978), 126–44.

Janssens, G. A. M. "The Present State of American Poetry: Robert Bly and James Wright," *English Studies*, 51 (1971), 112–37.

Kinnell, Galway. "Poetry, Personality, and Death," *Field*, 4 (Spring 1971).

Lacey, Philip. "That Scarred Truth of Wretchedness," *The Inner Way*. Philadelphia: Fortress Press, 1972.

Landness, Thomas S. "New Urns for Old," *Sewanee Review*, 81 (Winter 1973), 137–57.

Lensing, George S., and Ronald Moran. *Four Poets and the Emotive Imagination: Robert Bly, James Wright, Louis Simpson, and William Stafford*. Baton Rouge: Louisiana State University Press, 1976.

Lieberman, Laurence. *Unassigned Frequencies*. Urbana: University of Illinois Press, 1978.

Logan, John. "The Prose of James Wright," *Ironwood 10* (1977), 154–55.

Malkoff, Karl. *Crowell's Handbook of Contemporary American Poetry*. New York: T. Y. Crowell Co., 1974.

Martin, Philip. "A Dungeon with the Door Open," *Carleton Miscellany*, 17 (Winter 1977), 30–33.

Martz, William. *The Distinctive Voice*. Glenview, Ill.: Scott Foresman, and Co., 1966.

Matthews, William, "The Continuity of James Wright's Poems," *Ohio Review*, 18 (Spring–Summer 1977), 44–57.

McElarth, Joseph R., ed. "Something to Be Said for the Light: A Conversation with James Wright," *Southern Humanities Review*, 6 (1973), 134–53.

McMaster, Belle M. "James Arlington Wright: A Checklist," *Bulletin of Bibliography*, 31 (1974), 71–82.

McPherson, Sandra. "You Can Say That Again," *Iowa Review*, 13 (Spring 1972), 70–77.

Mills, Ralph, Jr. *Contemporary American Poetry*. New York: Random House, 1965.

———. *Creation's Very Self*. Fort Worth: Texas Christian University Press, 1969.

———. *Cry of the Human*. Urbana: University of Illinois Press, 1975.

———. "James Wright's Poetry: Introductory Notes," *Chicago Review*, 17, nos. 2–3 (1964), 128–43.

Molesworth, Charles. *The Fierce Embrace*. Columbia: University of Missouri Press, 1979.

———. "James Wright and the Dissolving Self," *Salmagundi*, 22–23 (1973), 222–33.

Moore, James. "American Poetry in and out of the Cave": Part I, "The Yenan Complex," *Lamp in the Spine*, no. 3 (Winter 1972), 12–27.

Moran, Ronald, and George Lensing. "The Emotive Imagination: A New Departure in American Poetry," *Southern Review*, 3 (1966), 51–67.

Nathan, Leonard. "The Private 'I' in Contemporary Poetry," *Shenandoah*, 22 (Summer 1971), 80–99.

———. "The Traditional James Wright," *Ironwood* 10 (1977), 131–37.

Oberg, Arthur. *Modern American Lyric.* New Brunswick, N.J.: Rutgers University Press, 1977.

Orlen, Steven. "The Green Wall," *Ironwood* 10 (1977), 5–12.

Pearce, Roy Harvey. "The Burden of Romanticism: Towards the New Poetry," *Iowa Review*, 2 (Spring 1971), 109–28.

Perloff, Marjorie G. "Poetry Chronicle: 1970–71," *Contemporary Literature*, 14 (Winter 1973), 97–131.

———. "Roots and Blossoms," *Book World—Washington Post*, Sept. 16, 1973, pp. 6–7.

Pinsky, Robert. *The Situation of Poetry.* Princeton, N.J.: Princeton University Press, 1976.

Plumly, Stanley. "Sentimental Forms," *Antaeus*, 30–31 (1978), 321–28.

Pritchard, William H. "Poetry Matters," *Hudson Review*, 26 (1973), 579–97.

Rexroth, Kenneth. *American Poetry in the Twentieth Century.* New York: Herder and Herder, 1971.

Robinett, Jane. "Two Poems and Two Poets," *Ironwood* 10 (1977), 38–44.

Rosenthal, M. L. *The New Modern Poetry.* New York: Oxford University Press, 1967.

———. *The New Poets: American and British Poetry since World War II.* New York: Oxford University Press, 1967.

Saunders, William S. *James Wright: An Introduction.* Columbus: State Library of Ohio, 1979.

Scott, Shirley Clay. "Surrendering the Shadow," *Ironwood* 10 (1977), 46–63.

Smith, Dave. "Chopping the Distance on James Wright," *Back Door*, nos. 7 & 8 (Spring 1975), 89–95.

———, ed. "James Wright: The Pure Clear Word," *American Poetry Review*, 9, no. 3 (1980), 19–30.

———. "That Halting, Stammering Movement," *Ironwood* 10 (1977), 111–30.

Spendal, R. J. "Wright's 'Lying in a Hammock at William Duffy's Farm in Pine Island, Minnesota,'" *Explicator*, 34 (May 1976), 34.

Spender, Stephen. "The Last Ditch," *New York Review of Books*, July 22, 1971, pp. 3–4.

Stephanchev, Stephen. *American Poetry since 1945.* New York: Harper and Row, 1965.

Stilwell, Robert. "Samples," *Michigan Quarterly Review*, 7 (Fall 1969), 278–82.

Stitt, Peter A. "James Wright and Robert Bly," *Hawaii Review*, 3 (Spring 1975), 89–94.

———. "James Wright: Poetry of the Present," *Ironwood* 10 (1977), 140–53.

———. "The Poetry of James Wright," *Minnesota Review*, 12 (Winter 1972), 13–32.

Stryk, Lucien. "Zen Buddhism and Modern American Poetry," *Yearbook of Comparative and General Literature*, 15 (1966), 186–91.

Taylor, Henry. "Eight Poets," *Michigan Quarterly Review*, 14 (Winter 1975), 92–100.

Thompson, Phyllis Hoge. "James Wright: His Kindliness," *Ironwood* 10 (1977), 97–100.

Tisdale, Bob. "Blood Relations," *Carleton Miscellany*, 17 (Winter 1977), 12–27.

Toole, William B., III. "Wright's 'At the Slackening of the Tide,'" *Explicator*, 22, no. 4 (1962), 13–15.

Van Den Heuvel, Cor. "The Poetry of James Wright," *Mosaic*, 7 (Spring 1973), 163–70.

Wallace-Crabbe, Chris. "Mendeleef, Grass Roots and the Wombat Mandala," *Carleton Miscellany*, 17 (Winter 1977), 37–40.

Whittemore, Reed. *From Zero to the Absolute*. New York: Crown, 1967.

Williamson, Alan. "History Has to Live with What Was Here," *Shenandoah*, 25 (Winter 1974), 85–91.

———. "Language against Itself: The Middle Generation of Contemporary Poets," *American Poetry since 1960*, ed. Robert B. Shaw. London: Carcanet Press, 1973.

———. "Silence, Surrealism, and Allegory," *Kayak 40* (1975), 57–67.

Wright, Annie. "A Horse Grazes in My Long Shadow: A Short Biography of James Wright," *Envoy*, Spring–Summer 1981, pp. 1–5.

Yenser, Stephen. "Open Secrets," *Parnassus*, 6 (Spring–Summer 1978), 125–42.

B. Book Reviews:

1. *The Green Wall:*

Booth, Phillip. "World Redeemed," *Saturday Review*, July 20, 1957, p. 18.

Fitts, Dudley. "Five Young Poets," *Poetry*, 94 (Aug. 1959), 333–39.

Nemerov, Howard. "Younger Poets: The Lyric Difficulty," *Kenyon Review*, 20 (Winter 1958), 25–37.

Palmer, J. E. "The Poetry of James Wright: A First Collection," *Sewanee Review*, 65 (Autumn 1957), 687–93.

Simpson, Louis. "Poets in Isolation," *Hudson Review*, 10 (1957), 458–64.

2. *Saint Judas:*

Booth, Philip. "Four Modern Poets," *New York Times Book Review*, Sept. 27, 1959, p. 22.

Deutsch, Babette. *New York Herald Tribune Book Review*, Nov. 15, 1959, p. 8.

Galler, David. "Three Poets," *Poetry*, 96 (June 1960), 185–90.

Gunn, Thom. "Excellence and Variety," *Yale Review*, 49 (Winter 1960), 295–305.

Hecht, Anthony. "The Anguish of the Spirit and the Letter," *Hudson Review*, 12 (1959–60), 593–603.

Hoffman, Daniel G. "Between New Voice and Old Master," *Sewanee Review*, 68 (Autumn 1960), 674–80.

Scott, Winfield T., "Four New Voices in Verse," *Saturday Review*, May 21, 1960, pp. 39–40.

3. *The Branch Will Not Break:*

Baro, Gene. "Curiosity and Illumination," *New York Times Book Review*, Sept. 1, 1963, p. 5.

Gunn, Thom. "Modes of Control," *Yale Review*, 53 (Spring 1964), 447–58.

Hartman, Geoffrey. "Beyond the Middle Style," *Kenyon Review*, 25 (Autumn 1963), 751–57.

Judson, Jerome. "For Summer, a Wave of New Verse," *Saturday Review*, July 6, 1963, pp. 30–32.

Logan, John. "Poetry Shelf," *The Critic*, 22 (Aug.–Sept. 1963), 85–86.

Rubin, Larry. "Revelations of What Is Present," *The Nation*, July 13, 1963, pp. 38–39.

Strickhausen, H. "In the Open," *Poetry*, 102 (Sept. 1963), 391–92.

Weeks, Robert. "The Nature of the 'Academic'," *Chicago Review*, 16, no. 3 (1963), 138–44.

4. *Shall We Gather at the River:*

Brownjohn, Alan. "Dark Forces," *New Statesman*, Sept. 12, 1969, 346–47.

Dickey, William. "A Place in the Country," *Hudson Review*, 22 (1969), 347–68.

French, Roberts. "Shall We Gather at the River," *Minnesota Review*, 8 (Fall 1968), 382–83.

Ignatow, David. "Shall We Gather at the River," *New York Times Book Review*, Mar. 9, 1969, p. 31.

Kessler, Jascha. "The Caged Sybil," *Saturday Review*, Dec. 14, 1968, pp. 34–46.

Lieberman, Lawrence. "A Confluence of Poets," *Poetry*, 115 (Apr. 1969), 40–58.

Matthews, William. "Entering the World," *Shenandoah*, 20 (Summer 1969), 80–93.

Meyers, Bert. "Our Inner Life," *Kayak 18* (1969), 71–74.

Moss, Stanley. "Joy out of Terror," *New Republic*, Mar. 29, 1969, pp. 30–32.

Zweig, Paul. "Pieces of a Broken Mirror," *The Nation*, July 7, 1969, pp. 20–22.

5. *Collected Poems:*

Carruth, Hayden. "Poetry Chronicle," *Hudson Review*, 24 (1971), 320–26.

Davidson, Peter. "Three Visionary Poets," *Atlantic Monthly*, 229 (Feb. 1972), 106–7.

Deutsch, Babette. "A Fashionable Poet?" *New Republic*, July 17, 1971, p. 27.

Ditsky, John M. "James Wright Collected: Alterations on the Monument," *Modern Poetry Studies*, 2 (1973), 252–59.

Hecht, Roger. "Poems from a Dark Country," *The Nation*, Aug. 2, 1971, p. 88.

Hughes, John W. "Humanism and the Orphic Voice," *Saturday Review*, May 22, 1971, pp. 31–33.

Seay, James. "A World Immeasurably Alive and Good: A Look at James Wright's *Collected Poems*," *Georgia Review*, 27 (1973), 71–81.

Stitt, Peter. *New York Times Book Review*, May 16, 1971, pp. 1–2.

Williamson, Alan. "Pity for the Clear Word," *Poetry*, 119 (Feb. 1972), 296–98.

Zweig, Paul. "Making and Unmaking," *Partisan Review*, 15, no. 2 (1973), 271–79.

6. *Two Citizens:*

Bedient, Calvin. "*Two Citizens*," *New York Times Book Review*, Aug. 11, 1974, p. 6.

Cooney, Seamus. *Library Journal*, Apr. 15, 1973, p. 1291.

Deutsch, Babette. "Chiefly Ironists," *New Republic*, Apr. 28, 1973, p. 25.

Engelberg, Edward. "Discovering America and Asia: The Poetry of Wright and Merwin," *Southern Review*, 11 (1975), 440–43.

Henry, Gerritt. "Starting from Scratch," *Poetry*, 124 (Aug. 1974), 293–95.

Lieberman, Laurence. "The Shocks of Normality," *Yale Review*, 113 (Spring 1974), 453–73.

Perloff, Marjorie G. "The Corn-Pone Lyric: Poetry 1972–73," *Contemporary Literature*, 15 (Winter 1975), 84–125.

Ramsey, Paul. "American Poetry in 1973," *Sewanee Review*, 82 (Spring 1974), p. 394.

7. *Moments of the Italian Summer:*

Dodd, Wayne. "That Same Bodily Curve of the Spirit," *Ohio Review*, 18 (Spring–Summer 1977), 59–62.

8. *To a Blossoming Pear Tree:*

Carruth, Hayden. *Harper's*, 256 (June 1978), 86.

Kazin, Alfred. "James Wright: The Gift of Feeling," *New York Times Book Review*, July 20, 1980, p. 13.

Kinzie, Mary. "Through the Looking Glass," *Ploughshares*, 5, no. 1 (1979), 202–40.

Pinsky, Robert. "Light, Motion, Life," *Saturday Review*, Jan. 21, 1978, pp. 47–49.

Serchuk, Peter. "James Wright: The Art of Survival," *Hudson Review*, 31 (1978), 546–50.

Stitt, Peter. "Poetry Chronicle," *Georgia Review*, 32 (1978), 691–99.

Contributors

W. H. Auden, who was the judge for the Yale University Series of Younger Poets and who chose James Wright's first collection, *The Green Wall*, as a winner, published his own first poems in 1928. The third edition of *Contemporary Poets* lists fifty-five collections of poetry by Auden, the most recent being *Selected Poems*, edited by Edward Mendelson, in 1979, two years after Auden's death.

Henry Taylor teaches at American University. A translator and a poet, his most recent collection is *An Afternoon of Pocket Billiards*.

Peter Stitt teaches at the University of Houston. He is the poetry critic for the *Georgia Review*. His essays have appeared in the *New York Times Book Review*, *Poetry*, *Southern Review*, and elsewhere.

Robert Bly lives in Minnesota and is a familiar reader at American universities. He is editor of Odin House Press, author of many books of poetry and criticism, and has most recently published *News of the Universe: Poems of Twofold Consciousness* and *Talking All Morning*.

William Matthews is Director of the Creative Writing Program at the University of Washington. He is a past editor of *Lillabulero* and the *Iowa Review*. His most recent books are *A World Rich in Anniversaries*, translations of the poems of Jean Follain, and *Rising and Falling*, new poems.

James Seay teaches at the University of North Carolina. His collections of poems are *Let Not Your Hart*, *Water Tables*, and *Where Our Voices Broke Off*.

Edward Butscher is a critic whose books include *Sylvia Plath: Method and Madness*.

Stephen Yenser teaches at the University of California at Los Angeles. He received *The Nation*'s Discovery Award for his poetry in 1979. He is the author of *Circle to Circle: The Poetry of Robert Lowell*.

Leonard Nathan teaches at the University of California at Berkeley. Among his books are *The Tragic Drama of W. B. Yeats* and numerous collections of poetry, including most recently *Dear Blood*.

DAVE SMITH is Director of Creative Writing at the University of Florida. He is a poetry critic for the *American Poetry Review*. His first novel, *Onliness*, and his tenth collection of poems, *Homage to Edgar Allan Poe*, were published in 1981.

ROBERT HASS teaches at St. Mary's College (California). He has held a Guggenheim Fellowship and numerous other awards. His first collection of poems, *Field Guide*, won the Yale Younger Poets Award, and his second collection is *Praise*.

BONNIE COSTELLO teaches at Boston University. She is a poet and critic whose first book is *Marianne Moore: Imaginary Possessions*.

MILLER WILLIAMS is Director of the MFA Program in Translation at the University of Arkansas and also Director of the University of Arkansas Press. His most recent collection of poems is *Distractions*. He is also the translator of Nicanor Parra and many others.